Ubuntu 18.04 Essentials

Ubuntu 18.04 Essentials

ISBN-13: 978-1-951442-16-3

Rev: 1.0

Contents

Table of Contents

Chapter 1

1. Introduction

Ubuntu is arguably one of the most highly regarded and widely used Linux distributions available today. Praised both for its ease of use and reliability, Ubuntu also has a loyal following of Linux users and an active community of developers.

Ubuntu 18.04 Essentials is designed to provide detailed information on the installation, use and administration of the Ubuntu 18.04 distribution. For beginners, the book covers topics such as operating system installation, the basics of the GNOME desktop environment, configuring email and web servers and installing packages and system updates. Additional installation topics such as dual booting with Microsoft Windows are also covered, together with all important security topics such as configuring a firewall and user and group administration.

For the experienced user, topics such as remote desktop access, the Cockpit web interface, logical volume management (LVM), disk partitioning, swap management, KVM virtualization, Secure Shell (SSH), Linux Containers and file sharing using both Samba and NFS are covered in detail to provide a thorough overview of this enterprise class operating system.

1.1 Superuser Conventions

Ubuntu, in common with Linux in general, has two types of user account, one being a standard user account with restricted access to many of the administrative files and features of the operating system, and the other a superuser (*root*) account with elevated privileges. Typically, a user can gain root access either by logging in as the root user, or using the *su -* command and entering the root password. In the following example, a user is gaining root access via the *su -* command:

```
[neil@demo-server ~]$ su -
Password:
[root@demo-server ~]#
```

Note that the command prompt for a regular user ends with a $ sign while the root user has a # character. When working with the command-line, this is a useful indication as to whether or not you are currently issuing commands as the root user.

If the *su -* command fails, the root account on the system has most likely been disabled for security reasons. In this case, the *sudo* command can be used instead as outlined below.

Alternatively, a single command requiring root privileges may be executed by a non-root user via the *sudo* command. Consider the following attempt to update the operating system with the latest patches and packages:

```
$ apt update
Reading package lists... Done
E: Could not open lock file /var/lib/apt/lists/lock - open (13: Permission denied)
```

Optionally, user accounts may be configured so that they have access to root level privileges. Instead of using the *su* - command to first gain root access, user accounts with administration privileges are able to run otherwise restricted commands using *sudo*.

```
$ sudo apt update
[sudo] password for demo:
Hit:1 http://us.archive.ubuntu.com/ubuntu bionic InRelease
.
.
```

To perform multiple commands without repeatedly using the sudo command, a command prompt with persistent super-user privileges may be accessed as follows:

```
[neil@demo-server]$ sudo su -
[neil@demo-server]#
```

The reason for raising this issue so early in the book is that many of the command-line examples outlined in this book will require root privileges. Rather than repetitively preface every command-line example with directions to run the command as root, the command prompt at the start of the line will be used to indicate whether or not the command needs to be performed as root. If the command can be run as a regular user, the command will be prefixed with a $ command prompt as follows:

```
$ date
```

If, on the other hand, the command requires root privileges, the command will be preceded by a # command prompt:

```
# apt install openssh-server
```

1.2 Opening a Terminal Window

If you are running Ubuntu with the GNOME desktop and need to access a command-prompt you will need to open a terminal window. This can be achieved by right-clicking on the desktop background and selecting the Open Terminal menu option as shown in Figure 1-1:

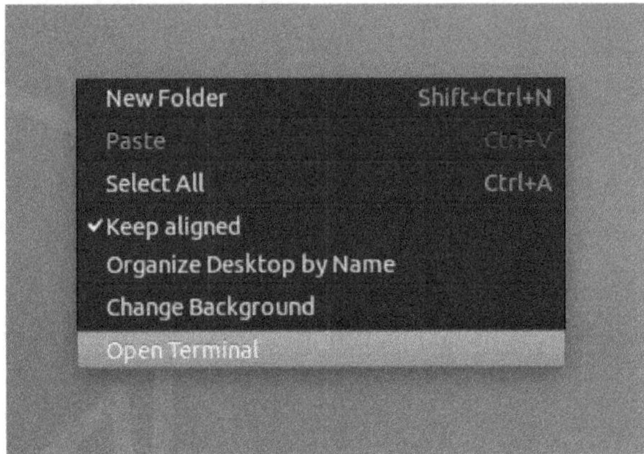

Figure 1-1

A terminal window may also be opened within the GNOME desktop using the Ctrl-Alt-T keyboard accelerator.

1.3 Editing Files

Configuring a Linux system typically involves editing files. For those new to Linux it can be unclear which editor to use. If you are running a terminal session and do not already have a preferred editor we recommend using the *nano* editor. To launch *nano* in a terminal window simply enter the following command:

```
# nano <file>
```

Where <file> is replaced by the path to the file you wish to edit. For example:

```
# nano /etc/passwd
```

Once loaded, *nano* will appear as illustrated in Figure 1-2:

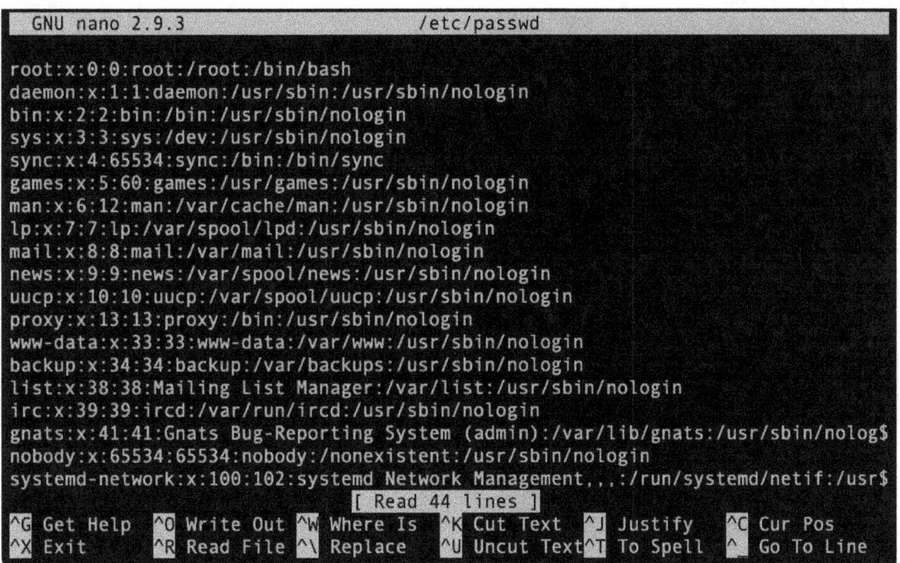

Figure 1-2

To create a new file simply run *nano* as follows:

```
# nano
```

When you have finished editing the file, type Ctrl-S to save the file followed by Ctrl-X to exit. To open an existing file, use the Ctrl-R keyboard shortcut.

If you prefer to use a graphical editor within the GNOME desktop environment *gedit* is a useful starting point for basic editing tasks. To launch *gedit* from the desktop press Alt-F2 to display the Enter a Command window as shown in Figure 1-3:

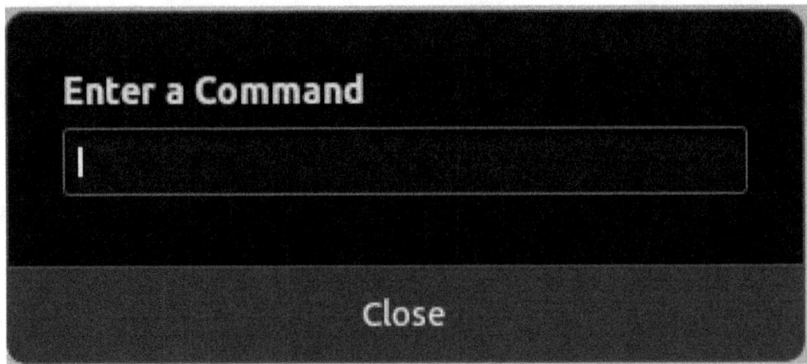

Figure 1-3

Enter gedit into the text field and press the Enter key. After a short delay, gedit will load ready to open, create and edit files:

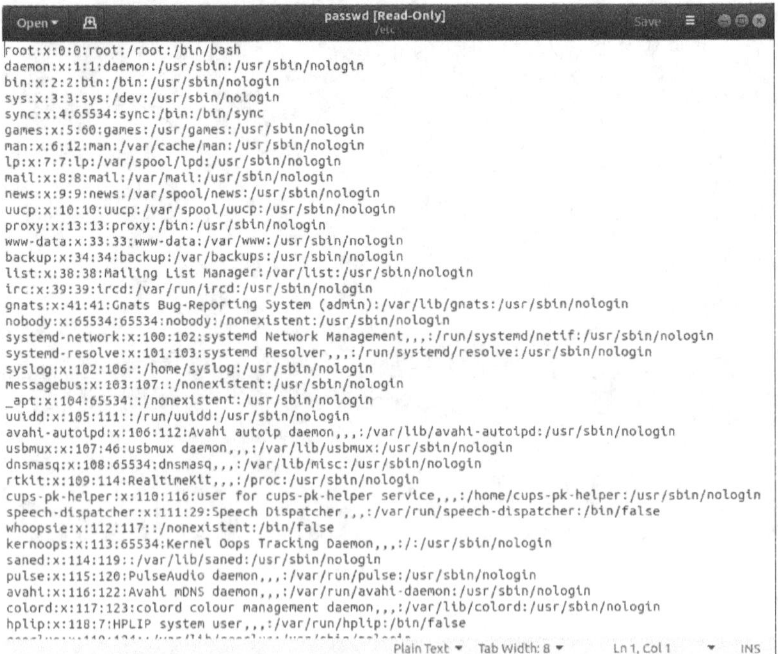

Figure 1-4

Alternatively, launch gedit from a terminal window either with or without the path to the file to open:

```
# gedit
```

```
# gedit /etc/passwd
```

1.4 Feedback

We want you to be satisfied with your purchase of this book. If you find any errors in the book, or have any comments, questions or concerns please contact us at *feedback@ebookfrenzy.com.*

1.5 Errata

While we make every effort to ensure the accuracy of the content of this book, it is inevitable that a book covering a subject area of this size and complexity may include some errors and oversights. Any known issues with the book will be outlined, together with solutions, at the following URL:

https://www.ebookfrenzy.com/errata/ubuntu1804.html

In the event that you find an error not listed in the errata, please let us know by emailing our support team at *feedback@ebookfrenzy.com*.

Chapter 2

2. A Brief History of Linux

Ubuntu Linux is one of a number of variants (also referred to as *distributions*) of the Linux operating system and is the product of a U.K. company named Canonical Ltd. The company was founded in 1994 by Mark Shuttleworth. The origins of Linux, however, go back even further. This chapter will outline the history of both the Linux operating system and Ubuntu.

2.1 What exactly is Linux?

Linux is an operating system in much the same way that Windows is an operating system (and there any similarities between Linux and Windows end). The term operating system is used to describe the software that acts as a layer between the hardware in a computer and the applications that we all run on a daily basis. When programmers write applications, they interface with the operating system to perform such tasks as writing files to the hard disk drive and displaying information on the screen. Without an operating system, every programmer would have to write code to directly access the hardware of the system. In addition, the programmer would have to be able to support every single piece of hardware ever created to be sure the application would work on every possible hardware configuration. Because the operating system handles all of this hardware complexity, application development becomes a much easier task. Linux is just one of a number of different operating systems available today.

2.2 UNIX Origins

To understand the history of Linux, we first have to go back to AT&T Bell Laboratories in the late 1960s. During this time AT&T had discontinued involvement in the development of a new operating system named Multics. Two AT&T engineers, Ken Thompson and Dennis Ritchie, decided to take what they had learned from the Multics project and create a new operating system named UNIX which quickly gained popularity and wide adoption both with corporations and academic institutions.

A variety of proprietary UNIX implementations eventually came to market including those created by IBM (AIX), Hewlett-Packard (HP-UX) and Sun Microsystems (SunOS and Solaris). In addition, a UNIX-like operating system named MINIX was created by Andrew S. Tanenbaum designed for educational use with source code access provided to universities.

2.3 Who Created Linux?

The origins of Linux can be traced back to the work and philosophies of two people. At the heart of the Linux operating system is something called the kernel. This is the core set of features necessary for the operating system to function. The kernel manages the system's resources and handles communication between the hardware and the applications. The Linux kernel was developed by Linus Torvalds who, taking a dislike to MS-DOS, and impatient for the availability of MINIX for the new Intel 80386 microprocessor, decided to write his own UNIX-like kernel.

When he had finished the first version of the kernel, he released it under an open source license that enabled anyone to download the source code and freely use and modify it without having to pay Linus any money.

Around the same time, Richard Stallman at the Free Software Foundation, a strong advocate of free and open source software, was working on an open source operating system of his own. Rather than focusing initially on the kernel, however, Stallman decided to begin by developing open source versions of all the UNIX tools, utilities and compilers necessary to use and maintain an operating system. By the time he had finished developing this infrastructure it seemed like the obvious solution was to combine his work with the kernel Linus had written to create a full operating system. This combination became known as GNU/Linux. Purists insist that Linux always be referred to as GNU/Linux (in fact, at one time, Richard Stallman refused to give press interviews to any publication which failed to refer to Linux as GNU/Linux). This is not unreasonable given that the GNU tools developed by the Free Software Foundation make up a significant and vital part of GNU/Linux. Unfortunately, most people and publications simply refer to Linux as Linux and this will probably always continue to be the case.

2.4 The History of Ubuntu

As mentioned previously, Ubuntu is one of a number of Linux distributions. The source code that makes up the Ubuntu distribution originates from a highly regarded Linux distribution known as Debian created Ian Murdoch.

A South African internet mogul named Mark Shuttleworth (who made his fortune selling his company to VeriSign for around $500 million) decided it was time for a more user friendly Linux. He took the Debian distribution and worked to make it a more human friendly distribution which he called Ubuntu. He subsequently formed a company called Canonical Ltd to promote and provide support for Ubuntu.

If you are new to Linux, or already use Linux and want to try a different Linux distribution it is unlikely you will find a better option than Ubuntu.

2.5 What does the word “Ubuntu” Mean?

The word “Ubuntu” is an ancient Zulu and Xhosa word that means “humanity to others”. Ubuntu also means “I am what I am because of who we all are”. It was chosen because these sentiments precisely describe the spirit of the Ubuntu distribution.

2.6 Summary

The origins of the Linux operating system can be traced back to the work of Linus Torvalds and Richard Stallman in the form of the Linux kernel combined with the tools and compilers built by the GNU project.

Over the years, the open source nature of Linux has resulted in the release of a wide range of different Linux distributions. One such distribution is Ubuntu, based on the Debian Linux distribution and created by Canonical Ltd, a company founded by Mark Shuttleworth.

Chapter 3

3. Installing Ubuntu on a Clean Disk Drive

There are now two ways in which an Ubuntu system can be deployed. One method is to either purchase new hardware or re-purpose an existing computer system on which to install and run the operating system. Another option is to create a cloud-based operating system instance using services such as Amazon AWS, Google Cloud or Microsoft Azure (to name but a few). Since cloud-based instances are typically created by selecting a pre-configured, ready to run operating system image that is already optimized for the cloud platform, and using that as the basis for the Ubuntu system, there is no need to perform a manual operating system installation in this situation.

If, on the other hand, you plan to install Ubuntu on your own hardware, the first step on the path to learning about Ubuntu involves installing the operating system.

Ubuntu can be installed either in a clean disk environment (where an entire disk is cleared of any existing partitions and dedicated entirely to Ubuntu) or in a dual boot environment where Ubuntu co-exists with another operating system on the disk (typically a member of the Microsoft Windows family of operating systems).

In this chapter we will be covering the clean disk approach to installation from local or remote installation media. Dual boot installation with a Windows 10 system will be covered in *"Dual Booting Ubuntu with Windows"*.

3.1 Ubuntu Installation Options

Ubuntu can be downloaded free of charge from the following web page:

https://ubuntu.com/download

This page provides a number of download options depending on how the operating system is to be installed and used:

- **Ubuntu Desktop** - Downloads the installation media for the desktop edition of the operating system. This edition is intended for use on desktop and laptop systems where a graphical desktop environment is needed and is only available for 64-bit x86 systems. The desktop edition can be downloaded in the form of an ISO image which you can then write to a USB drive using the steps outlined later in this chapter. When booted, the desktop media will allow you to test out Ubuntu by running a Live Ubuntu session prior to performing the installation.
- **Ubuntu Server** - Downloads the installation media for the server edition of the operating system. This image is intended for performing an installation on servers on which the graphical

desktop environment is not required and is available for x86, ARM, IBM POWER (PowerPC) and s390x (IBM System z mainframe) systems. The installation media does not include the option to try Ubuntu before installing and uses the text based installer instead of the graphical installer used for Ubuntu Desktop. This allows Ubuntu to be installed on systems without a graphical console.

When downloading Ubuntu Server edition, the following options are available:

- **Standard ISO Image** - Contains everything to install Ubuntu Server. This allows the installation to be performed without needing a network or internet connection.
- **Network Installer ISO Image** - Contains the minimum needed to begin the installation process during which additional packages are downloaded based on choices made during the configuration phase. The Network installer will be covered in detail in the chapter entitled *"Installing Ubuntu with the Network Installer"*.

3.2 Server vs. Desktop Editions

Clearly a decision between the Desktop and the Server Edition images needs to be made before installation can begin. If you would like to try Ubuntu before installing it, then the Desktop option is the best solution since it allows you to boot Ubuntu from the installation media without first installing it on a disk drive. As shown in Figure 3-1, this option also allows the installation to be initiated from within the live session:

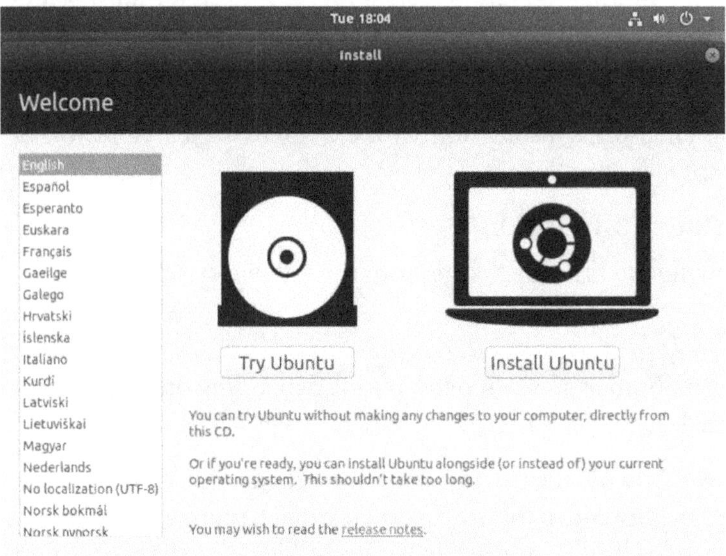

Figure 3-1

If the graphical desktop environment is not required, and the destination system does not have internet access then the Server Edition Standard ISO image is recommended since this allows a fully functional server to be built without the need to download any additional packages.

Regardless of the chosen installation method, packages can be added to and removed from the system after installation to configure the system to specific needs.

3.3 Obtaining the Ubuntu Installation Media

For the purposes of this chapter, the Ubuntu Desktop environment will be installed using the graphical installer. Begin, therefore, by downloading the Ubuntu Desktop 18.10.4 ISO image from the following URL:

https://ubuntu.com/download/desktop

The DVD ISO image is self-contained including all of the packages necessary to install an Ubuntu system and is named using the following convention:

```
ubuntu-<version>-<edition>-<architecture>.iso
```

For example, the Ubuntu 18.10.4 Desktop ISO image for 64-bit Intel/AMD systems is named as follows:

```
ubuntu-18.04.4-desktop-amd64.iso
```

Having downloaded the image, either burn it to disk or use the steps in the next section to write the media to a USB drive and configure your virtualization environment to treat it as a DVD drive.

3.4 Writing the ISO Installation Image to a USB Drive

These days it is more likely that an operating system installation will be performed from a USB drive than from a DVD. Having downloaded the ISO installation image for Ubuntu, the steps to write that image to a USB drive will differ depending on whether the drive is attached to a Linux, macOS or Windows system. The steps outlined in the remainder of this section assume that the USB drive is new, or has been reformatted to remove any existing data or partitions:

3.4.1 Linux

The first step in writing an ISO image to a USB drive on Linux is to identify the device name. Before inserting the USB drive, identify the storage devices already detected on the system by listing the devices in */dev* as follows:

```
# ls /dev/sd*
/dev/sda   /dev/sda1   /dev/sda2
```

Attach the USB drive to the Linux system and run the *dmesg* command to get a list of recent system messages, one of which will be a report that the USB drive was detected and will be similar to the following:

```
[445597.988045] sd 6:0:0:0: [sdb] Attached SCSI removable disk
```

This output tells us that we should expect the device name to include "sdb" which we can confirm by listing device names in */dev* again:

```
# ls /dev/sd*
/dev/sda    /dev/sda1    /dev/sda2    /dev/sdb
```

From this output we can tell that the USB drive has been assigned to /dev/sdb. The next step before writing the ISO image to the device is to run the *findmnt* command to make sure it has not been auto-mounted:

```
# findmnt /dev/sdb?
TARGET                     SOURCE    FSTYPE OPTIONS
/media/demo/C24E-6727 /dev/sdb1 vfat   rw,nosuid,nodev, ...
```

If the *findmnt* command indicates that the USB drive has been mounted, unmount it before continuing:

```
# umount /media/demo/C24E-6727
```

Once the filesystem has been unmounted, use the *dd* command as follows to write the ISO image to the drive:

```
# dd if=/path/to/iso/<image name>.iso of=/dev/sdb bs=512k
```

The writing process can take some time (as long as 10 - 15 minutes) to complete depending on the image size and speed of the system on which it is running. Once the image has been written, output similar to the following will appear and the USB drive is ready to be used to install Ubuntu:

```
4056+1 records in
4056+1 records out
2126544896 bytes (2.1 GB, 2.0 GiB) copied, 625.911 s, 3.4 MB/s
```

3.4.2 macOS

The first step in writing an ISO image to a USB drive attached to a macOS system is to identify the device using the *diskutil* tool. Before attaching the USB device, open a Terminal window and run the following command:

```
$ diskutil list
/dev/disk0 (internal, physical):
   #:                       TYPE NAME                    SIZE       IDENTIFIER
   0:      GUID_partition_scheme                        *1.0 TB     disk0
   1:                        EFI EFI                     209.7 MB   disk0s1
   2:                 Apple_APFS Container disk2         1000.0 GB  disk0s2

/dev/disk1 (internal):
   #:                       TYPE NAME                    SIZE       IDENTIFIER
   0:      GUID_partition_scheme                         28.0 GB    disk1
   1:                        EFI EFI                     314.6 MB   disk1s1
   2:                 Apple_APFS Container disk2         27.7 GB    disk1s2

/dev/disk2 (synthesized):
   #:                       TYPE NAME                    SIZE       IDENTIFIER
   0:      APFS Container Scheme -                      +1.0 TB     disk2
                                 Physical Stores disk1s2, disk0s2
   1:                APFS Volume Macintosh HD            473.6 GB   disk2s1
   2:                APFS Volume Preboot                 42.1 MB    disk2s2
```

```
   3:                APFS Volume Recovery              517.0 MB   disk2s3
   4:                APFS Volume VM                    1.1 GB     disk2s4
```

Having established a baseline of detected devices, insert the USB drive into a port on the macOS system and run the command again. The same results should appear with one additional entry for the USB drive resembling the following:

```
/dev/disk3 (external, physical):
   #:                       TYPE NAME                  SIZE       IDENTIFIER
   0:                                                 *16.0 GB    disk3
```

In the above example, the USB drive has been assigned to /dev/disk3. Before proceeding, unmount the disk as follows:

```
$ diskutil unmountDisk /dev/disk3
Unmount of all volumes on disk3 was successful
```

Finally, use the *dd* command to write the ISO image to the device, taking care to reference the raw disk device (/dev/**r**disk3) and entering your user password when prompted:

```
$ sudo dd if=/path/to/iso/image.iso of=/dev/rdisk3 bs=1m
```

Once the image has been written, the USB drive is ready.

3.4.3 Windows

A number of free tools are available for Windows that will write an ISO image to a USB drive, but one written specifically for writing Linux ISO images is the Fedora Media Writer tool which can be downloaded from the following URL:

https://getfedora.org/en/workstation/download/

Once installed, launch the writer tool and select the *Custom image* option as highlighted in Figure 3-2:

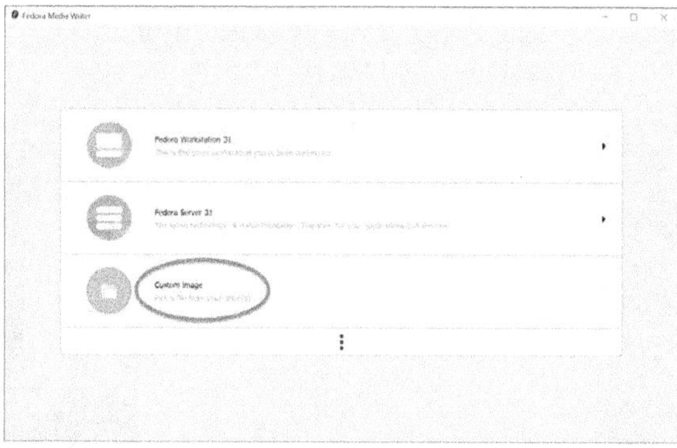

Figure 3-2

In the resulting file selection dialog, navigate to and select the Ubuntu installation ISO image and click on the *Open* button. After selecting the image, a dialog will appear within which the image can be written to the USB drive. Select the target USB drive from the device menu before clicking on the *Write to Disk* button:

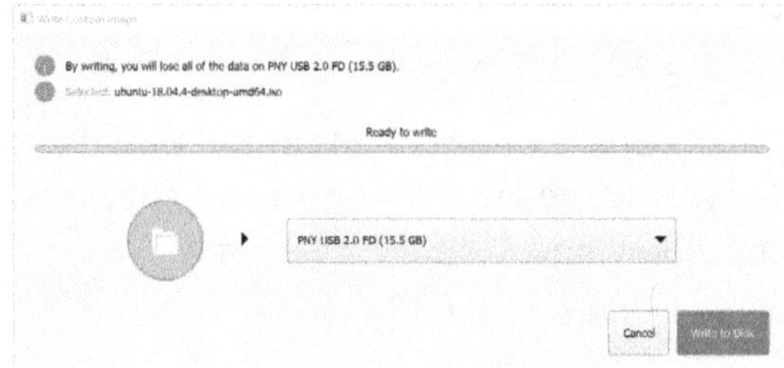

Figure 3-3

Once the image has been written to the device, the device is ready to be used to perform the installation.

3.5 Booting from the Ubuntu USB Image

Insert the Ubuntu installation media into the appropriate drive and power on the system. If the system tries to boot from the hard disk drive you will need to enter the BIOS set up for your computer and change the boot order so that it boots from the installation media drive first. For the first few seconds of the boot process a largely blank screen will appear with the following image located along the bottom edge:

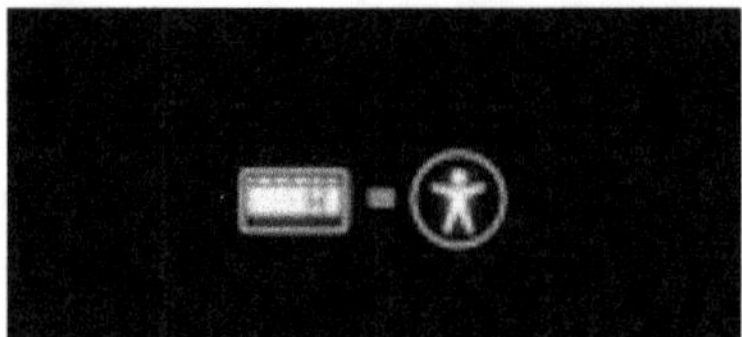

Figure 3-4

If no action is taken at this point, Ubuntu will boot into the Live session and provide the option to either try Ubuntu without installing, or to begin the installation process as shown in Figure 3-1 above. Alternatively, pressing the keyboard Esc key will enter the boot menu system beginning with the language selection screen shown in Figure 3-5:

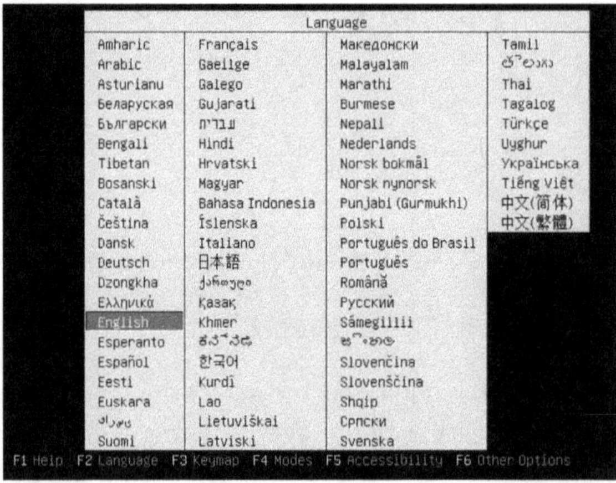

Figure 3-5

Navigate using the keyboard arrow keys and press the Enter key to select a language at which point the Ubuntu boot menu screen will appear as shown below:

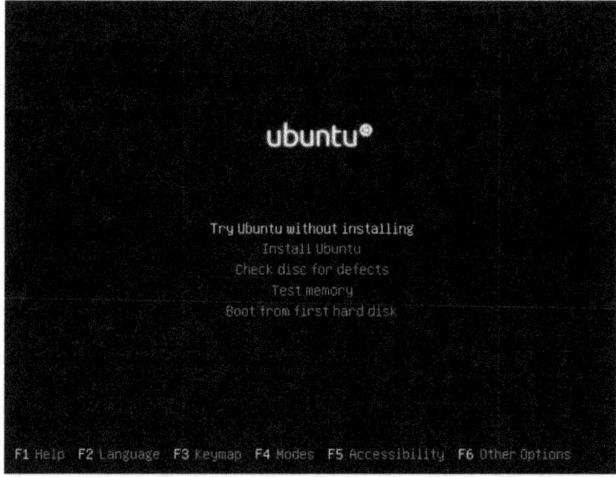

Figure 3-6

Once again, options are provided to either try the Ubuntu Live session, or to begin the installation process. The installation media and system memory may also be checked for defects, or the system booted from the primary hard disk drive installed in the computer system (assuming it contains a bootable operating system image). A range of Function key options provide access to settings such as changing the accessibility options, accessing help and specifying special boot parameters.

3.6 Installing Ubuntu

From within either the live session or the boot menu, select the option to begin the Ubuntu installation and wait for the initial screen of the installer to appear:

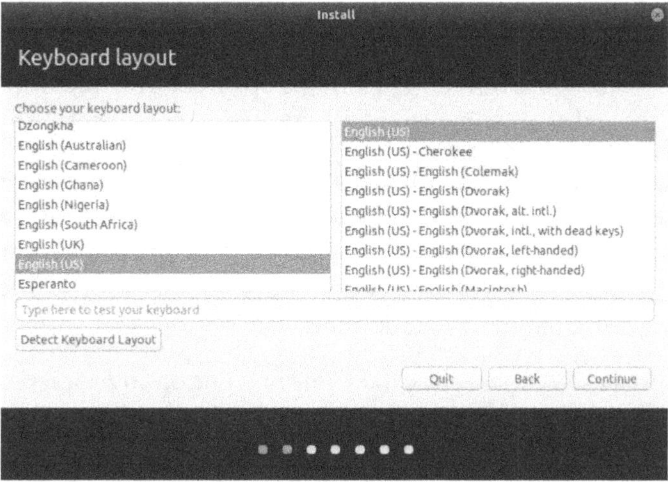

Figure 3-7

Either select your keyboard layout or, if you are unsure, click on the Detect Keyboard Layout button to work through some steps to identify your keyboard before clicking on Continue. On the next screen, choose whether to perform the Normal or Minimal installation:

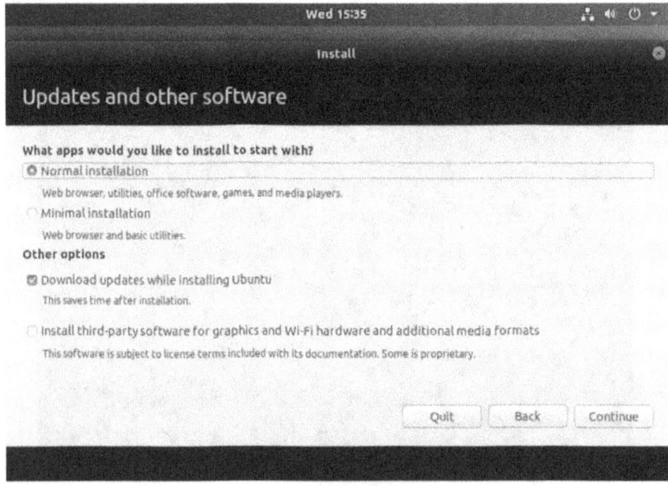

Figure 3-8

Select the Normal option if you have plenty of disk space and want to explore the main applications and utilities included with Ubuntu without having to manually install them later. Alternatively, to avoid cluttering the system with software you may never need, select the Minimal option. Regardless of the choice made here, all of the software provided with Ubuntu can be easily installed or removed at any point in the future if needed.

The option is also available to update the software packages that comprise the Ubuntu distribution during the installation. Ubuntu, as with most actively supported operating systems, continues to be updated with bug fixes and security patches long after it has been released to the public. If this option is selected and the system is connected to the internet, the installer will download any updates issued since the Ubuntu installation image was released and applies them to the system during installation. If you choose not to perform this update during the installation process these updates may still be applied at any time after the installation completes.

A second option provides the choice of whether to install 3rd party non-open source software to support specific hardware devices and the playback of proprietary media files on the system. Some users object fervently to using any software which is not published under a public license. If you are one of those people then do not select this option. If, on the other hand, you just want the best experience from your Ubuntu installation then this option is recommended.

Having made appropriate selections, click the Continue button to proceed to the disk allocation screen:

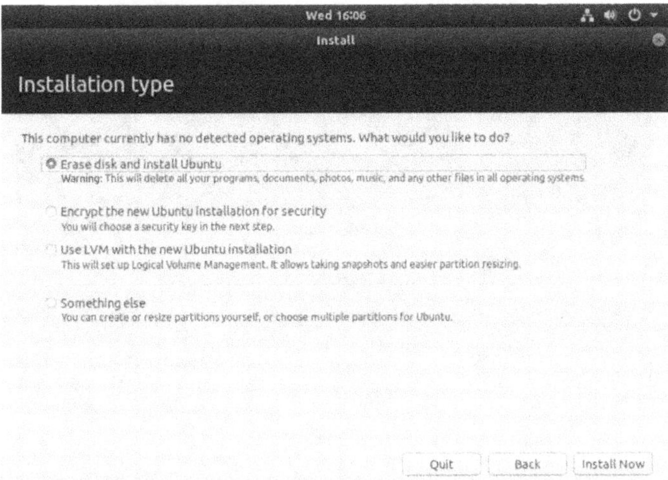

Figure 3-9

Assuming that this is a new disk on which an existing operating system is not present, the installer will provide the option to erase the entire disk and use it for Ubuntu (in which case the installer will calculate and implement a typical and recommended partition layout). Alternatively, to define your own custom disk layout, select the *Something else* option to manually create and size the disk partitions that will contain the operating system and your data.

If the security of the data stored on the disk is of paramount concern, select the option to encrypt the Ubuntu installation. If this option is selected the next screen will prompt you to choose a security key which will then need to be entered each time the system starts.

The option to use Logical Volume Management (LVM) is also strongly recommended to make the management of the disks and partitions on the system easier, a topic covered in detail in the chapter entitled *"Adding a New Disk to an Ubuntu Volume Group and Logical Volume"*.

Once the selections have been made, click on the Install Now button to begin the installation process at which point the system will seek confirmation that the changes are to be made to the disk drive:

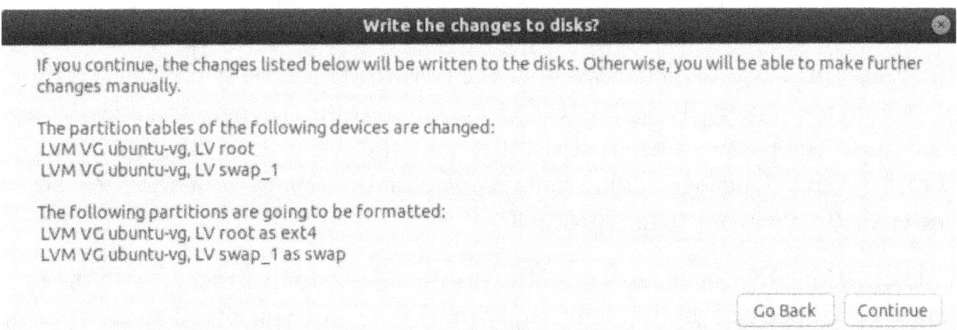

Figure 3-10

While the installation is in progress, the installer will ask for information about your geographical location in order to configure time zone settings:

Figure 3-11

Next, the installer will ask you to provide a user name and password for the first account on the system:

Wed 13:21
Install
Who are you?
Your name:
Your computer's name:
The name it uses when it talks to other computers.
Pick a username:
Choose a password:
Confirm your password:
Log in automatically
Require my password to log in
Back
Continue

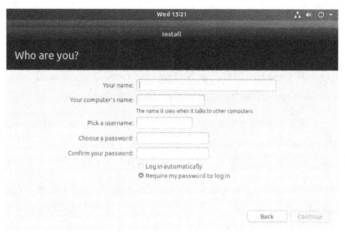

Figure 3-12

The option is also provided to dictate whether the password must be specified each time the user wishes to log into the system. By default, each time Ubuntu starts a login screen will be presented seeking username and password credentials. If you are the sole user of the system and would like to bypass this screen and be logged in automatically each time the system boots, be sure to set the *Log in automatically* checkbox before proceeding.

Once all the questions have been answered, the installer will simply proceed with the installation. Depending on the speed of your system, and whether or not you opted to download updates during the installation, this process can take some time. For a more detailed view of the steps being performed by the installer, click on the status title located above the progress bar:

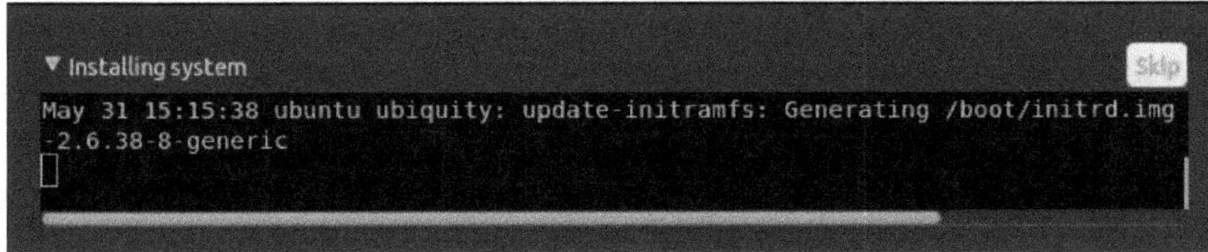

Figure 3-13

When the installation is complete, a dialog will appear to inform you the system is ready to be restarted:

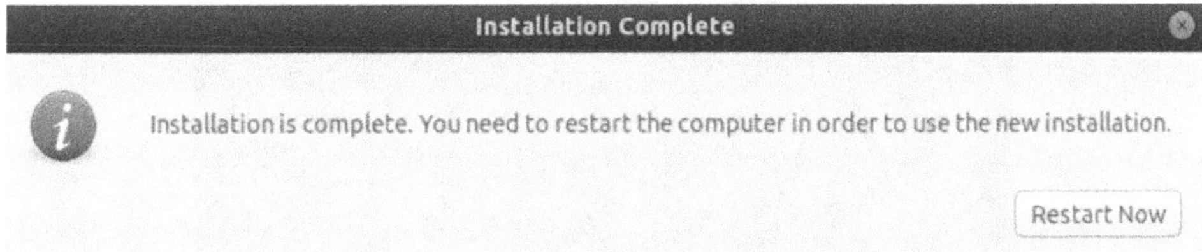

Figure 3-14

When you are ready to reboot, press the Restart Now button. The installer may prompt you to remove the installation media and the system will take a few moments to shut down. At this point remove the USB flash drive and press the Enter key to proceed.

3.7 Accessing the Ubuntu Desktop

Once the system has started, if the password requirement option was enabled the GNOME Display Manager (GDM) login screen (Figure 3-15) will appear. To access the system, select the user name and enter the password specified during installation:

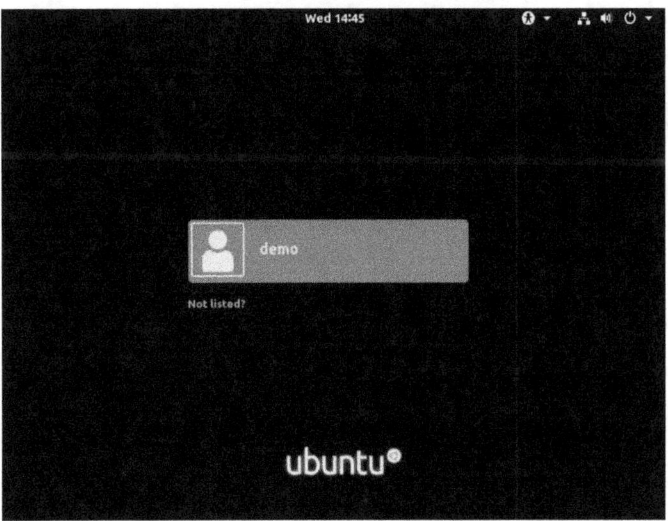

Figure 3-15

Alternatively, if the installation was configured to log directly into the desktop, the GNOME desktop (Figure 3-16) will appear after the system has restarted:

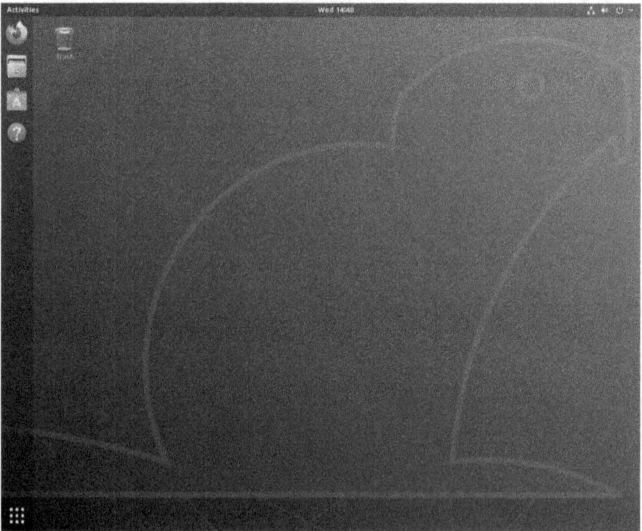

Figure 3-16

The GNOME Display Manager (GDM) login screen will appear and the system is ready to use.

3.8 Installing Updates

As with most operating systems today, each particular release of the Ubuntu distribution continues to evolve after it has been released. This generally takes the form of bug fixes and security updates and, occasionally, new features that may be downloaded over the internet and installed on your system.

Best practices dictate that the first step after installing Ubuntu is to make sure any available updates are applied to the system. This can be achieved via the command-line prompt in a Terminal window using the *apt* package manager tool. To check for the availability of updates, right-click on the desktop background and, from the resulting menu, select the Open Terminal option:

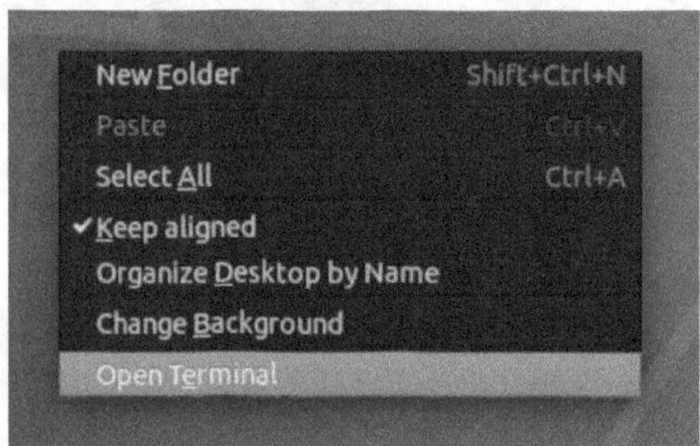

Figure 3-17

Within the Terminal window, run the following commands to gain root privileges and update the package list:

```
# sudo su -
# apt update
```

If updated packages are available, the command will display output similar to the following:

```
.
.
.
Reading package lists... Done
Building dependency tree
Reading state information... Done
103 packages can be upgraded. Run 'apt list --upgradable' to see them.
```

Any pending updates may be applied using the *apt* tool:

```
# apt upgrade
```

Upon execution, the *apt* tool will provide a list of packages that are available for update and prompt for permission to perform the update

```
103 upgraded, 7 newly installed, 0 to remove and 0 not upgraded.
Need to get 75.2 MB/286 MB of archives.
After this operation, 352 MB of additional disk space will be used.
Do you want to continue? [Y/n]
```

Once the upgrade is complete the installation is essentially finished.

3.9 Displaying Boot Messages

During the boot process, the system will display the Ubuntu splash screen which hides from view all of the boot messages generated by the system as it loads. To make these messages visible during the boot process (as shown in Figure 3-18), simply press the keyboard Esc key while the system is starting:

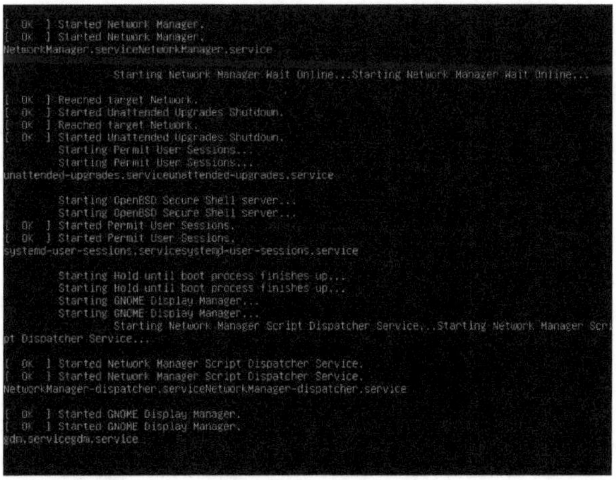

Figure 3-18

The default behavior can be changed so that messages are always displayed by default by editing the */etc/default/grub* file and changing the GRUB_CMDLINE_LINUX setting which, by default, will resemble the following:

```
GRUB_CMDLINE_LINUX="... rhgb quiet"
```

If you are new to Linux and are not familiar with the editors available, refer to the editor recommendations outlined in the *"Introduction"* chapter. For example, to use the nano editor, enter the following command to start the editor and load the *grub* file:

```
# nano /etc/default/grub
```

To remove the graphical boot screen so that messages are visible without pressing the Esc key, remove the "splash" and "quiet" options from the setting:

```
GRUB_CMDLINE_LINUX="quiet splash"
```

This change will cause the system to display all of the boot messages generated by the system.

Once the changes have been made, run the following command to generate a new boot configuration to take effect next time the system starts:

```
# grub-mkconfig --output=/boot/grub/grub.cfg
```

3.10 Summary

The first step in working with Ubuntu is to install the operating system. In the case of a cloud-based server, this task is typically performed automatically when an operating system image is selected for the system based on a range of options offered by the cloud service provider. Installation on your own hardware, however, involves downloading the installation media in the form of an ISO image, writing that image to suitable storage such as a DVD or USB drive and booting from it. Once installation is complete, it is important to install any operating system updates that may have been released since the original installation image was created.

Chapter 4

4. Installing Ubuntu with the Network Installer

The previous chapter explored the different options available when installing Ubuntu with a particular emphasis on using the graphical installer. This chapter will go into more detail regarding the use of the Network installer image to install Ubuntu.

4.1 Network Installer Advantages

The Network installer (also referred to as Netboot) image provides a small image (approximately 50Mb in size compared to more than 2Gb for the Desktop image) that can be used to install either the server or desktop-based Ubuntu environments. This option requires an internet connection to download additional packages during installation and uses the text-based installer.

While the Server and Desktop images provide very little choice in terms of configuration options during installation, the Network installer provides an extensive list of pre-defined software collections from which to choose during installation. The Ubuntu Desktop ISO image, for example, will only install the GNOME desktop environment. The Network installer, on the other hand, lets you install various desktop environments including KDE Plasma (Kubuntu) and LXQt (Lubuntu). Options are also available to install a basic server environment with optional additional server related packages such as web server, mail server and database software.

All of these packages can, of course, be added or removed after installation is complete when using the Server and Desktop images, but if you want to use a small installation image that can be quickly written to a USB drive and allows you to pre-install many software dependencies, the Network installer is an ideal option.

4.2 Obtaining the Network Installer Image

Network installer images for most Ubuntu versions can be downloaded from the following web page:

https://ubuntu.com/download/alternative-downloads

From this page, select the required Ubuntu version followed by the CPU architecture. Finally, download the image file named *mini.iso* and follow the steps in the chapter entitled *"Installing Ubuntu on a Clean Disk Drive"* to write the image to a USB drive.

4.3 Booting from the Installer Image

Insert the Ubuntu installation media and power on the system. If the system tries to boot from the hard disk drive you will need to enter the BIOS set up for your computer and change the boot order so that it boots from the installation media drive first. Once the system has booted, the screen shown in Figure 4-1 will appear:

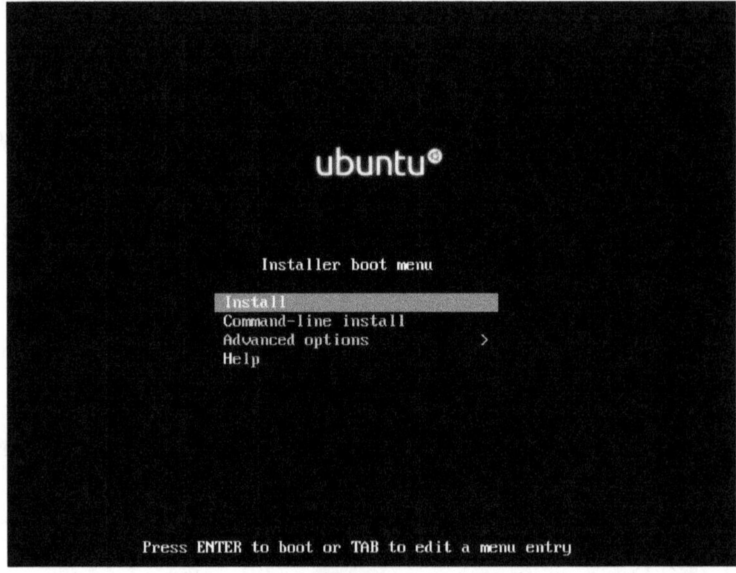

Figure 4-1

4.4 Performing the Installation

From the menu, select the Install option and tap the keyboard Enter key to start the installation process. On the next few screens, use the keyboard arrow keys and the Enter key to select your preferred language and keyboard type.

After making the configuration selections, the installer will scan the device hardware in search of a network interface:

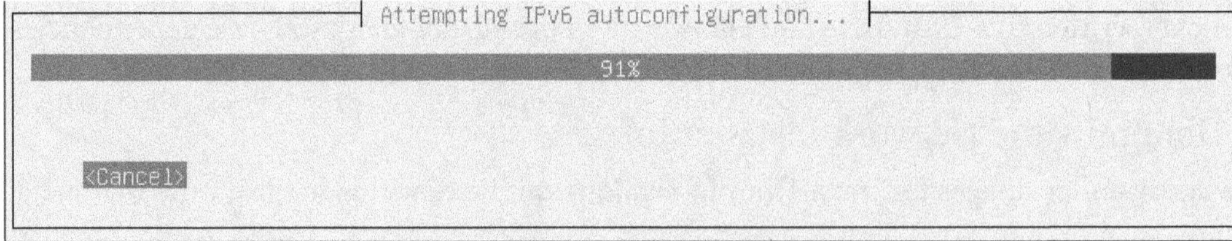

Figure 4-2

Once a network connection has been detected, the system will need to be assigned a host name by which it will appear on the network. When prompted, enter a host name then use the Tab key to navigate to the Continue button before tapping the Enter key to move to the next screen.

During the installation, the installer will download only the packages that are needed to match the software selections you make during the installation process. These Ubuntu software packages are hosted on mirror servers throughout the world. To ensure optimal download performance select the country in which the system is located:

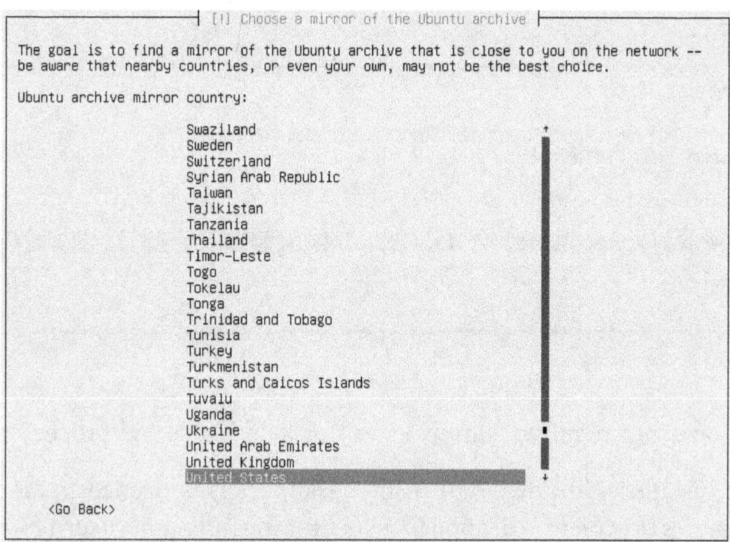

Figure 4-3

On the next screen select a mirror server before continuing:

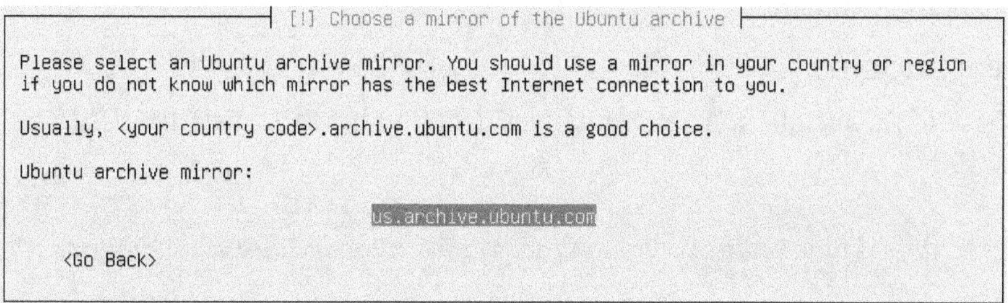

Figure 4-4

If the computer on which the installation is being performed is located behind a proxy based firewall, enter the information for the proxy on the screen shown in Figure 4-5. A proxy service firewall is placed between the internet and an internal network of computers and acts as a go-between for the two environments. With a proxy service in place, internal client computers do not connect directly to outside resources. Instead they connect to the proxy server which in turn connects with the external resource on behalf of the client, thereby masking the internal IP address of the client. Any responses from the external resources are handled by the proxy service which passes them along to the client that originally requested the data:

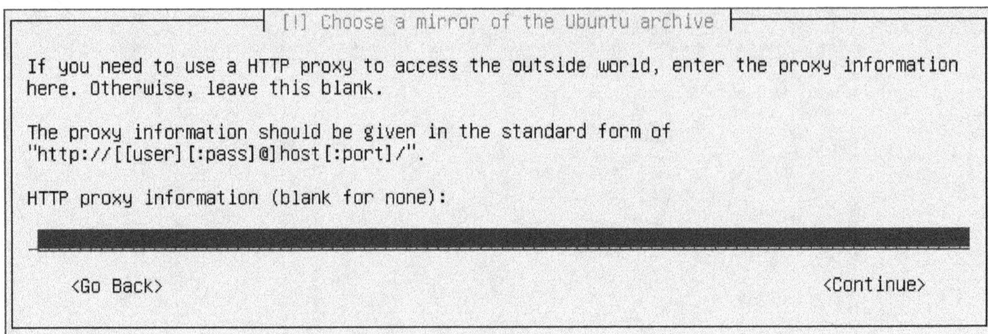

Figure 4-5

If proxy information is not required, simply leave this field blank and proceed to the next screen.

At this point, the installer will download some basic packages needed to start the installation. Once complete, a series of screens will appear asking for the full name, username and password for the first user to be added to the system. Once this information has been provided, the installer will identify the geographical location of the system based on the external IP address of the internet connection. If the installer has detected the location correctly, accept the location, otherwise make the selection manually.

4.5 Disk Partitioning

The next phase of the installation setup involves deciding how the disk drive is to be partitioned and managed:

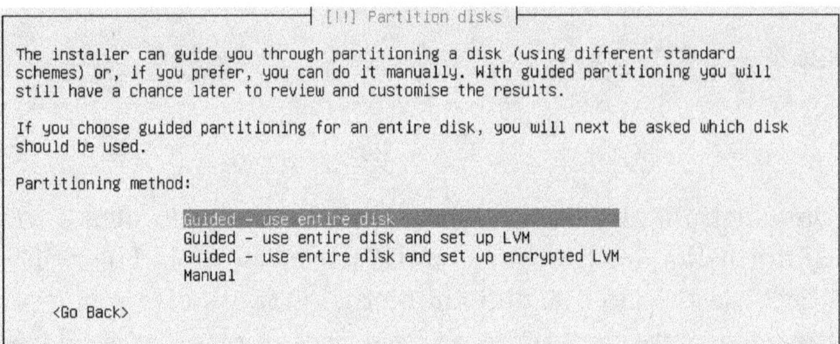

Figure 4-6

Assuming that this is a new disk on which an existing operating system is not present, the installer will provide the option to erase the entire disk and use it for Ubuntu (in which case the installer will calculate and implement a typical and recommended partition layout). If the security of the data stored on the disk is of paramount concern, select the option to encrypt the Ubuntu installation. If this option is selected a later screen will prompt you to choose a security key which will then need to be entered each time the system starts.

The option to use Logical Volume Management (LVM) is also strongly recommended to make the management of the disks and partitions on the system easier, a topic covered in detail in the chapter entitled *"Adding a New Disk to an Ubuntu Volume Group and Logical Volume"*.

Alternatively, to define your own custom disk layout or to implement more advanced configurations such as RAID, select the Manual option:

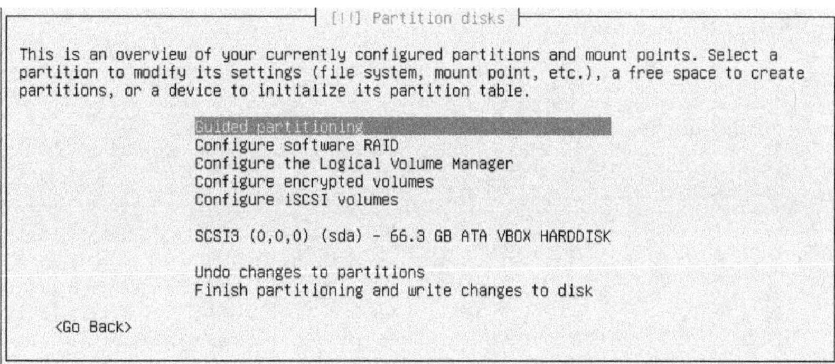

Figure 4-7

Unless you have a specific requirement, select the option to perform a guided LVM installation and follow the steps to confirm the target disk drive and to select the amount of available space to be allocated to the partition. Finally, review the partition configuration summary and select the *Finish partitioning and write changes to disk* menu option as shown in Figure 4-8:

```
[!!] Partition disks

This is an overview of your currently configured partitions and mount points. Select a
partition to modify its settings (file system, mount point, etc.), a free space to create
partitions, or a device to initialize its partition table.

    Guided partitioning
    Configure software RAID
    Configure the Logical Volume Manager
    Configure encrypted volumes
    Configure iSCSI volumes

    LVM VG ubuntu-desktop-vg, LV root - 65.3 GB Linux device-mapper (linear)
         #1           65.3 GB     f  ext4     /
    LVM VG ubuntu-desktop-vg, LV swap_1 - 1.0 GB Linux device-mapper (linear)
         #1            1.0 GB     f  swap     swap
    SCSI3 (0,0,0) (sda) - 66.3 GB ATA VBOX HARDDISK
         #1  primary  66.3 GB     K  lvm

    Undo changes to partitions
    Finish partitioning and write changes to disk

  <Go Back>
```

Figure 4-8

Provide a final confirmation and then wait while the partition is created and the base system installed.

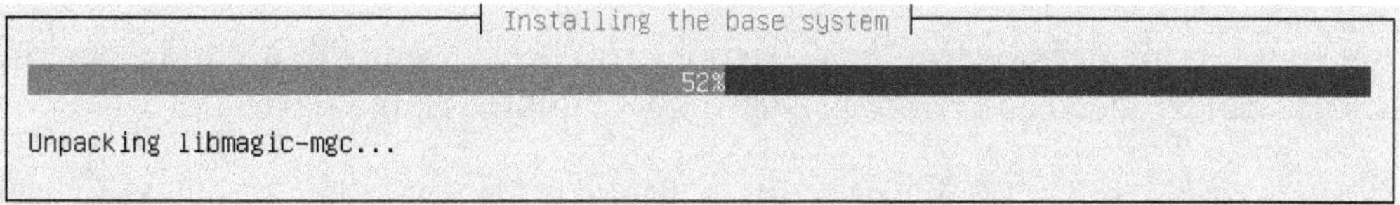

Figure 4-9

On the next screen, select your preferred option for installing updates on the running system. It is generally recommended to have updates installed automatically, though the manual option is also available if you prefer to control when updates are installed. If, on the other hand, you are managing multiple Ubuntu systems using the Landscape web management environment, select the Landscape option from the menu:

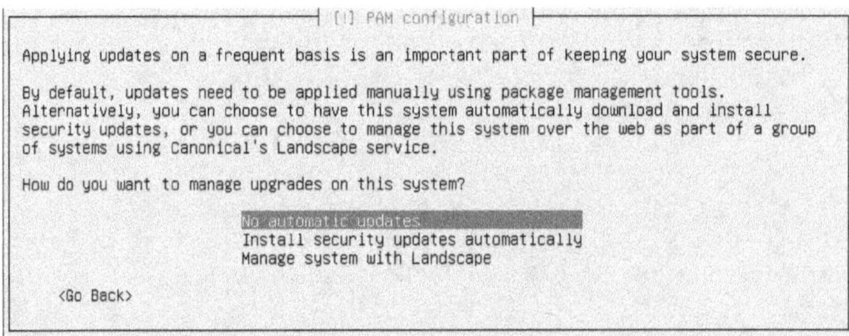

Figure 4-10

4.6 Software Collection Selection

The final step in the network installation is to choose the software collections to be installed. This is performed in the screen shown in Figure 4-11:

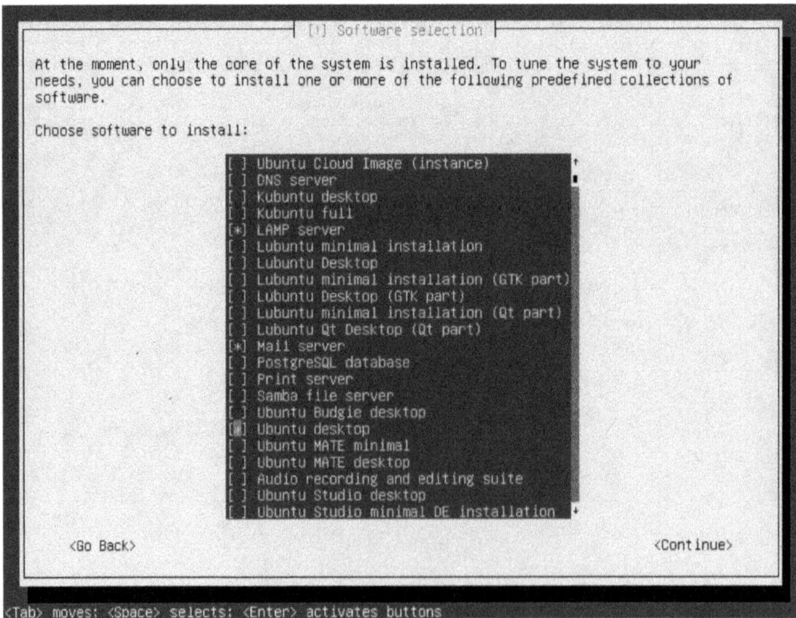

Figure 4-11

Based on your requirements, select the collections you believe you will need (keeping in mind that packages can be added and removed later from within the running system).

Once you have placed asterisks next to all of the items you need, select the Continue option and wait while the selected packages are downloaded and installed. Once the software has been installed, a screen will appear seeking confirmation that the master boot record on the disk can be modified to add the Ubuntu boot options. Finally, the installer will seek confirmation that the system is to use Coordinated Universal Time (UTC). Accept the use of UTC unless the system is dual booting with Windows, in which case this option should not be selected.

Once the installation is complete, remove the installation media, press the Enter key and wait while the system reboots.

4.7 Installing Software Collections After System Setup

Once the system is up and running, any of the software collections listed in the dialog in Figure 4-11 above can be installed manually from within a running Ubuntu system using the *tasksel* tool. This tool can be installed in a terminal window using the following command:

```
# apt install tasksel
```

Once installed, run the command as follows:

```
# tasksel
```

Once tasksel starts, the screen shown in Figure 4-12 will appear from which collections may be selected and installed:

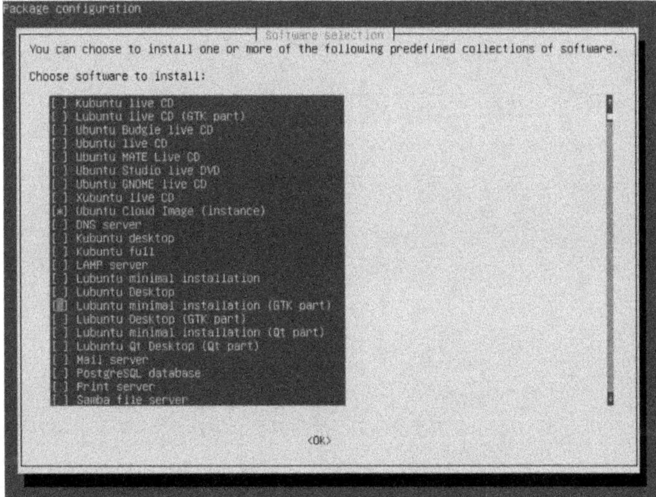

Figure 4-12

4.8 Summary

The Ubuntu Network installation provides a way to install Ubuntu using a relatively small ISO image. This requires that the target system has an active network connection that will be used to install the software packages during the installation process, and limits the installation to being performed in text mode (though the graphical desktop can still be installed). Unlike the desktop and server installation images, the Network installer also allows different software collections to be selected for installation, providing greater control over the installation process and resulting in a more finely configured operating system.

Chapter 5

5. Dual Booting Ubuntu with Windows

Ubuntu, just like most Linux distributions, will happily co-exist on a hard disk drive with just about any version of Windows. This is a concept known as dual-booting. Essentially, when you power up your PC you will be presented with a menu providing the option to boot either Ubuntu or Windows. Obviously you can only run one operating system at a time, but it is worth noting that the files on the Windows partition of your disk drive will be available to you from Ubuntu regardless of whether your Windows partition was formatted using NTFS, FAT16 or FAT32.

During the installation process the Ubuntu installer will detect the Windows installation on the drive and provide the option of deleting it and using the entire disk for Ubuntu, or sharing the disk with Windows. In the latter case you will be able to specify the percentage of the disk to be used for Ubuntu.

According to the Ubuntu documentation, a minimum of 25 GB of disk space is required for a full Ubuntu Desktop Edition installation, and more space to store any files you may subsequently create. Once the disk space for Ubuntu has been selected, the installer will resize the Windows partition (without destroying any data) and use the remainder of the disk for Ubuntu.

This chapter will demonstrate how to set up a dual boot system with Ubuntu and Windows 10, change the system that boots by default when the computer system is powered on, and outline how to access files located on the Windows partition of the disk from within Ubuntu.

Within this chapter the assumption is made that the steps outlined in the previous chapter have been followed to create a bootable Ubuntu installation USB drive using the Ubuntu Desktop installation image and that the system has been configured to boot from the USB drive when started.

5.1 Beginning the Ubuntu Installation

To start the installation, insert the Ubuntu USB drive and reboot your computer system. If the system loads Windows again you will need to change the boot order in your system settings. Details on how to do this will be system specific and were covered briefly in the previous chapter,

Once Ubuntu has loaded you will be presented with the screen shown in Figure 5-1.

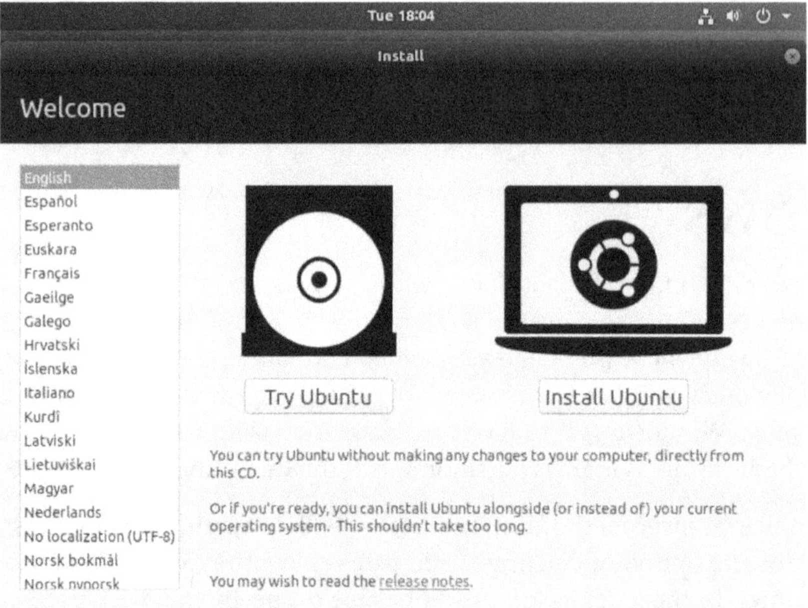

Figure 5-1

Begin the installation by clicking on the Install Ubuntu button and wait for the initial screen of the installer to appear as shown in Figure 5-2:

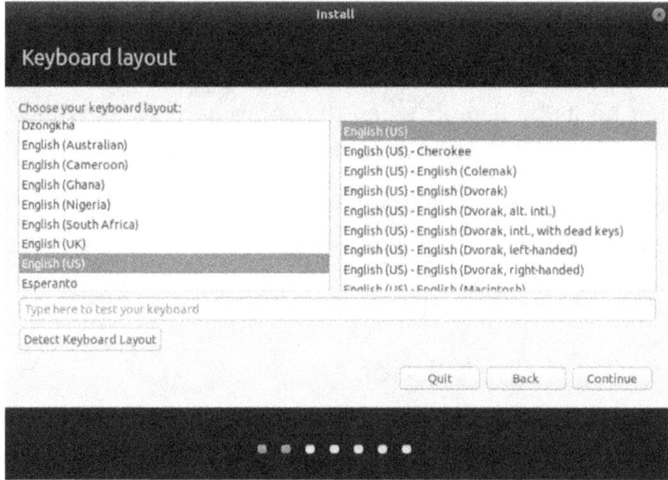

Figure 5-2

Either select your keyboard layout or, if you are unsure, click on the Detect Keyboard Layout button to work through some steps to identify your keyboard before clicking on Continue. On the next screen, choose whether to perform the Normal or Minimal installation:

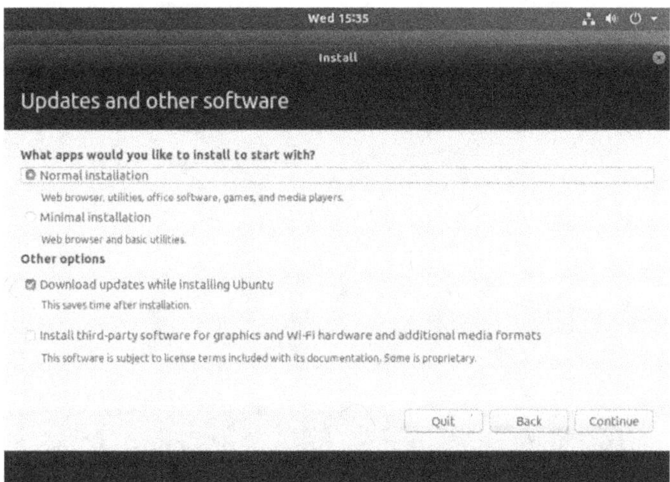

Figure 5-3

Select the Normal option if you have plenty of disk space and want to explore the main applications and utilities included with Ubuntu without having to manually install them later, otherwise use the Minimal option.

The option is also available to update the software packages that comprise the Ubuntu distribution during the installation. Ubuntu, as with most actively supported operating systems, continues to be updated with bug fixes and security patches long after it has been released to the public. If this option is selected and the system is connected to the internet, the installer will download any updates issued since the Ubuntu installation image was released and applies them to the system during installation. If you choose not to perform this update during the installation process these updates may still be applied at any time after the installation completes.

A second option provides the choice of whether to install 3rd party non-open source software to support specific hardware devices and the playback of proprietary media files on the system. Some users object fervently to using any software which is not published under a public license. If you are one of those people then do not select this option. If, on the other hand, you just want the best experience from your Ubuntu installation then this option is recommended.

Having made appropriate selections, click the Continue button to proceed to the disk allocation screen. At this point, the installer will have detected the presence of an existing Windows operating system on the target disk drive and will provide a number of options in terms of how the disk should be used to accommodate the Ubuntu installation:

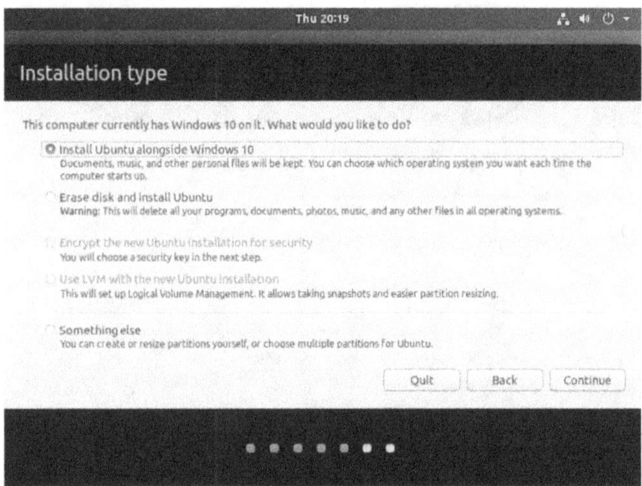

Figure 5-4

Given that it is our intention to configure a dual boot system, the option to Install Ubuntu alongside Windows is the desired choice. With this option selected, click the Continue button to proceed. The subsequent screen allows the amount of disk space allocated to each operating system (in this case Windows and Ubuntu) to be configured:

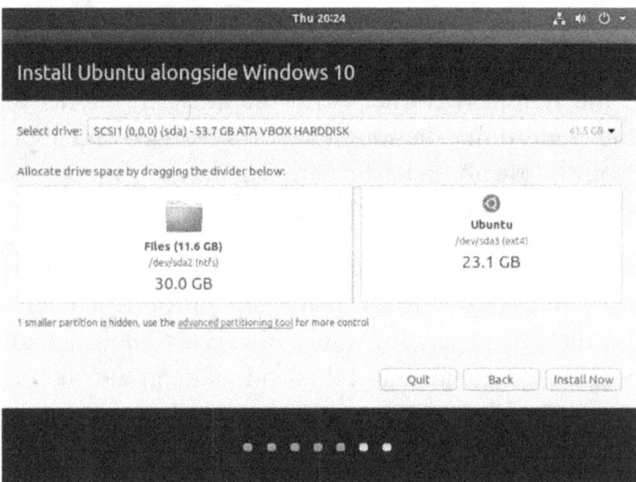

Figure 5-5

At this point it is necessary to decide how much of your Windows partition you wish to donate to the Ubuntu installation. Move the slider (positioned between the Windows and Ubuntu partitions in the diagram) until the Ubuntu partition allocation is a size you are comfortable with. At least 25Gb of space should be made available for a full Ubuntu Desktop installation.

When you have selected the size of the Ubuntu partition, click the Install Now button to proceed with the installation. When the warning dialog appears read it carefully and click Continue if you are sure you wish to proceed.

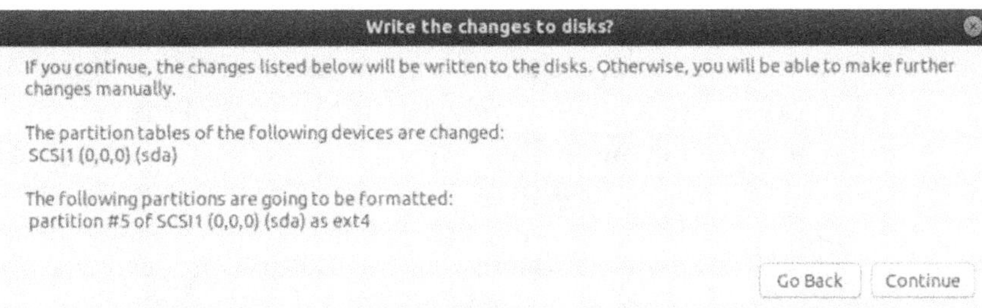

Figure 5-6

While the installation is in progress, the installer will ask for information about your geographical location in order to configure time zone settings:

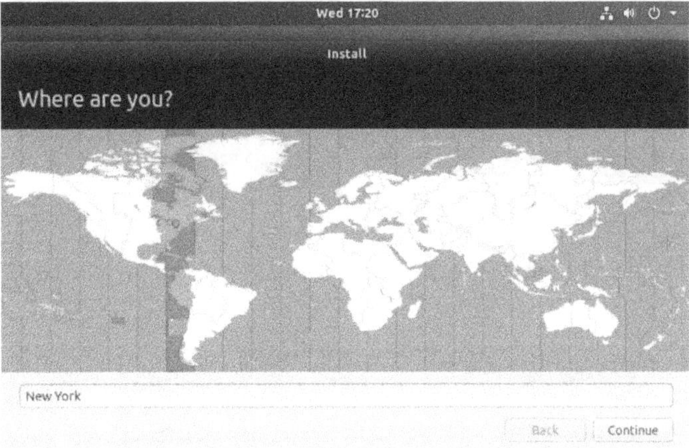

Figure 5-7

Next, the installer will ask you to provide a user name and password for the first account on the system:

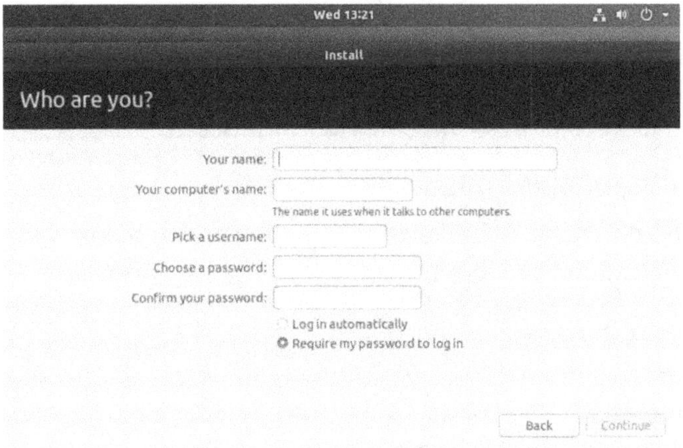

Figure 5-8

The option is also provided to dictate whether the password must be specified each time the user wishes to log into the system. By default, each time Ubuntu starts a login screen will be presented seeking username and password credentials. If you are the sole user of the system and would like to bypass this screen and be logged in automatically each time the system boots, be sure to set the Log in automatically checkbox before proceeding.

Once all the questions have been answered, the installer will simply proceed with the installation. Depending on the speed of your system, and whether or not you opted to download updates during the installation, this process can take some time. For a more detailed view of the steps being performed by the installer, click on the status title located above the progress bar:

▼ Installing system Skip

```
May 31 15:15:38 ubuntu ubiquity: update-initramfs: Generating /boot/initrd.img
-2.6.38-8-generic
```

Figure 5-9

When the installation is complete, a dialog will appear to inform you the system is ready to be restarted:

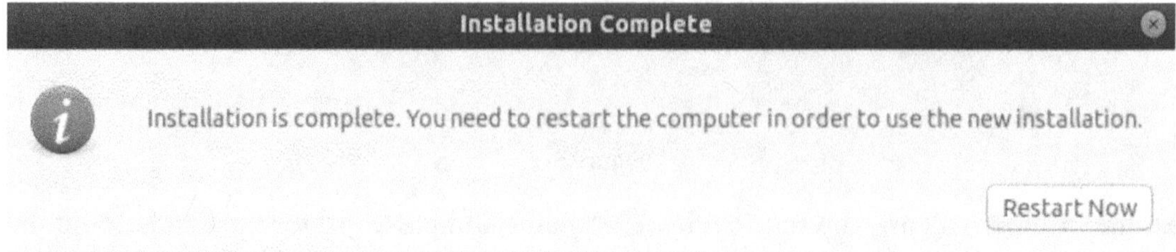
Installation Complete
Installation is complete. You need to restart the computer in order to use the new installation.
Restart Now

Figure 5-10

When you are ready to reboot, press the Restart Now button. The installer may prompt you to remove the installation media and the system will take a few moments to shut down. At this point remove the USB flash drive and press the Enter key to proceed.

5.2 Booting Ubuntu for the First Time

When the system reboots a screen similar to the one illustrated below will appear providing the option to boot either Windows or Ubuntu:

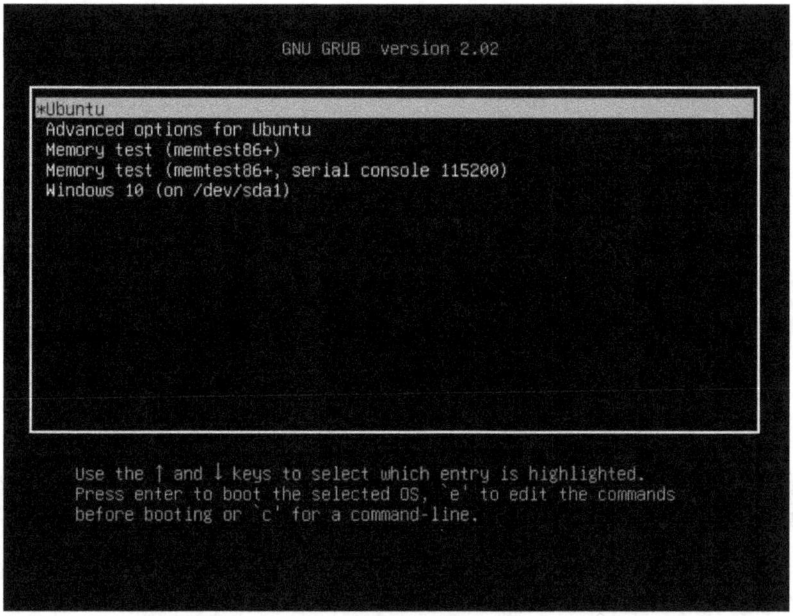

Figure 5-11

Press Enter to boot Ubuntu. If you wish to boot Windows use the keyboard arrow keys to select the Windows option. If you choose to boot Ubuntu the operating system will load and the Ubuntu login screen will appear (unless the automatic login option was selected). Enter the user name and password you set up during the installation process and you will be logged into the Ubuntu Desktop environment.

5.3 Changing the Default Boot Option

When the system starts, the boot options screen will appear and wait 10 seconds for the user to make an operating system choice. If no selection has been made before the timeout elapses, the default operating system will be started. On a newly configured system, the default operating system will be the standard Ubuntu image. This default can, however, be changed from within Ubuntu.

A range of boot configuration options (including the 10 second timeout and the boot settings outlined in "*Installing Ubuntu on a Clean Disk Drive*") are declared in the */etc/default/grub* file which reads as follows on a new installation:

```
GRUB_DEFAULT=0
GRUB_TIMEOUT_STYLE=hidden
GRUB_TIMEOUT=10
GRUB_DISTRIBUTOR=`lsb_release -i -s 2> /dev/null || echo Debian`
GRUB_CMDLINE_LINUX_DEFAULT="quiet splash"
GRUB_CMDLINE_LINUX=""
```

The first step in changing the default boot system is to declare the GRUB_SAVEDEFAULT setting within this file and to change the GRUB_DEFAULT setting to *saved*:

```
GRUB_DEFAULT=saved
GRUB_SAVEDEFAULT=true
GRUB_TIMEOUT_STYLE=hidden
GRUB_TIMEOUT=10
.
.
```

This setting allows a new default value to be saved within the boot configuration. Next, run the *grub-set-default* command to change the default setting using a numbering system that counts the first option as 0. For example, if the Windows 10 option is position 5 in the menu, the command to make Windows 10 the default boot option would read as follows:

```
# grub-set-default 4
```

Check that the new setting has taken effect by running the following command:

```
# grub-editenv list
saved_entry=4
```

Note that the *saved_entry* value is now set to 4. After changing the default, regenerate the boot configuration file as follows:

```
# grub-mkconfig --output=/boot/grub/grub.cfg
```

Reboot the system and verify that the boot menu defaults to the Windows 10 option and that Windows loads after the timeout expires.

5.4 Accessing the Windows Partition from the Command-line

When running Ubuntu in a dual boot configuration it is still possible to access files located on the Windows partition. This can be achieved by manually mounting the partition from the command-line or from the desktop using the Disks (*gnome-disks)* graphical utility.

When working from the command-line, the first step in this process is to create a directory to use as the mount point for our Windows partition. In this example we will create a directory named */mnt/windows*:

```
# mkdir /mnt/windows
```

In order to identify the device name that has been assigned to the Windows partition, use the *fdisk* command as follows:

```
# fdisk -l
.
.
Disk /dev/sda: 50 GiB, 53687091200 bytes, 104857600 sectors
Units: sectors of 1 * 512 = 512 bytes
Sector size (logical/physical): 512 bytes / 512 bytes
I/O size (minimum/optimal): 512 bytes / 512 bytes
Disklabel type: dos
Disk identifier: 0x7ef44412
```

```
Device     Boot    Start       End  Sectors  Size Id Type
/dev/sda1  *        2048   1187839  1185792  579M  7 HPFS/NTFS/exFAT
/dev/sda2        1187840  59770533 58582694   28G  7 HPFS/NTFS/exFAT
/dev/sda3       59770878 104855551 45084674 21.5G  5 Extended
/dev/sda5       59770880 104855551 45084672 21.5G 83 Linux
.
.
```

In the above output, the main Windows partitions can be identified from the NTFS entry in the type column. In the above example output the system contains one physical disk drive referenced by device name. The first is the Windows system partition while the second, much larger, NTFS partition is the Windows boot partition containing the Windows operating system and user data. This partition contains the files we need access to and is represented by */dev/sda2*.

With this knowledge, we need to run the *mount* command (assuming the Windows partition is /dev/sda2) as follows:

```
# mount /dev/sda2 /mnt/windows
```

Check that the mount was successful by listing the contents of the top level directory of the mount point:

```
# ls /mnt/windows
'$Recycle.Bin'             ProgramData              swapfile.sys
'Documents and Settings'  'Program Files'          'System Volume Information'
 pagefile.sys             'Program Files (x86)'     Users
 PerfLogs                  Recovery                 Windows
```

To automate the mount each time the system is booted, simply add the appropriate mount line to the */etc/fstab* file:

```
/dev/sda2 /mnt/windows ntfs defaults 0 0
```

To unmount the Windows file system at any time:

```
# umount /mnt/windows
```

5.5 Accessing the Windows Partition from the Desktop

The first step in mounting a partition using the desktop environment is to launch the disks utility. With the desktop loaded, right-click on the desktop background and select Open Terminal from the resulting menu. Within the terminal window, gain root privileges before launching the Disks utility as follows:

```
# gnome-disks
```

Once the disks tool has launched, a window similar to that shown in Figure 5-12 will appear:

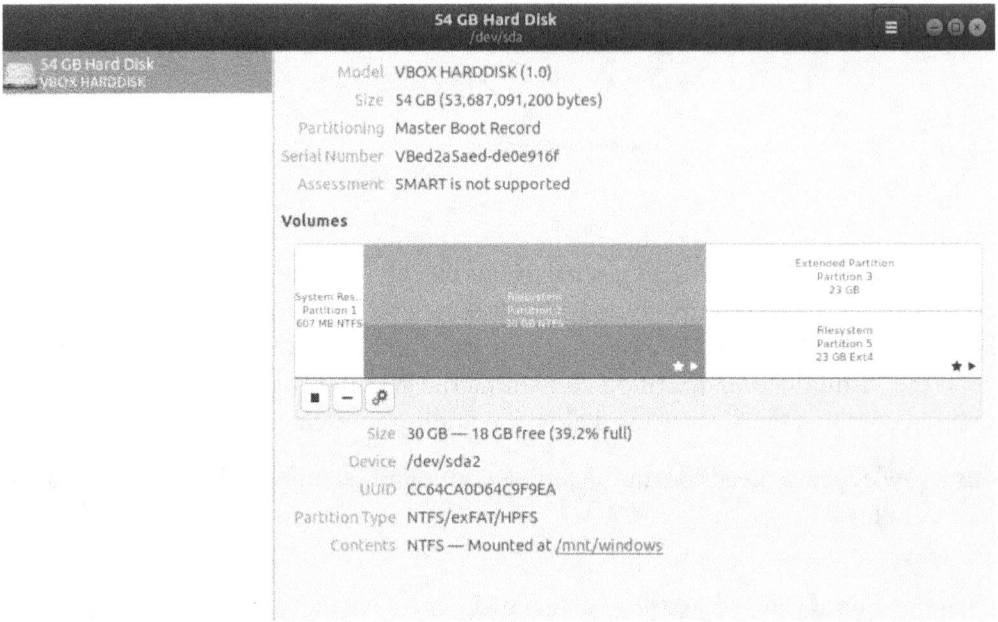

Figure 5-12

To view information about a partition, select it from the graphical representation in the Volumes section of the dialog. In the above example, the Windows system partition is selected and highlighted. To mount the partition so that the contents can be accessed from within Ubuntu, select the partition and click on the options button indicated in Figure 5-13 to display the menu:

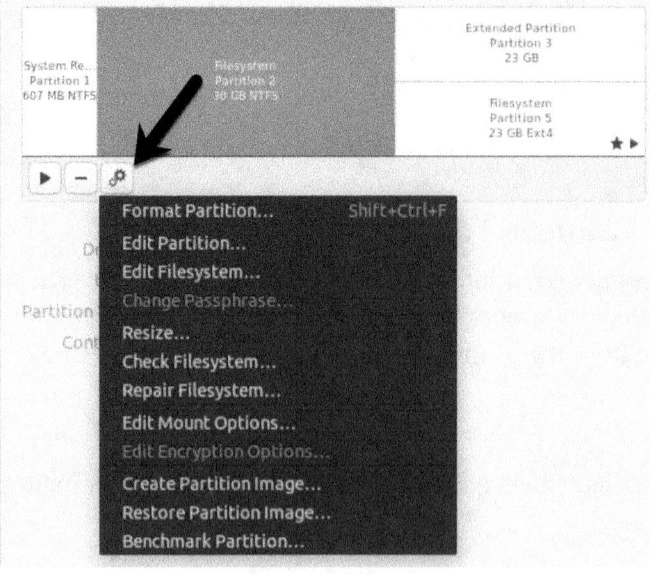

Figure 5-13

From the menu, select *Edit Mount Options...* to display the dialog shown in Figure 5-14. Turn off the User Session Defaults switch and make sure that both the *Mount at system startup* and *Show in user interface* options are enabled. Within the Mount Point text field, change the path to */mnt/windows*. If the partition needs to be automatically mounted each time the system reboots, also enable the *Mount at system startup* option:

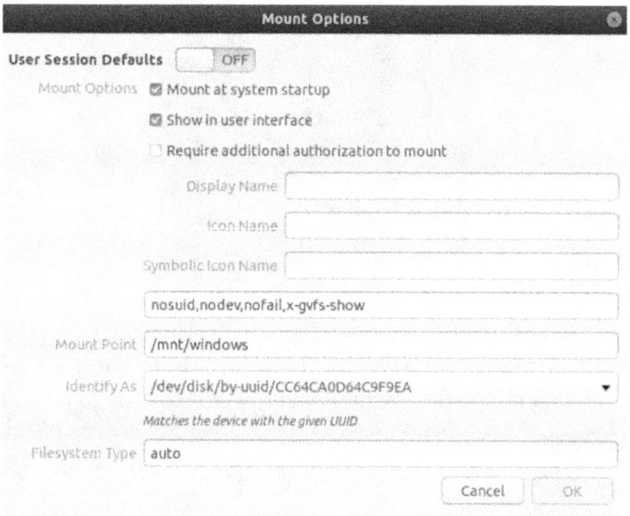

Figure 5-14

With the changes made, click on the OK button to return to the main dialog. To mount the partition, simply click on the mount button highlighted in Figure 5-15 below:

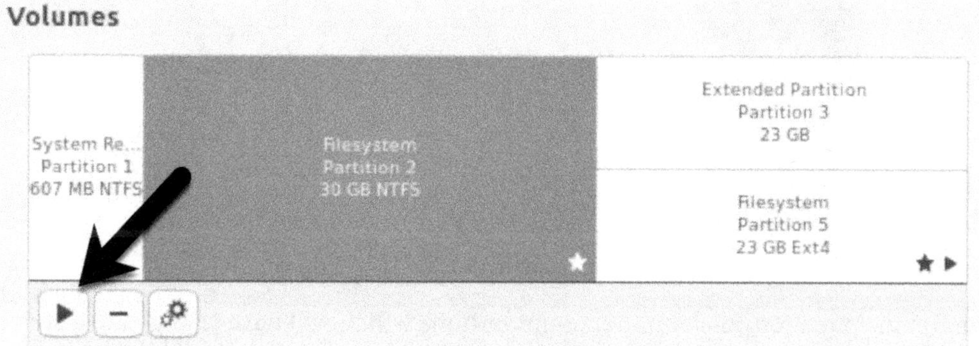

Figure 5-15

Once the partition is mounted, exit from gnome-disks and note that an icon for the volume has appeared in the desktop (note that if the *Show in user interface* option has been disabled this icon would not be present):

Figure 5-16

Double click on the icon to browse the partition using the Files tool:

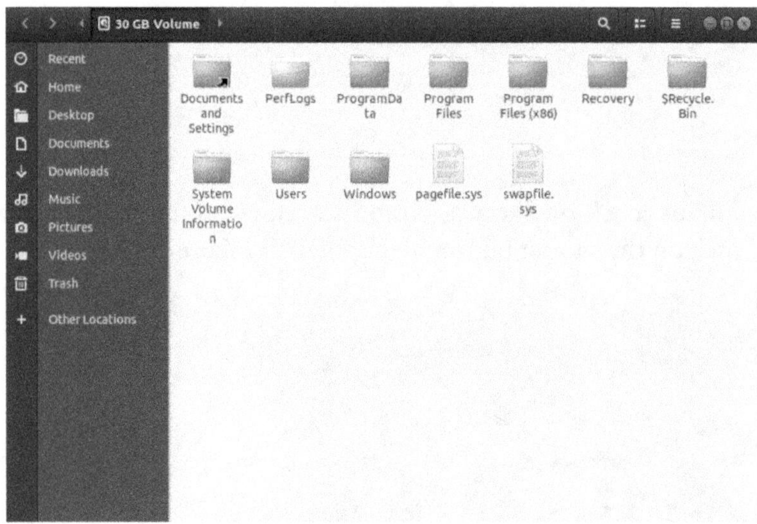

Figure 5-17

To unmount the partition, click on the mount button (which will have changed to a stop button) as shown in Figure 5-15 above.

5.6 Summary

Ubuntu can safely co-exist on the same disk drive as a Windows operating system by creating a dual boot environment. This involves shrinking the amount of space occupied by the Windows system to make room for Ubuntu during the installation. Once Ubuntu has been installed, the boot menu configuration can be modified to change the default operating system. The Windows partition on the disk drive may be accessed from Ubuntu either via the command-line or using the Disks desktop utility.

Chapter 6

6. Allocating Windows Disk Partitions to Ubuntu

In the previous chapter we looked at how to install Ubuntu on the same disk as Windows. This so called "dual boot" configuration allows the user to have both operating systems installed on a single disk drive with the option to boot one or the other when the system is powered on.

This chapter is intended for users who have decided they like Ubuntu enough to delete Windows entirely from the disk, and use the resulting space for Linux. In the following sections we will work through this process step by step.

6.1 Unmounting the Windows Partition

If the steps in the *"Dual Booting Ubuntu with Windows"* chapter were followed to mount the Windows partition from within Ubuntu, steps should be taken to unmount the partition before continuing with this chapter. Assuming that the Windows partition was mounted as */mnt/windows*, it can be unmounted as follows:

```
# umount /mnt/windows
```

The */etc/fstab* file should also be edited to remove the */mnt/windows* auto-mount if it was previously added.

6.2 Deleting the Windows Partitions from the Disk

The first step in freeing up the Windows partition for use by Ubuntu is to delete that partition. Before doing so, however, it is imperative that any data you need to keep is backed up from both the Windows and Ubuntu partitions. Having done that, it is safe to proceed with this chapter.

In order to remove the Windows partitions we first need to identify the disk on which they reside using the *fdisk* tool:

```
# fdisk -l
Disk /dev/loop0: 3.7 MiB, 3862528 bytes, 7544 sectors
Units: sectors of 1 * 512 = 512 bytes
Sector size (logical/physical): 512 bytes / 512 bytes
I/O size (minimum/optimal): 512 bytes / 512 bytes
.
.
Device     Boot    Start       End  Sectors  Size Id Type
/dev/sda1  *        2048   1187839  1185792  579M  7 HPFS/NTFS/exFAT
/dev/sda2        1187840  59770533 58582694   28G  7 HPFS/NTFS/exFAT
/dev/sda3       59770878 104855551 45084674 21.5G  5 Extended
/dev/sda5       59770880 104855551 45084672 21.5G 83 Linux
```

.

.

In the above example output the system contains one physical disk drive referenced by device name */dev/sda*. On that disk drive are five partitions accessed via the device names */dev/sda1* through */dev/sda5* respectively. Based on the values in the System column, there are two NTFS partitions. The first is the Windows system partition while the second, much larger, NTFS partition is the Windows boot partition containing the Windows operating system and user data. On some systems, an additional Windows Recovery partition may be listed and may also be deleted to free up space for Ubuntu. If such a partition exists, it will likely be listed as follows::

```
/dev/sda3        967012352 976771071    9758720    4.7G 27 Hidden NTFS WinRE
```

To remove the partitions, start the *fdisk* tool using the device name of the disk containing the partition (*/dev/sda* in this instance) and follow the instructions to once again display the partition and sector information:

```
# fdisk /dev/sda

Welcome to fdisk (util-linux 2.31.1).
Changes will remain in memory only, until you decide to write them.
Be careful before using the write command.

Command (m for help): p
Disk /dev/sda: 50 GiB, 53687091200 bytes, 104857600 sectors
Units: sectors of 1 * 512 = 512 bytes
Sector size (logical/physical): 512 bytes / 512 bytes
I/O size (minimum/optimal): 512 bytes / 512 bytes
Disklabel type: dos
Disk identifier: 0x7ef44412

Device     Boot     Start       End  Sectors  Size Id Type
/dev/sda1  *         2048   1187839  1185792  579M  7 HPFS/NTFS/exFAT
/dev/sda2         1187840  59770533 58582694   28G  7 HPFS/NTFS/exFAT
/dev/sda3        59770878 104855551 45084674 21.5G  5 Extended
/dev/sda5        59770880 104855551 45084672 21.5G 83 Linux

Command (m for help):
```

Currently, the Windows system partition is listed as being the bootable partition. Since we will be deleting this partition, the Linux boot partition needs to be marked as bootable. In the above configuration, this is represented by */dev/sda3*. Remaining within the *fdisk* tool, make this the bootable partition as follows:

```
Command (m for help): a
Partition number (1,3-5, default 5): 3
The bootable flag on partition 3 is enabled now.
```

Before proceeding, make a note of the start and end addresses of the partitions we will be deleting (in other words the start of */dev/sda1* and the sector before the start of */dev/sda3*).

At the command prompt, delete the Windows partitions (these being partitions 1 and 2 on our example system):

```
Command (m for help): d
Partition number (1-5, default 5): 1

Partition 1 has been deleted.

Command (m for help): d
Partition number (2-5, default 5): 2

Partition 2 has been deleted.
```

Now that we have deleted the Windows partitions we need to create the new partition in the vacated disk space. The partition number must match the number of the partition removed (in this case 1) and is going to be a primary partition. It will also be necessary to enter the Start and End sectors of the partition exactly as reported for the old partition (*fdisk* will typically offer the correct values by default, though it is wise to double check). If you are prompted to remove the NTFS signature, enter Y:

```
Command (m for help): n
Partition type
   p   primary (0 primary, 1 extended, 3 free)
   l   logical (numbered from 5)
Select (default p): p
Partition number (1,2,4, default 1): 1
First sector (2048-104857599, default 2048):
Last sector, +sectors or +size{K,M,G,T,P} (2048-59770877, default 59770877):

Created a new partition 1 of type 'Linux' and of size 28.5 GiB.
Partition #1 contains a ntfs signature.

Do you want to remove the signature? [Y]es/[N]o: Y

The signature will be removed by a write command.
```

Having made these changes the next step is to check that the settings are correct (taking this opportunity to double check that the Linux boot partition is bootable):

```
Command (m for help): p
Disk /dev/sda: 50 GiB, 53687091200 bytes, 104857600 sectors
Units: sectors of 1 * 512 = 512 bytes
Sector size (logical/physical): 512 bytes / 512 bytes
I/O size (minimum/optimal): 512 bytes / 512 bytes
Disklabel type: dos
```

```
Disk identifier: 0x7ef44412

Device     Boot    Start       End  Sectors  Size Id Type
/dev/sda1           2048  59770877 59768830 28.5G 83 Linux
/dev/sda3  *    59770878 104855551 45084674 21.5G  5 Extended
/dev/sda5       59770880 104855551 45084672 21.5G 83 Linux

Filesystem/RAID signature on partition 1 will be wiped.
```

To commit the changes we now need to write the new partition information to disk and quit from the *fdisk* tool:

```
Command (m for help): w
The partition table has been altered.
Syncing disks.
```

6.3 Formatting the Unallocated Disk Partition

In order to make the new partition suitable for use by Ubuntu, it needs to have a file system created on it. The default file system type for the current release of Ubuntu is XFS and will be covered in greater detail in the chapter entitled *"Adding a New Disk Drive to an Ubuntu System"*. Creation of the file system is performed using the *mkfs.xfs* command as follows (installing the xfsprogs package if necessary):

```
# apt install xfsprogs
# mkfs.xfs /dev/sda1
meta-data=/dev/sda1              isize=512    agcount=4, agsize=1867776 blks
         =                       sectsz=512   attr=2, projid32bit=1
         =                       crc=1        finobt=1, sparse=0, rmapbt=0,
reflink=0
data     =                       bsize=4096   blocks=7471103, imaxpct=25
         =                       sunit=0      swidth=0 blks
naming   =version 2              bsize=4096   ascii-ci=0 ftype=1
log      =internal log           bsize=4096   blocks=3647, version=2
         =                       sectsz=512   sunit=0 blks, lazy-count=1
realtime =none                   extsz=4096   blocks=0, rtextents=0
```

6.4 Mounting the New Partition

Next, we need to mount the new partition. In this example we will mount it in a directory named */data*. You are free, however, to mount the new partition using any valid mount point you desire or to use it as part of a logical volume (details of which are covered in the chapter entitled *"Adding a New Disk to an Ubuntu Volume Group and Logical Volume"*). First we need to create the directory to act as the mount point:

```
# mkdir /data
```

Secondly, we need to edit the mount table in */etc/fstab* so that the partition is automatically mounted each time the system starts. At the bottom of the */etc/fstab* file, add the following line to mount the new partition (modifying the */dev/sda1* device to match your environment):

```
/dev/sda1 /data xfs  defaults 0 0
```

Finally, we can manually mount the new partition (note that on subsequent reboots this will not be necessary as the partition will automount as a result of the setting we added to the */etc/fstab* file above).

```
# mount /data
```

To check the partition, run the following command to display the available space:

```
# df -h /data
Filesystem       Size  Used Avail Use% Mounted on
/dev/sda1         29G   62M   29G   1% /data
```

6.5 Editing the Boot Menu

The next step is to modify the Ubuntu boot menu. Since this was originally a dual boot system, the menu is configured to provide the option of booting either Windows or Ubuntu. Now that the Windows partition is gone, we need to remove this boot option. On Ubuntu this can be achieved by running the *update-grub* command as follows:

```
# update-grub
Sourcing file `/etc/default/grub'
Generating grub configuration file ...
Found linux image: /boot/vmlinuz-5.3.0-42-generic
Found initrd image: /boot/initrd.img-5.3.0-42-generic
Found linux image: /boot/vmlinuz-5.3.0-28-generic
Found initrd image: /boot/initrd.img-5.3.0-28-generic
Found memtest86+ image: /boot/memtest86+.elf
Found memtest86+ image: /boot/memtest86+.bin
```

Since there is now only one operating system to boot, the system will automatically boot Ubuntu on the next restart without displaying the boot menu. If you need to access this boot menu, for example to use the advanced boot options, simply press the Esc key during the initial stages of the startup process.

6.6 Using GNOME Disks Utility

The gnome-disks utility provides a user-friendly graphical alternative to reclaiming the Windows partitions from the command-line. Since the example used here will convert the Windows NTFS partitions to XFS format, the first step us to install the xfsprogs package as follows:

```
# apt install xfsprogs
```

Once the package has been installed, open a terminal window and launch the gnome-disks utility:

```
# gnome-disks
```

After a short delay, the gnome-disks tool will appear as shown in Figure 6-1:

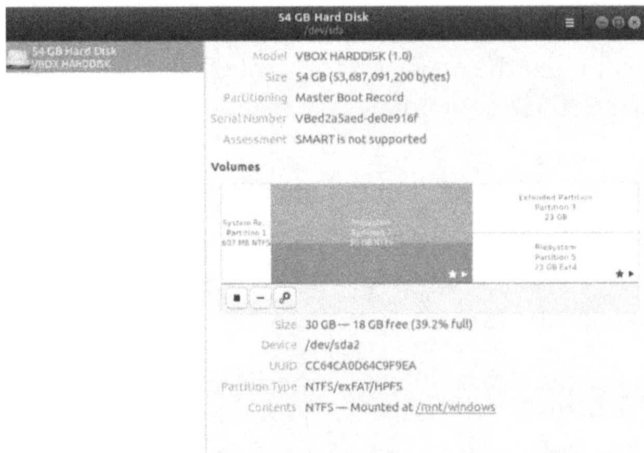

Figure 6-1

In the above example, the disk contains two Windows NTFS partitions which will need to be deleted. Any NTFS partitions with a star shown in the disk map (as is the case for the highlighted partition in the above figure) will need to be unmounted before they can be deleted. This can be achieved by selecting the partition and clicking on the unmount button as indicated in Figure 6-2 below:

Figure 6-2

With all the NTFS partitions unmounted, the next step is to delete them. Select the left-most partition in the disk map and click on the Delete button as shown in Figure 6-3:

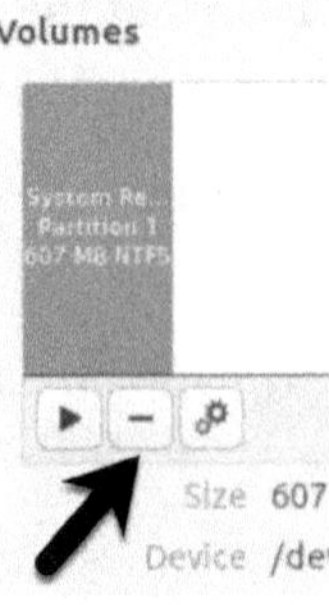

Figure 6-3

Review the information in the confirmation dialog before clicking on the Delete button to commit the change. Once the first partition has been deleted, repeat this step for any remaining NTFS partitions.

Once the NTFS partitions have been removed, the space should now be shown as being free within the disk map.

A new partition now needs to be created to make use of this free space. With the space selected, click on the new partition button (indicated by the arrow in Figure 6-4):

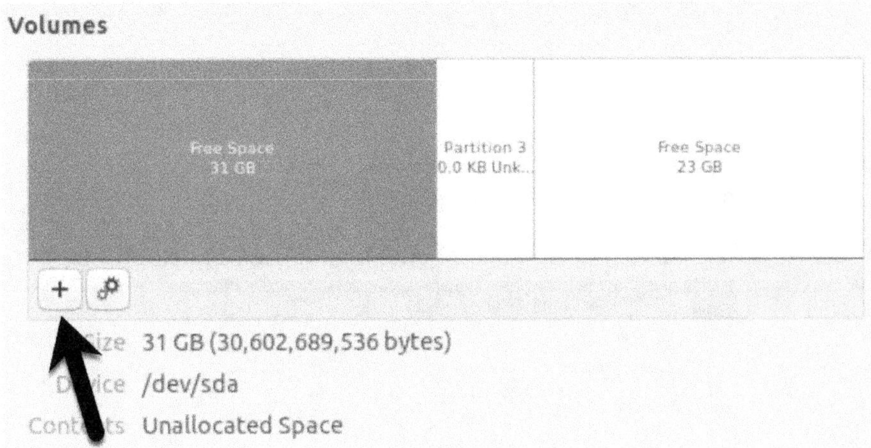

Figure 6-4

In the Create Partition dialog, choose whether the partition is to occupy all of the available space, or reduce the size if you plan to use the space for more than one partition:

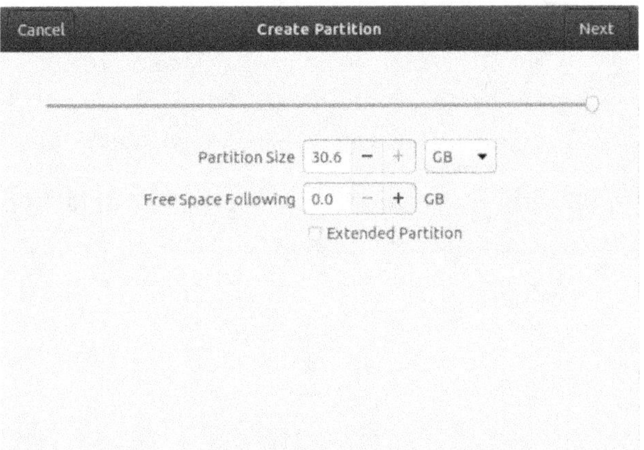

Figure 6-5

Click next and, on the subsequent screen, enter a name for the new partition and choose whether the partition should be erased during creation. This causes the creation process to take more time but is a recommended option. Finally, choose a filesystem type for the partition. This will typically be either ext4 or XFS. Given the benefits of XFS, select Other before clicking the Next button.

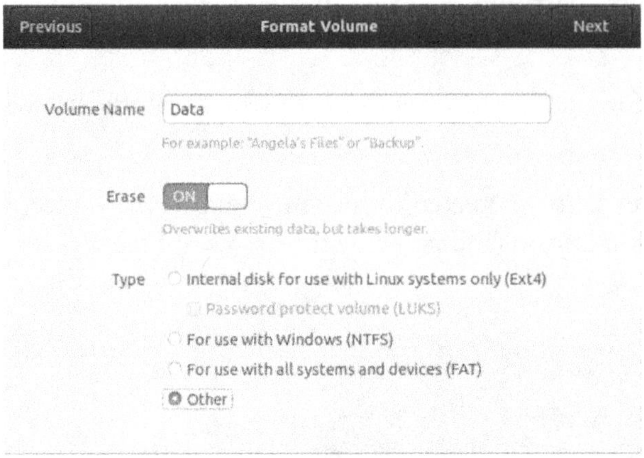

Previous Format Volume Next

Volume Name Data

For example: "Angela's Files" or "Backup".

Erase ON

Overwrites existing data, but takes longer.

Type Internal disk for use with Linux systems only (Ext4)

Password protect volume (LUKS)

For use with Windows (NTFS)

For use with all systems and devices (FAT)

Other

Figure 6-6

On the next screen, select the XFS option before clicking on the Create button:

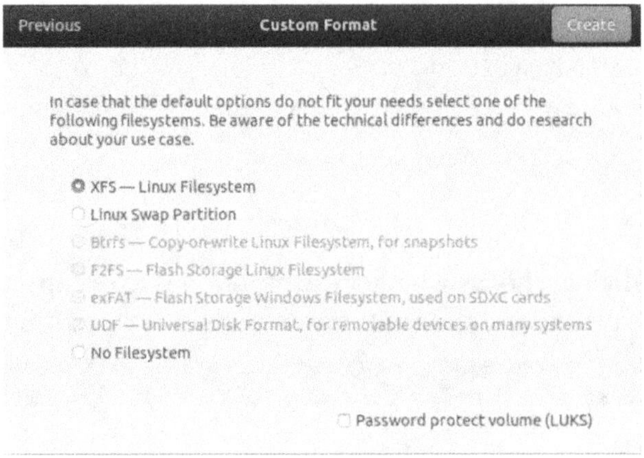

Previous Custom Format Create

In case that the default options do not fit your needs select one of the following filesystems. Be aware of the technical differences and do research about your use case.

XFS — Linux Filesystem

Linux Swap Partition

Btrfs — Copy-on-write Linux Filesystem, for snapshots

F2FS — Flash Storage Linux Filesystem

exFAT — Flash Storage Windows Filesystem, used on SDXC cards

UDF — Universal Disk Format, for removable devices on many systems

No Filesystem

Password protect volume (LUKS)

Figure 6-7

The gnome-disks utility will begin the formatting process and display the status of the process:

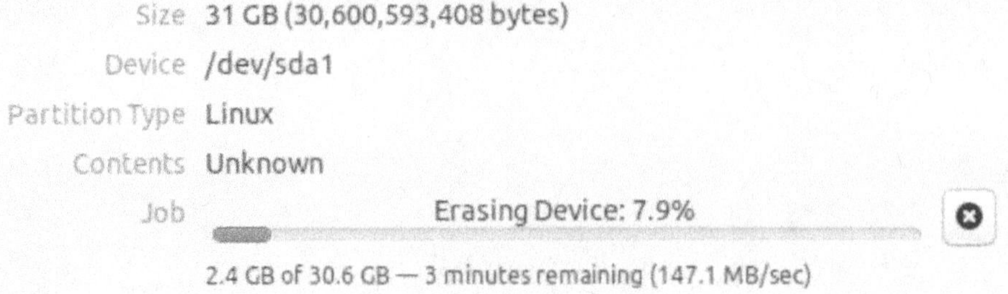

Figure 6-8

Once the partition is ready, it can be mounted either from the command-line or using the gnome-disks utility. To configure a mount point, select the partition and click on the settings button as shown in Figure 6-9:

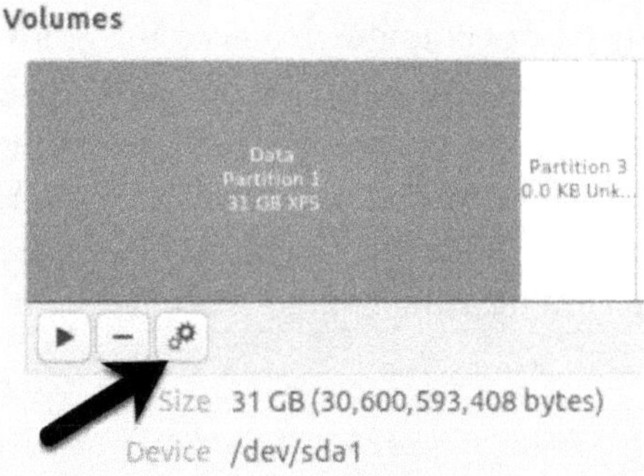

Figure 6-9

From the settings menu, select the *Edit Mount Options...* item to display the dialog shown in Figure 6-10.

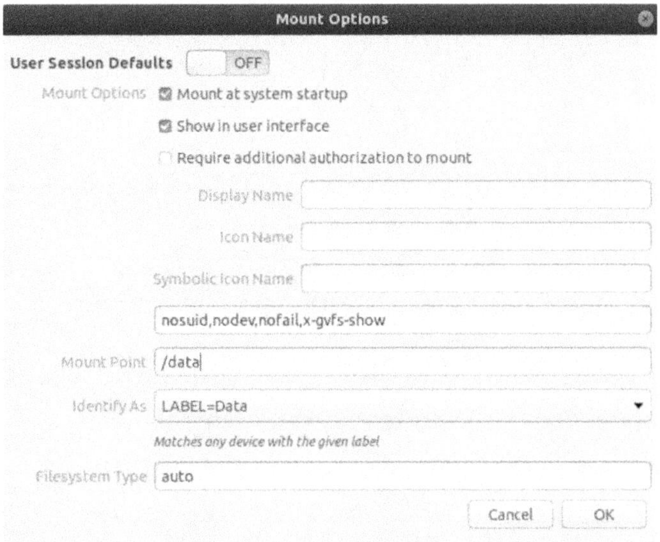

Figure 6-10

Turn off the User Session Defaults switch and configure the mount point to your requirements. In the above figure, the partition is mounted at */data* at system startup and is configured to be identified by the label "Data".

Once the settings are complete, click on OK. The volume is now mounted and ready for use:

```
$ df -h /mnt/Data
Filesystem       Size  Used Avail Use% Mounted on
/dev/sda1         29G   62M   29G   1% /data
```

Finally, update the boot menu to remove the Windows option using the steps outlined in section

6.5 above.

6.7 Summary

The Windows partitions in a dual boot configuration can be removed at any time to free up space for a Ubuntu system by identifying which partitions belong to Windows and then deleting them. Once deleted, the unallocated space can be used to create a new filesystem and mounted to make it available to the Ubuntu system. The final task is to remove the Windows option from the boot menu configuration. These tasks can be performed either from the command-line using *fdisk*, or from within the desktop environment using *gnome-disks*.

Chapter 7

7. A Guided Tour of the GNOME 3 Desktop

Ubuntu 18.04 includes the GNOME 3 desktop environment. Although lacking the complexity of Windows and macOS desktops, GNOME 3 provides an uncluttered and intuitive desktop environment that provides all of the essential features of a windowing environment with the added advantage that it can be learned quickly.

In this chapter, the main features of the GNOME desktop will be covered together with an outline of how basic tasks are performed.

7.1 Installing the GNOME Desktop

If the Ubuntu Desktop image was used for the Ubuntu 18.04 installation process, the GNOME desktop will already be installed and will automatically launch each time the system starts.

If any other software configuration was selected during the Ubuntu 18.04 installation process, the GNOME desktop will not have been included in the packages installed on the system. On server-based systems without a display attached, the idea of installing a graphical desktop environment may seem redundant. It is worth noting, however, that remote access to the GNOME desktop is also possible so, even on so called *headless servers* (i.e. servers lacking a monitor, keyboard and mouse) it may still be beneficial to install the GNOME desktop packages. The topic of establishing remote desktop access will be covered in detail in the *"Ubuntu Remote Desktop Access with Vino"* chapter of this book.

If the installation configuration did not include the GNOME desktop, it may be installed at any time using the following command:

```
# apt install tasksel
# tasksel install ubuntu-desktop
```

Once the installation is complete, the desktop login screen will appear next time the system restarts.

7.2 An Overview of the GNOME 3 Desktop

The screen shown in Figure 7-1 below shows the appearance of a typical, newly launched GNOME desktop session before any other programs have been launched or configuration changes made.

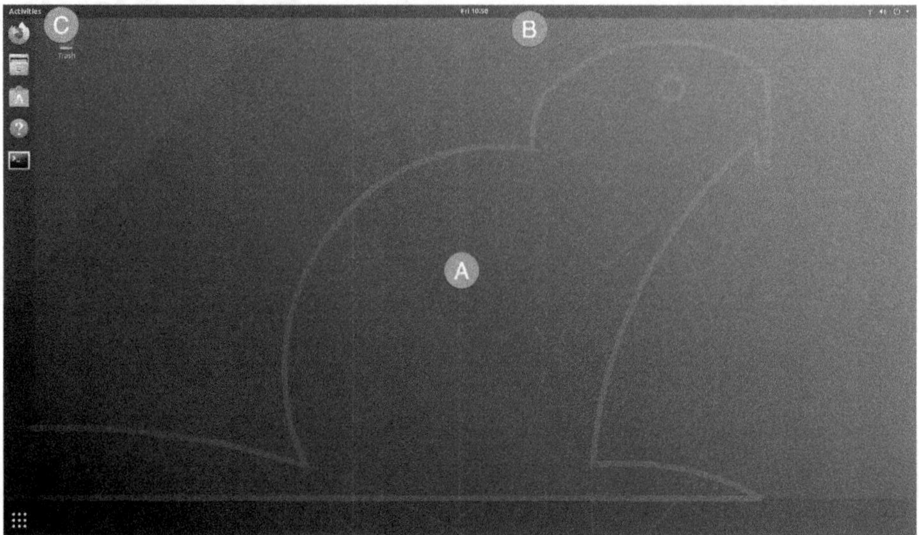

Figure 7-1

The main desktop area (marked A) is where windows will appear when applications and utilities are launched.

The bar at the top of the screen (B) is called the *top bar* and includes the Activities menu (C), the day and time and a collection of buttons and icons including network status, audio volume, battery power and other status and account settings. The application menu for the currently active application running on the desktop will also appear in the top bar. Figure 7-2, for example, shows the application menu for the Terminal program:

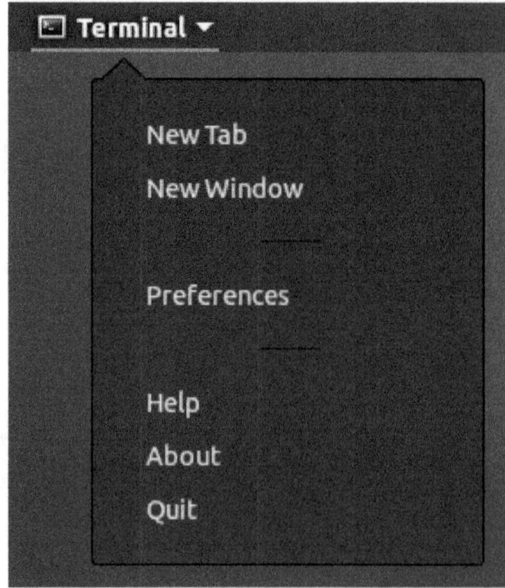

Figure 7-2

7.3 Launching Activities

Applications and utilities are launched using the Activities overview dashboard (referred to as the *dash)* which may be displayed either by clicking on the Activities button in the top bar or pressing the *special key* on the keyboard. On Windows keyboards this is the Windows key, on macOS the Command key and on Chromebooks the key displaying a magnifying glass.

When displayed, the dash will appear as shown in Figure 7-3 below:

Figure 7-3

By default the dash will display an icon for a predefined set of commonly used applications and will also include an icon for any applications that are currently running. If the application is currently running it will appear with a dot marker to the left of the icon and if multiple copies are running a dot will appear for each instance.

To launch an application, simply click on the icon in the dash.

To find an application not included on the dash, one option is to select the bottom most icon (the square comprising nine dots) to display a browsable list of applications as shown in Figure 7-4:

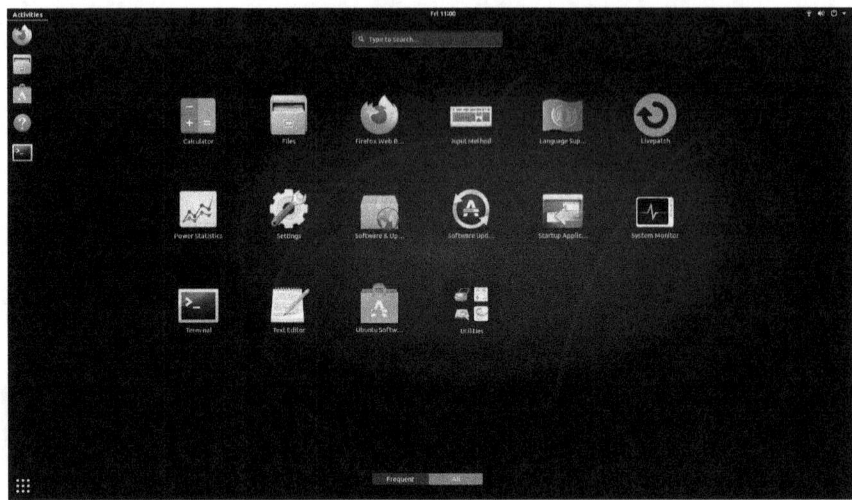

Figure 7-4

Note that the list can be filtered to display all applications or only those used frequently by selecting the buttons at the bottom center of the screen. It is also important to be aware that some entries in the list are actually folders holding addtional applications. In the above screenshot, for example, the *Utilities* entry provides access to a collection of other tools such as the system monitor and disk management tools and the Terminal window application.

An alternative to browsing the applications is to perform a search using the search bar which appears when the dash is displayed as shown in Figure 7-5:

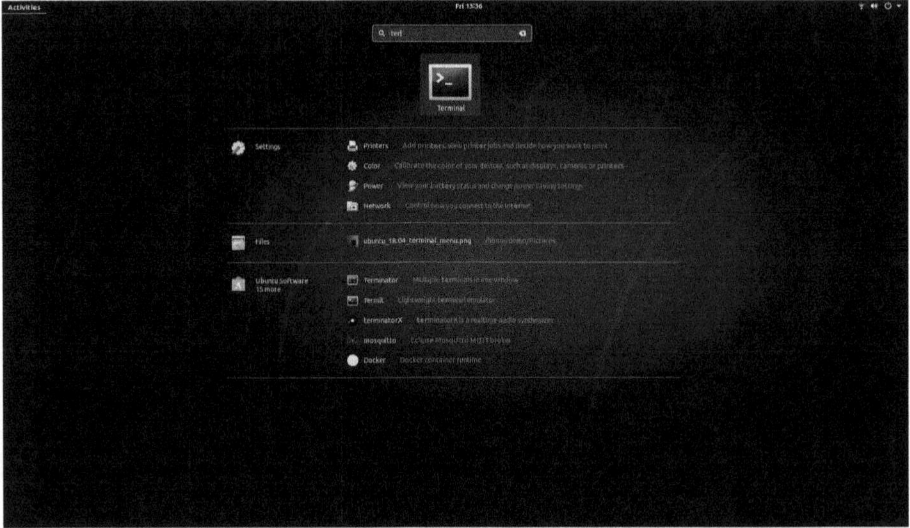

Figure 7-5

As text is typed into the search box, the list of possible matches will be refined.

To add an application to the dash for more convenient access, locate the icon for the application, right-click on it and select the *Add to Favorites* menu option:

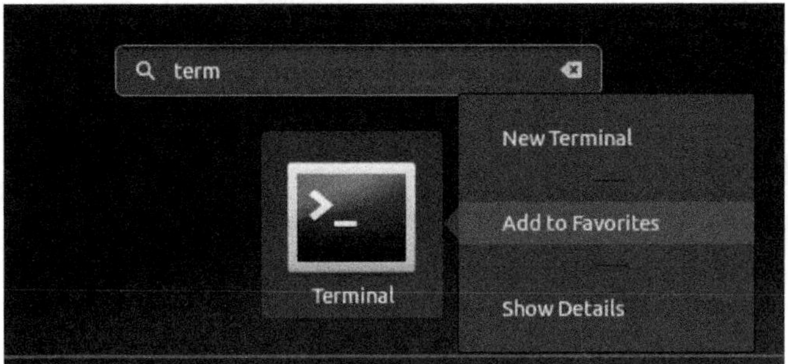

Figure 7-6

To remove an app from the dash, right-click on the icon in the dash and select *Remove from Favorites.*

7.4 Managing Windows

As with other desktop environments, applications run on GNOME in windows. When multiple application windows are open, the Super + Tab keyboard shortcut will display the switcher panel (Figure 7-7) allowing a different window to be chosen as the currently active window (the Super key is either the Windows key or, in the case of a Mac keyboard, the Cmd key):

Figure 7-7

If a single application has more than one window open, the switcher will display those windows in a second panel so that a specific window can be selected:

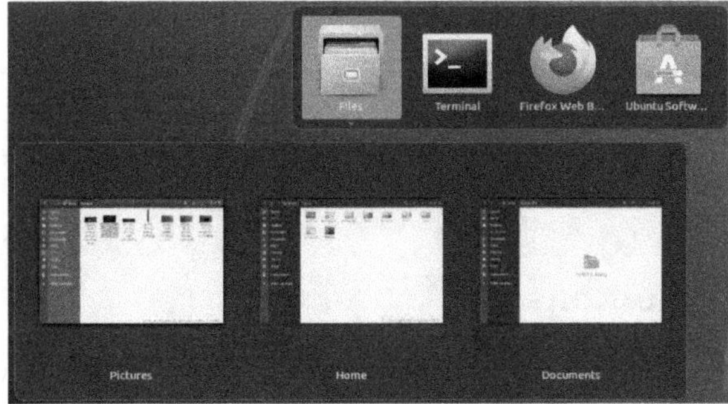

Figure 7-8

To cycle backwards through the icons in the switcher, use the Shift + Tab keyboard shortcut.

To maximize a window so that it fills the entire screen click the title bar and drag the window to the top of the screen. To return the window to its original size, click on the title bar and drag downwards. Alternatively, simply double-click on the title bar to toggle between window sizes. Similarly, dragging a window to the left or right side of the screen will cause the window to fill that half of the screen.

7.5 Using Workspaces

The area of the screen where the application windows appear is referred to as the *workspace* and GNOME 3 allows multiple workspaces to be configured. To create a new workspace, display the Activities overview and move the mouse pointer to the far right of the screen to display the work spaces panel:

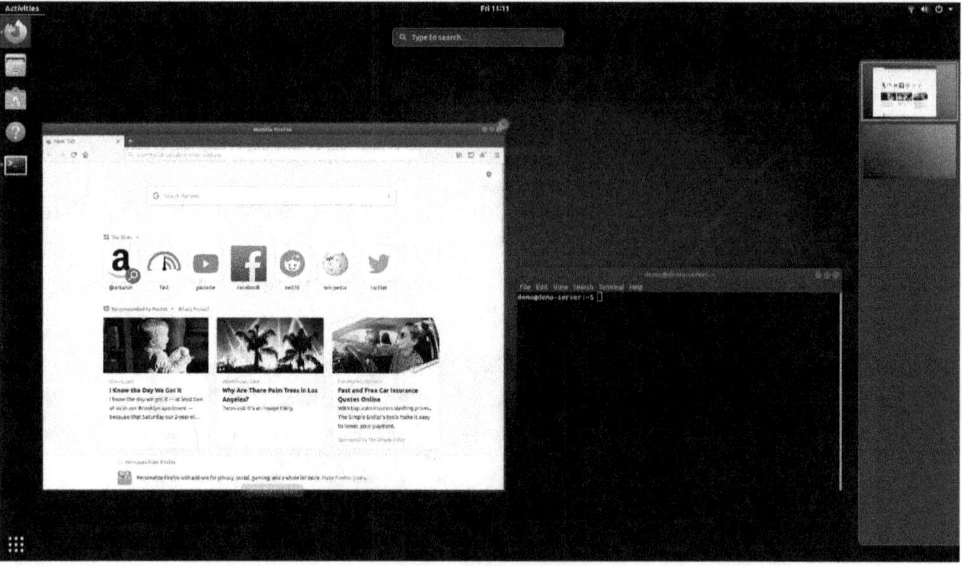

Figure 7-9

To switch to a different panel, simply select it from the list. To move a window from one workspace to another, display the workspaces panel and drag and drop the application window (either the actual window from the current workspace or the thumbnail window in the workspaces panel) onto the destination workspace. When a window is added to a blank workspace, another blank workspace is added to the workspace panel, allowing multiple workspaces to be created.

To remove a workspace either close all the windows on that workspace, or move them to another workspace.

7.6 Calendar and Notifications

When the system needs to notify you of an event (such as the availability of system or application updates), a popup panel will appear at the top of the workspace. Access to the calendar and any previous notifications is available by clicking on the day and time in the top bar as shown in

Figure 7-10:

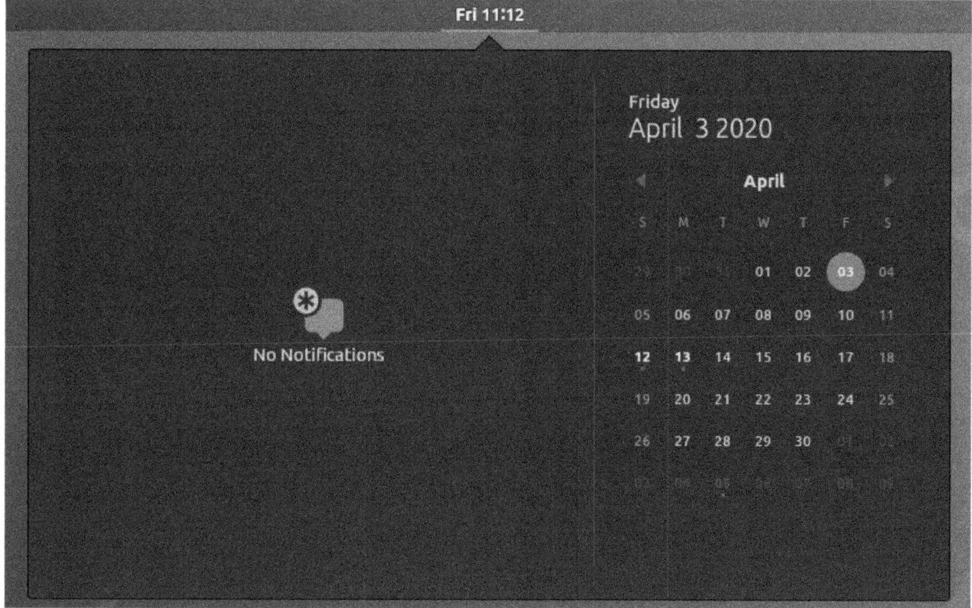

Figure 7-10

7.7 Desktop Settings

To access the Settings application, click on the down arrow on the far right of the top bar and select the button with the tools icon as highlighted in Figure 7-11:

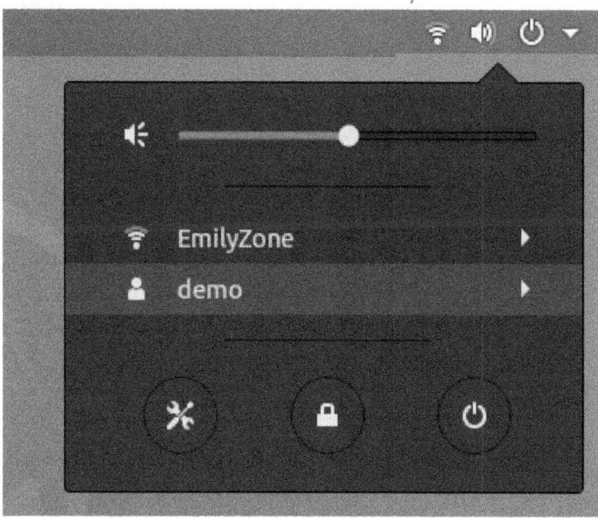

Figure 7-11

The Settings application provides a wide range of options such as Ethernet and WiFi connections, screen background customization options, screen locking and power management controls and language preferences. To explore the settings available in each category, simply select an option from the left-hand panel in the Settings window:

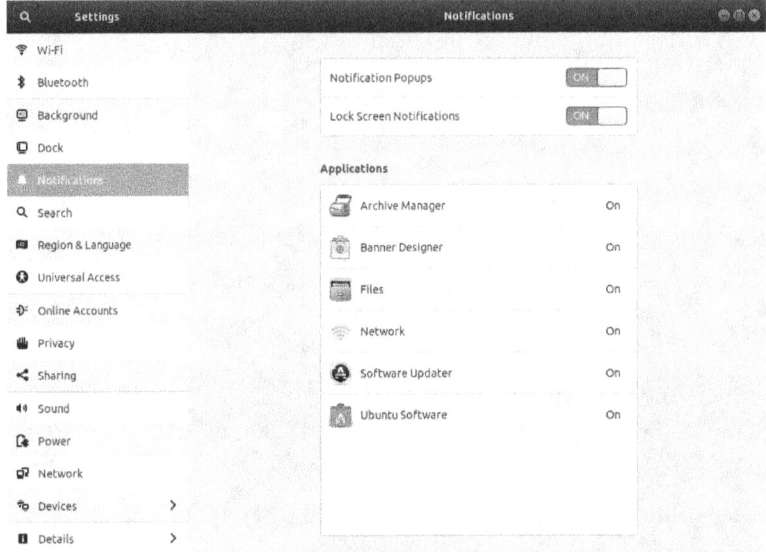

Figure 7-12

The menu shown in Figure 7-11 above also includes options to switch user, adjust audio volume, change to a different WiFi network and to log out, restart or power off the system.

7.8 Customizing the Dash

The size, position and behavior of the dash (also referred to as the dock) may be changed from within the Settings app by selecting the Dock option as shown in Figure 7-13:

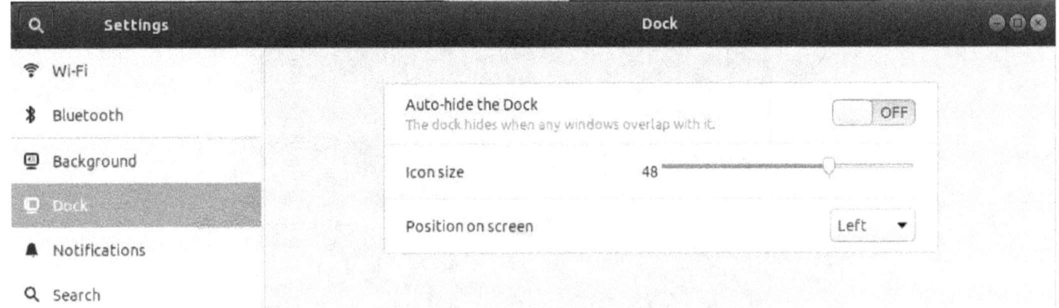

Figure 7-13

The position can be set to any of the four sides of the screen while the Icon size can be used to reduce the size of the dock. Finally, the auto-hide dock option, if enabled, will cause the dock to recede from view until the mouse pointer moves to the edge of the screen where it is currently located.

7.9 Installing Ubuntu Software

In common with other operating systems such as macOS, Windows, iOS and Android, Ubuntu has an "app store" in the form of the Ubuntu Software tool. An icon is usually placed in the dash as indicated in Figure 7-14:

Figure 7-14

Once loaded, the tool provides a list of applications available for installation on the system grouped together based on categories, recommendations and editor's picks. The library of available applications may also be search to find a specific item:

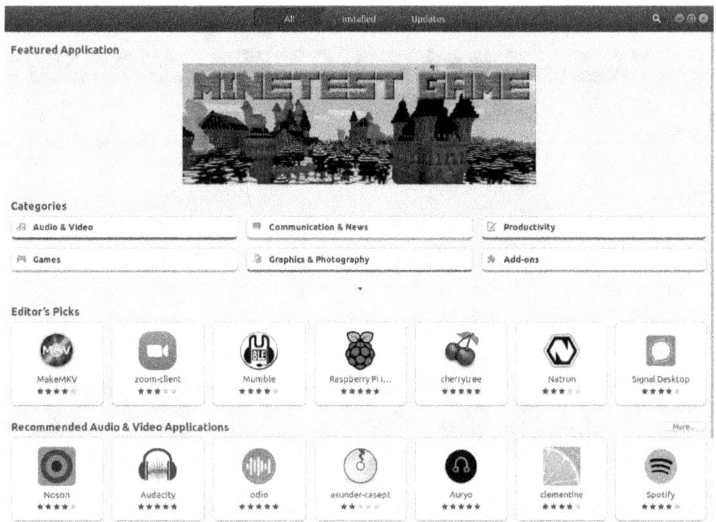

Figure 7-15

To install an application, simply select it in the Ubuntu Software window and click on the *Install* button:

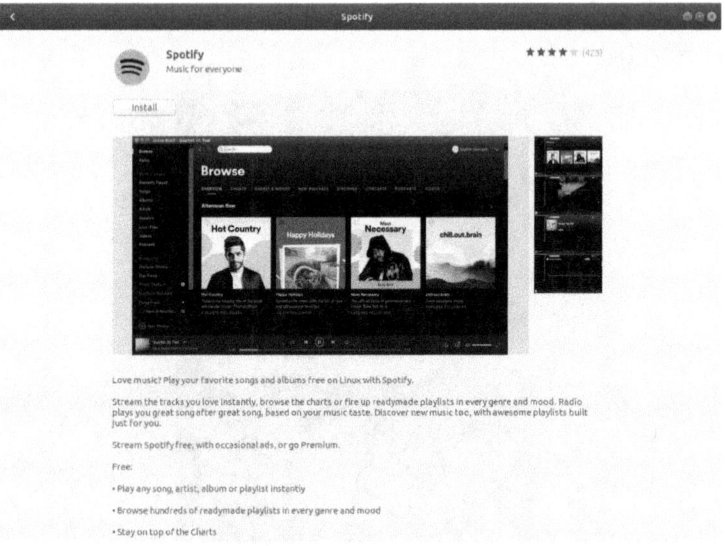

Figure 7-16

7.10 Beyond Basic Customization

The GNOME 3 desktop is, by design, a clean and uncluttered environment with minimal customization options. That does not mean, however, that it is not possible to make additional changes to the desktop. In fact, the GNOME Project has developed a tool called GNOME Tweaks for this very purpose. To install this tool, open the Ubuntu Software tool, search for and install the GNOME Tweaks application. Once installed, click on the Launch button to open the Tweaks interface:

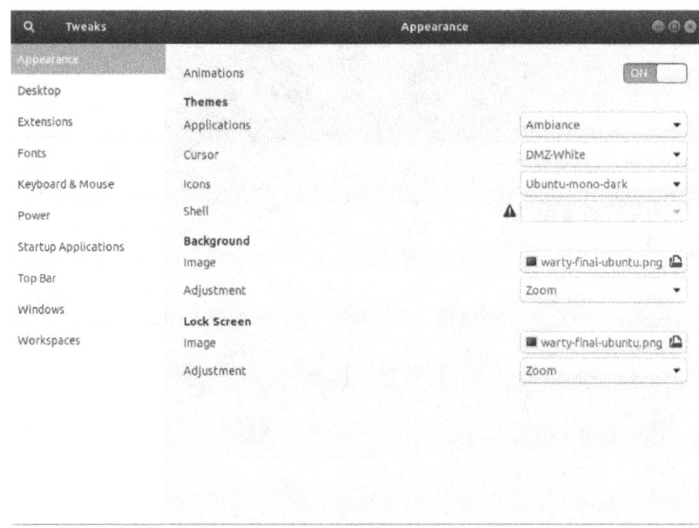

Figure 7-17

A wide range of options for customizing the desktop are now available. Too many, in fact, to cover in this chapter so take some time to experiment with these settings before proceeding to the next chapter.

7.11 Summary

Ubuntu includes the GNOME 3 desktop environment which may either be included during the initial installation or installed later using the *tasksel* command-line tool. Unlike most other desktop environments, GNOME 3 is intended to provide a clean and easy to use windowing user interface. Key areas of the GNOME 3 desktop include the top bar, Activities overview and dash. In addition, GNOME 3 supports multiple workspaces keeping running applications organized and the screen uncluttered. A variety of configuration options is also available within the Settings app including desktop background settings, audio, network configuration and WiFi network selection.

Chapter 8

8. An Overview of the Ubuntu Cockpit Web Interface

Although it comes equipped with the latest in Linux desktop environments, Ubuntu is very much a server operating system and, as such, the majority of Ubuntu deployments will either be to remote physical servers or as cloud-based virtual machine instances. Invariably, these systems run without a keyboard, mouse or monitor, with direct access only available via the command-prompt over a network connection. This presents a challenge in terms of administering the system from remote locations. While much can certainly be achieved via remote access to the command-line and desktop environments, this is far from a consistent and cohesive solution to the administrative and monitoring tasks that need to be performed on a daily basis on an enterprise level operating system such as Ubuntu.

This issue has been addressed with the introduction of the Cockpit web-based administration interface. This chapter will explain how to install, configure and access the Cockpit interface while also providing an overview of the key features of Cockpit, many of which will be covered in greater detail in later chapters.

8.1 An Overview of Cockpit

Cockpit is a light-weight, web-based interface that allows general system administrative tasks to be performed remotely. When installed and configured, the system administrator simply opens a local browser window and navigates to the Cockpit port on the remote server. After loading the Cockpit interface into the browser and logging in, a wide range of tasks can be performed visually using administration and monitoring tools.

Behind the scenes, Cockpit uses the same tools to perform tasks as would normally be used when working at the command-line, and updates automatically to reflect changes occurring elsewhere on the system. This allows Cockpit to be used in conjunction with other administration tools and techniques without the risk of one approach overriding another. Cockpit can also be configured to access more than one server, allowing multiple servers to be administered and monitored simultaneously through a single browser session.

Cockpit is installed by default with a wide range of tools already bundled. Cockpit also, however, allows additional extension plugins to be installed as needed. Cockpit is also designed so that you can create your own extensions using a combination of HTML and JavaScript to add missing or custom functionality.

Cockpit's modular design also allows many features to be embedded into other web-based applications.

8.2 Installing and Enabling Cockpit

Cockpit is generally not installed on Ubuntu by default, but can be set up and enabled in a few simple steps. The first step is to install the Cockpit package as follows:

```
# apt install cockpit
```

Next, the Cockpit socket service needs to be enabled:

```
# systemctl enable --now cockpit.socket
```

Finally, the necessary ports need to be opened on the firewall to allow remote browser connections to reach Cockpit if a firewall is enabled on your system (for details on firewalls, refer to the chapter entitled *"Ubuntu Firewall Basics"*).

If ufw is enabled:

```
# ufw allow 9090
```

If firewalld is enabled:

```
# firewall-cmd --add-service=cockpit --permanent
# firewall-cmd --reload
```

8.3 Accessing Cockpit

If you have access to the desktop environment of the server on which Cockpit has been installed, open a browser window and navigate to *https://localhost:9090* to access the Cockpit sign in screen. If, on the other hand, the server is remote, simply navigate to the server using the domain name or IP address (for example *https://myserver.com*:9090).

When the connection is established, the browser may issue a warning that the connection is not secure. This is because the Cockpit service is using a self-signed certificate. Either select the option to proceed to the web site or, to avoid this message in the future, select the advanced option and add an exception for the server address.

Once connected, the browser will load the log in page shown in Figure 8-1 below:

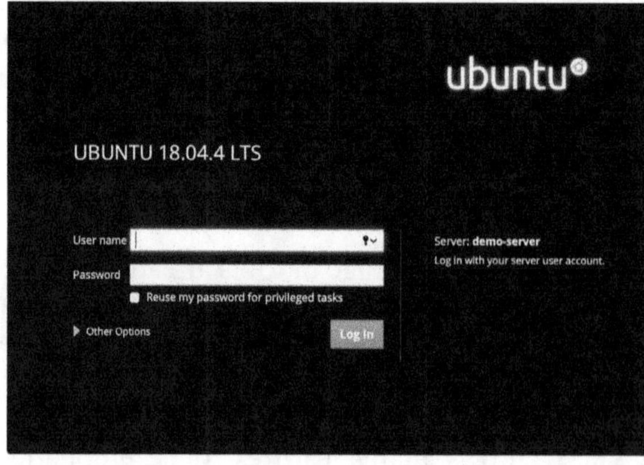

Figure 8-1

Sign in to the Cockpit interface either as root or with your a user account credentials. Note that when signed in as a user some tasks will be restricted within the Cockpit interface due to permission constraints unless you enable the *Reuse my password for privileged tasks option* prior to signing in. After signing in, Cockpit will display the System screen.

8.4 System

The System screen provides an overview of the current system including realtime performance metrics for CPU, memory, disk I/O and network usage. This screen also includes information about the system including the underlying hardware, host name, system time and whether the system software is up to date. Options are also provided to restart or shutdown the system.

Figure 8-2, for example, shows the system monitoring page of the Cockpit interface:

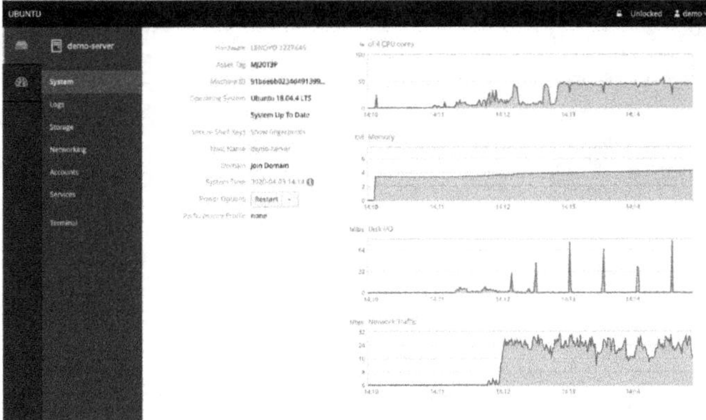

Figure 8-2

8.5 Logs

When the Logs category is selected, Cockpit displays the contents of the *systemd* journal logs. Selecting a log entry will display the entire log message. The log entries are ordered with the most recent at the top and menus are included to filter the logs for different time durations and based on message severity.

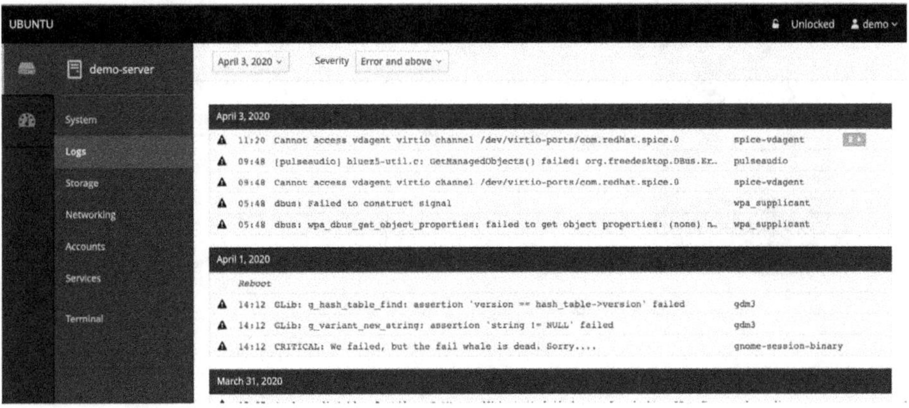

Figure 8-3

8.6 Storage

Select the Storage option to review and manage the storage on the system including disks, partitions and volume groups, Network File System (NFS) mounts and RAID storage. This screen also allows disk I/O activity to be monitored in realtime and lists log output from the system *udisksd* service used to query and manage storage devices.

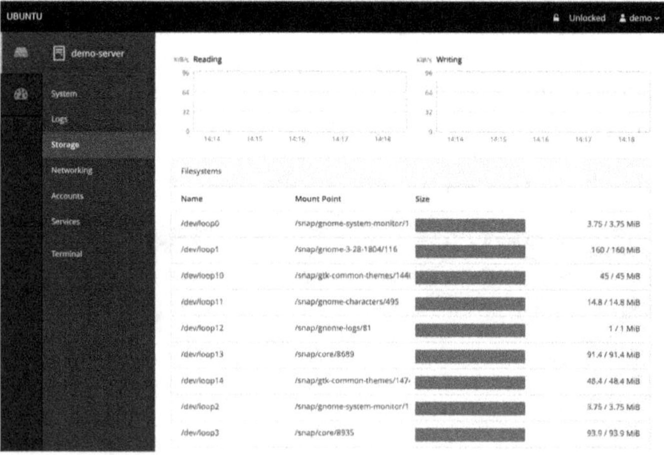

Figure 8-4

8.7 Networking

The Network screen provides information on a wide range of network related configurations and services including network interfaces and firewall settings and allows configuration changes to be made such as creating network bridges or setting up virtual networks.

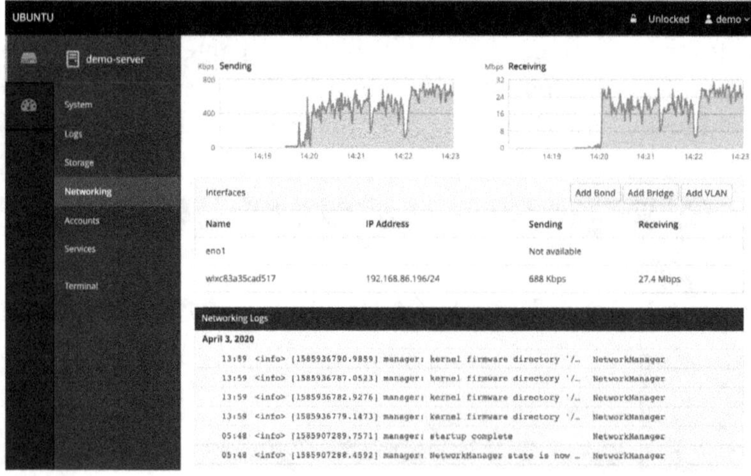

Figure 8-5

8.8 Accounts

Select this option to view the current user accounts configured on the system, and create accounts for additional users. The topic of user management will be covered later in the chapter entitled *"Managing Ubuntu Users and Groups"*.

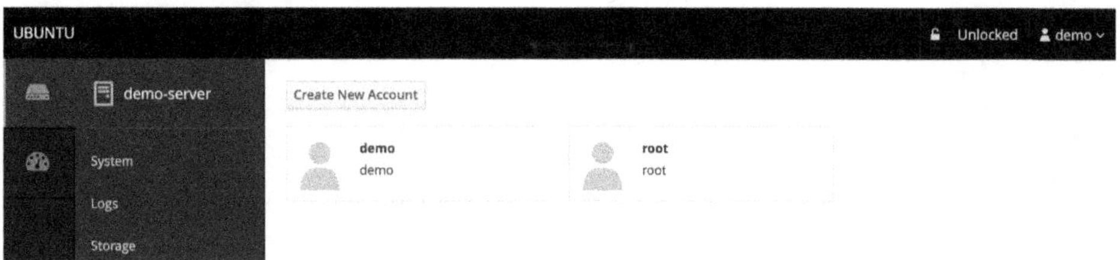

Figure 8-6

Click on an existing account to view details and make changes. The user account details page may also be used to review and add Public SSH keys to the user's account for remote access to the server as outlined in the chapter entitled *"Configuring SSH Key-based Authentication on Ubuntu"*.

8.9 Services

This screen displays a list of the system services running on the server and allows those services to be added, removed, stopped and started.

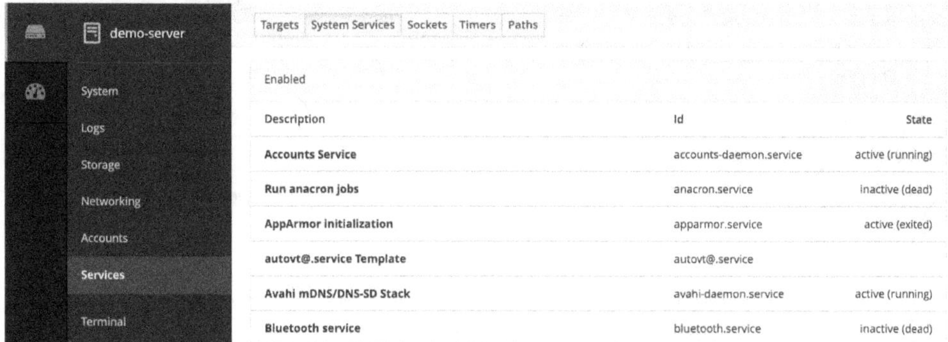

Figure 8-7

The topic of services will be covered in detail in the chapter entitled *"Configuring Ubuntu systemd Units"*.

8.10 Applications

As previously mentioned, additional functionality can be added to Cockpit in the form of extensions. These can either be self-developed extensions, or those provided by third parties. The Applications screen lists installed extensions and allows extensions to be added or deleted.

Figure 8-8

If the Applications option is not available within the cockpit interface, it can be installed as follows:

```
# apt install cockpit-packagekit
```

8.11 Virtual Machines

Virtualization allows multiple operating system instances to run simultaneously on a single computer system, with each system running inside its own *virtual machine*. The Virtual Machines Cockpit extension provides a way to create and manage the virtual machine guests installed on the server.

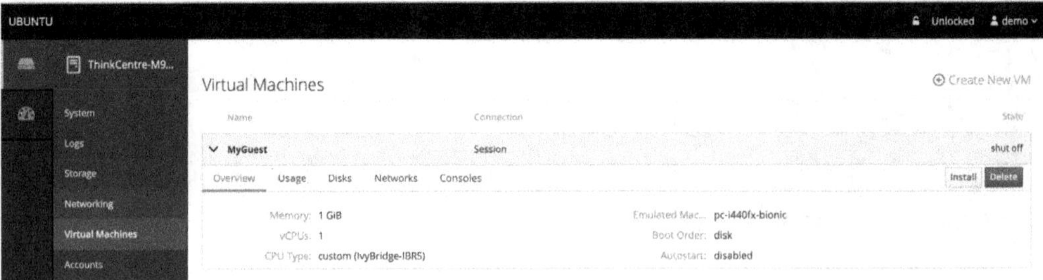

Figure 8-9

The Virtual Machines extension is not installed by default but can be added via the Cockpit Applications screen or by running the following command:

```
# apt install cockpit-machines
```

The use of virtualization with Ubuntu is covered starting with the chapter entitled *"An Overview of Virtualization Techniques"*.

8.12 Software Updates

If any software updates are available for the system they will be listed on this screen. If updates are available, they can be installed from this screen.

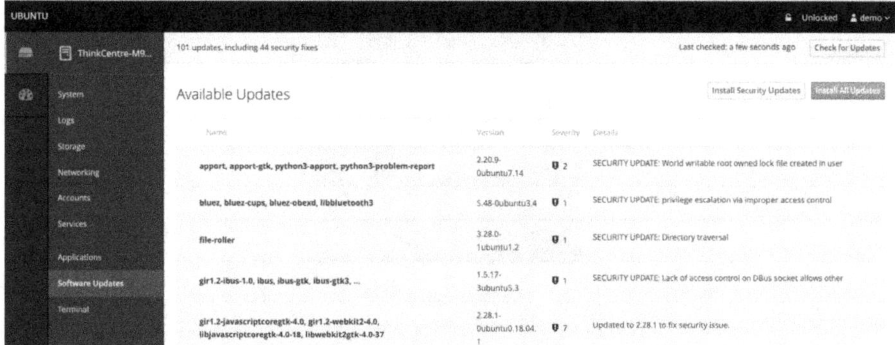

Figure 8-10

If the Cockpit Software Updates screen is not available, it can be installed as follows:

```
# apt install cockpit-packagekit
```

8.13 Terminal

As the name suggests, the Terminal screen provides access to the command-line prompt.

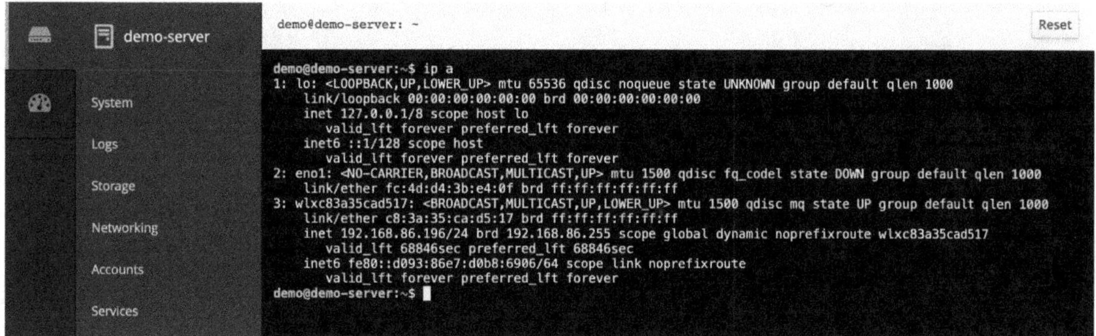

Figure 8-11

8.14 Connecting to Multiple Servers

Cockpit can be configured to administer multiple servers from within a single session. This requires that the Cockpit dashboard be installed on the primary system (in other words the system to which the initial Cockpit session will be established). If the dashboard is not already installed run the following command:

```
# apt install cockpit-dashboard
```

Once the dashboard has been installed, sign out of Cockpit and then sign in again. The dashboard will now appear in the Cockpit interface as highlighted in Figure 8-12:

Figure 8-12

When selected, the dashboard page will display performance graphs for the current system and provide a list of currently connected systems:

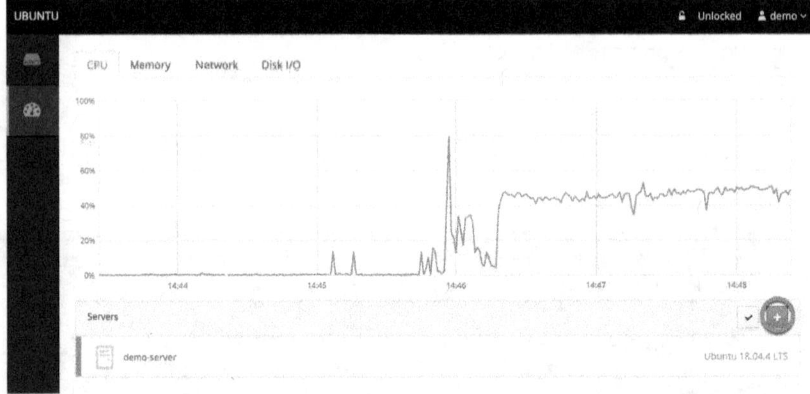

Figure 8-13

To add another system, click on the + button highlighted in Figure 8-13 above, enter the IP address or host name of the other system and select a color by which to distinguish this server from any others added to Cockpit before clicking on the Add button:

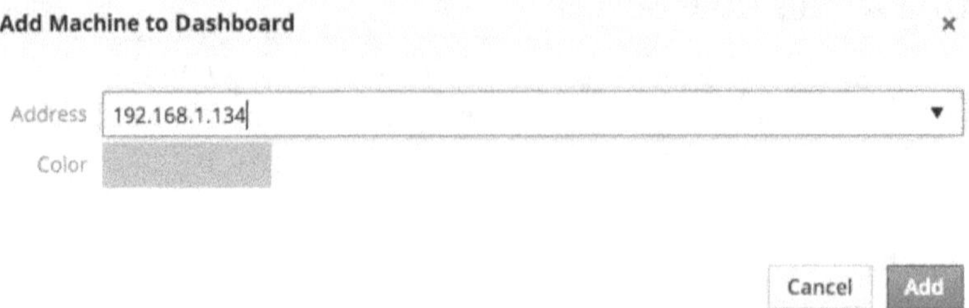

Figure 8-14

Enter the user name and password to be used when connecting to the other system, then click on the log in button. The newly added server will now be listed in the Cockpit dashboard and will appear in graphs represented by the previously selected color:

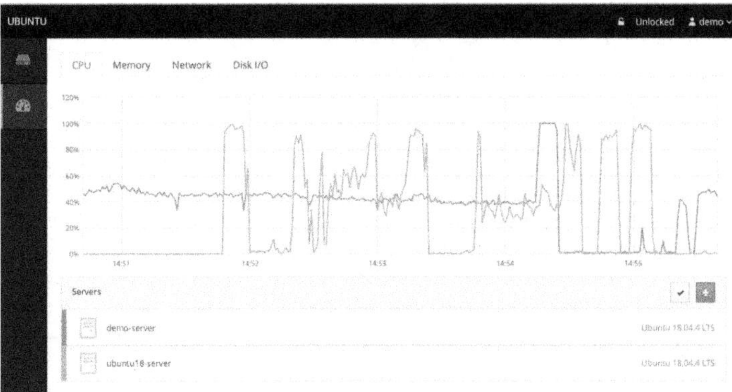

Figure 8-15

To switch between systems when using Cockpit, simply use the drop down menu shown in Figure 8-16 below:

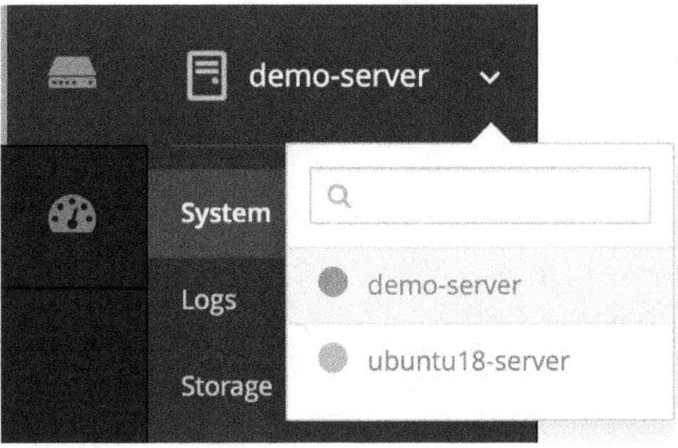

Figure 8-16

8.15 Summary

The Cockpit web interface allows remote system administration tasks to be performed visually from within a web browser without the need to rely on the command-prompt and command-line tools. Once installed and enabled, the system administrator simply opens a web browser, connects to the remote server and signs into the Cockpit interface. Behind the scenes, Cockpit uses the same command-line tools as those available via the command prompt, thereby allowing both options to be used without the risk of configuration conflicts. Cockpit uses a modular framework allowing additional extensions to be added, and for custom extensions to be developed and integrated. A Cockpit session can be used to administer a single server, or configured to access multiple servers simultaneously.

Chapter 9

9. Using the Bash Shell on Ubuntu

An important part of learning to work with Ubuntu, and Linux distributions in general, involves gaining proficiency in working in the shell environment. While the graphical desktop environments such as GNOME included with Linux provide a user friendly interface to the operating system, in practice the shell environment provides far greater capabilities, flexibility and automation than can ever be achieved using graphical desktop tools. The shell environment also provides a means for interacting with the operating system when a desktop environment is not available; a common occurrence when working with a server-based operating system such as Ubuntu or a damaged system that will not fully boot.

The goal of this chapter, therefore, is to provide an overview of the default shell environment on Ubuntu (specifically the Bash shell).

9.1 What is a Shell?

The shell is an interactive command interpreter environment within which commands may be typed at a prompt or entered into a file in the form of a script and executed. The origins of the shell can be traced back to the early days of the UNIX operating system. In fact, in the early days of Linux before the introduction of graphical desktops the shell was the only way for a user to interact with the operating system.

A variety of shell environments have been developed over the years. The first widely used shell was the Bourne shell, written by Stephen Bourne at Bell Labs.

Yet another early creation was the C shell which shared some syntax similarities with the C Programming Language and introduced usability enhancements such as command-line editing and history.

The Korn shell (developed by David Korn at Bell Labs) is based on features provided by both the Bourne shell and the C shell.

The default shell on Ubuntu is the Bash shell (shorthand for Bourne Again SHell). This shell, which began life as an open source version of the Bourne shell, was developed for the GNU Project by Brian Fox and is based on features provided by both the Bourne shell and the C shell.

9.2 Gaining Access to the Shell

From within the GNOME desktop environment, the shell prompt may be accessed from a Terminal window by selecting the Activities option in the top bar, entering Terminal into the search bar and clicking on the Terminal icon.

When remotely logging into an Ubuntu server, for example using SSH, the user is also presented with a shell prompt. Details on accessing a remote server using SSH will be covered in the chapter entitled *"Configuring SSH Key-based Authentication on Ubuntu"*. When booting a server-based system in which a desktop environment has not been installed, the shell is entered immediately after the user completes the login procedure at the physical console terminal or remote login session.

9.3 Entering Commands at the Prompt

Commands are entered at the shell command prompt simply by typing the command and pressing the Enter key. While some commands perform tasks silently, most will display some form of output before returning to the prompt. For example, the *ls* command can be used to display the files and directories in the current working directory:

```
$ ls
Desktop  Documents  Downloads  Music  Pictures  Public  Templates  Videos
```

The available commands are either built into the shell itself, or reside on the physical file system. The location on the file system of a command may be identified using the *which* command. For example, to find out where the *ls* executable resides on the file system:

```
$ which ls
alias ls='ls --color=auto'
	/usr/bin/ls
```

Clearly the *ls* command resides in the */usr/bin* directory. Note also that an alias is configured, a topic which will be covered later in this chapter. Using the *which* command to locate the path to commands that are built into the shell will result in a message indicating the executable cannot be found. For example, attempting to find the location of the *history* command (which is actually built into the shell rather than existing as an executable on the file system) will result in output similar to the following:

```
$ which history
/usr/bin/which: no history in (/home/demo/.local/bin:/home/demo/bin:/usr/share/
Modules/bin:/usr/local/bin:/usr/bin:/usr/local/sbin:/usr/sbin)
```

9.4 Getting Information about a Command

Many of the commands available to the Linux shell can seem cryptic to begin with. To find out detailed information about what a command does and how to use it, use the *man* command specifying the name of the command as an argument. For example, to learn more about the *pwd* command:

```
$ man pwd
```

When the above command is executed, a detailed description of the *pwd* command will be displayed. Many commands will also provide additional information when run with the *--help* command-line option:

```
$ wc --help
```

9.5 Bash Command-line Editing

Early shell environments did not provide any form of line editing capabilities. This meant that if you spotted an error at the beginning of a long command-line you were typing, you had to delete all the following characters, correct the error and then re-enter the remainder of the command. Fortunately Bash provides a wide range of command-line editing options as outlined in the following table:

Key Sequence	Action
Ctrl-b or Left Arrow	Move cursor back one position
Ctrl-f or Right Arrow	Move cursor forward one position
Delete	Delete character currently beneath the cursor
Backspace	Delete character to the left of the cursor
Ctrl-_	Undo previous change (can be repeated to undo all previous changes)
Ctrl-a	Move cursor to the start of the line
Ctrl-e	Move cursor to the end of the line
Meta-f or Esc then f	Move cursor forward one word
Meta-b or Esc then b	Move cursor back one word
Ctrl-l	Clear the screen of everything except current command
Ctrl-k	Delete to end of line from current cursor position
Meta-d or Esc then d	Delete to end of current word
Meta-DEL or Esc then DEL	Delete beginning to current word
Ctrl-w	Delete from current cursor position to previous white space

Table 9-1

9.6 Working with the Shell History

In addition to command-line editing features, the Bash shell also provides command-line history support. A list of previously executed commands may be viewed using the *history* command:

```
$ history
    1  ps
    2  ls
    3  ls -l /
    4  ls
    5  man pwd
    6  man apropos
```

In addition, Ctrl-p (or up arrow) and Ctrl-n (or down arrow) may be used to scroll back and forth through previously entered commands. When the desired command from the history is displayed, press the Enter key to execute it.

Another option is to enter the '!' character followed by the first few characters of the command to be repeated followed by the Enter key.

9.7 Filename Shorthand

Many shell commands take one or more filenames as arguments. For example, to display the content of a text file named *list.txt*, the *cat* command would be used as follows:

```
$ cat list.txt
```

Similarly, the content of multiple text files could be displayed by specifying all the file names as arguments:

```
$ cat list.txt list2.txt list3.txt list4.txt
```

Instead of typing in each name, pattern matching can be used to specify all files with names matching certain criteria. For example, the '*' wildcard character can be used to simplify the above example:

```
$ cat *.txt
```

The above command will display the content of all files ending with a *.txt* extension. This could be further restricted to any file names beginning with *list* and ending in *.txt*:

```
$ cat list*.txt
```

Single character matches may be specified using the '?' character:

```
$ cat list?.txt
```

9.8 Filename and Path Completion

Rather than typing in an entire file name or path, or using pattern matching to reduce the amount of typing, the shell provides the *filename completion* feature. In order to use filename completion, simply enter the first few characters of the file or path name and then press the Esc key twice. The shell will then complete the filename for you with the first file or path name in the directory that matches the characters you entered. To obtain a list of possible matches, press Esc = after entering the first few characters.

9.9 Input and Output Redirection

As previously mentioned, many shell commands output information when executed. By default this output goes to a device file called *stdout* which is essentially the terminal window or console in which the shell is running. Conversely, the shell takes input from a device file named *stdin*, which by default is the keyboard.

Output from a command can be redirected from stdout to a physical file on the file system using the '>' character. For example, to redirect the output from an *ls* command to a file named *files.txt*, the following command would be required:

```
$ ls *.txt > files.txt
```

Upon completion, *files.txt* will contain the list of files in the current directory. Similarly, the contents of a file may be fed into a command in place of stdin. For example, to redirect the contents of a file as input to a command:

```
$ wc -l < files.txt
```

The above command will display the number of lines contained in the *files.txt* file.

It is important to note that the '>' redirection operator creates a new file, or truncates an existing file when used. In order to append to an existing file, use the '>>' operator:

```
$ ls *.dat >> files.txt
```

In addition to standard output, the shell also provides standard error output using *stderr*. While output from a command is directed to stdout, any error messages generated by the command are directed to stderr. This means that if stdout is directed to a file, error messages will still appear in the terminal. This is generally the desired behavior, though stderr may also be redirected if desired using the '2>' operator:

```
$ ls dkjfnvkjdnf 2> errormsg
```

On completion of the command, an error reporting the fact that the file named *dkjfnvkjdnf* could not be found will be contained in the *errormsg* file.

Both stderr and stdout may be redirected to the same file using the &> operator:

```
$ ls /etc dkjfnvkjdnf &> alloutput
```

On completion of execution, the *alloutput* file will contain both a listing of the contents of the */etc* directory, and the error message associated with the attempt to list a non-existent file.

9.10 Working with Pipes in the Bash Shell

In addition to I/O redirection, the shell also allows output from one command to be piped directly as input to another command. A pipe operation is achieved by placing the '|' character between two or more commands on a command-line. For example, to count the number of processes running on a system, the output from the *ps* command can be piped through to the *wc* command:

```
$ ps -ef | wc -l
```

There is no limit to the number of pipe operations that can be performed on a command-line. For example, to find the number of lines in a file which contain the name Smith:

```
$ cat namesfile | grep Smith | wc -l
```

9.11 Configuring Aliases

As you gain proficiency with the shell environment it is likely that you will find yourself frequently issuing commands with the same arguments. For example, you may often use the *ls* command with the *l* and *t* options:

```
$ ls -lt
```

To reduce the amount of typing involved in issuing a command, it is possible to create an alias that maps to the command and arguments. For example, to create an alias such that entering the letter *l* will cause the *ls -lt* command to be executed, the following statement would be used:

```
$ alias l="ls -lt"
```

Entering *l* at the command prompt will now execute the original statement.

9.12 Environment Variables

Shell environment variables provide temporary storage of data and configuration settings. The shell itself sets up a number of environment variables that may be changed by the user to modify the behavior of the shell. A listing of currently defined variables may be obtained using the *env* command:

```
$ env
SSH_CONNECTION=192.168.0.19 61231 192.168.0.28 22
MODULES_RUN_QUARANTINE=LD_LIBRARY_PATH
LANG=en_US.UTF-8
HISTCONTROL=ignoredups
HOSTNAME=demo-pc.ebookfrenzy.com
XDG_SESSION_ID=15
MODULES_CMD=/usr/share/Modules/libexec/modulecmd.tcl
USER=demo
ENV=/usr/share/Modules/init/profile.sh
SELINUX_ROLE_REQUESTED=
PWD=/home/demo
HOME=/home/demo
SSH_CLIENT=192.168.0.19 61231 22
SELINUX_LEVEL_REQUESTED=
.
.
.
```

Perhaps the most useful environment variable is PATH. This defines the directories in which the shell will search for commands entered at the command prompt, and the order in which it will do so. The PATH environment variable for a user account on a newly installed Ubuntu system will likely be configured as follows:

```
$ echo $PATH
/home/demo/.local/bin:/home/demo/bin:/usr/share/Modules/bin:/usr/local/bin:/usr/
bin:/usr/local/sbin:/usr/sbin
```

Another useful variable is HOME which specifies the home directory of the current user. If, for example, you wanted the shell to also look for commands in the scripts directory located in your home directory, you would modify the PATH variable as follows:

```
$ export PATH=$PATH:$HOME/scripts
```

The current value of an existing environment variable may be displayed using the echo command:

```
$ echo $PATH
```

You can create your own environment variables using the *export* command. For example:

```
$ export DATAPATH=/data/files
```

A useful trick to assign the output from a command to an environment variable involves the use of back quotes (`) around the command. For example, to assign the current date and time to an environment variable called NOW:

```
$ export NOW=`date`
$ echo $NOW
Tue Apr 2 13:48:40 EDT 2019
```

If there are environment variable or alias settings that you need to be configured each time you enter the shell environment, they may be added to a file in your home directory named *.bashrc*. For example, the following *.bashrc* file is configured to set up the DATAPATH environment variable and an alias:

```
# .bashrc

# Source global definitions
if [ -f /etc/bashrc ]; then
        . /etc/bashrc
fi

# User specific environment
PATH="$HOME/.local/bin:$HOME/bin:$PATH"
export PATH

# Uncomment the following line if you don't like systemctl's auto-paging feature:
# export SYSTEMD_PAGER=

# User specific aliases and functions
export DATAPATH=/data/files
alias l="ls -lt"
```

9.13 Writing Shell Scripts

So far we have focused exclusively on the interactive nature of the Bash shell. By interactive we mean manually entering commands at the prompt one by one and executing them. In fact, this is only a small part of what the shell is capable of. Arguably one of the most powerful aspects of the shell involves the ability to create shell scripts. Shell scripts are essentially text files containing sequences of statements that can be executed within the shell environment to perform tasks. In addition to the ability to execute commands, the shell provides many of the programming constructs such as *for* and *do* loops and *if* statements that you might reasonably expect to find in a scripting language.

Unfortunately a detailed overview of shell scripting is beyond the scope of this chapter. There are, however, many books and web resources dedicated to shell scripting that do the subject much more justice than we could ever hope to achieve here. In this section, therefore, we will only be providing a very small taste of shell scripting.

The first step in creating a shell script is to create a file (for the purposes of this example we will name it *simple.sh*) and add the following as the first line:

```
#!/bin/sh
```

The #! is called the "shebang" and is a special sequence of characters indicating that the path to the interpreter needed to execute the script is the next item on the line (in this case the *sh* executable located in /bin). This could equally be, for example, */bin/csh* or */bin/ksh* if either were the interpreter you wanted to use.

The next step is to write a simple script:

```
#!/bin/sh
for i in *
do
     echo $i
done
```

All this script does is iterate through all the files in the current directory and display the name of each file. This may be executed by passing the name of the script through as an argument to *sh*:

```
$ sh simple.sh
```

In order to make the file executable (thereby negating the need to pass it through to the *sh* command) the *chmod* command can be used:

```
$ chmod +x simple.sh
```

Once the execute bit has been set on the file's permissions, it may be executed directly. For example:

```
$ ./simple.sh
```

9.14 Summary

In this chapter of Ubuntu Essentials we have taken a brief tour of the Bash shell environment. In the world of graphical desktop environments it is easy to forget that the true power and flexibility of an operating system can often only be utilized by dropping down below the user friendly desktop interface and using a shell environment. Moreover, familiarity with the shell is a necessity when required to administer and maintain server-based systems that do not have the desktop installed or when attempting to repair a system that is damaged to the point that the desktop or Cockpit interface will no longer launch.

The capabilities of the shell go far beyond the areas covered in this chapter. If you are new to the shell then we strongly encourage you to seek out additional resources. Once familiar with the concepts you will quickly find that it is quicker to perform many tasks using the shell in a terminal window than it is to wade through menus and dialogs on the desktop.

Chapter 10

10. Managing Ubuntu Users and Groups

During the installation of Ubuntu, the installer created a root, or superuser account, and required that a password be configured. The installer also provided the opportunity to create a user account for the system. We should not lose sight of the fact that Ubuntu is actually an enterprise class, multi-user and multi-tasking operating system. In order to use the full power of Ubuntu, therefore, it is likely that more than one user will need to be given access to the system. Each user should have his or her own user account login, password, home directory and privileges.

Users are further divided into groups for the purposes of easier administration and those groups can have different levels of privileges. For example, you may have a group of users who work in the Accounting department. In such an environment you may wish to create an accounts group and assign all the Accounting department users to that group.

In this chapter we will cover the steps to add, remove and manage users and groups on an Ubuntu system. There are a number of ways to manage users and groups on Ubuntu, the most common options being command-line tools and the Cockpit web interface. In this chapter we will look at both approaches.

10.1 User Management from the Command-line

New users may be added to an Ubuntu system via the command-line using the *useradd* utility. To create a new user account, enter a command similar to the following:

```
# adduser john
Adding user `john' ...
Adding new group `john' (1001) ...
Adding new user `john' (1001) with group `john' ...
The home directory `/home/john' already exists.  Not copying from `/etc/skel'.
Enter new UNIX password:
Retype new UNIX password:
passwd: password updated successfully
Changing the user information for john
Enter the new value, or press ENTER for the default
        Full Name []:
        Room Number []:
        Work Phone []:
        Home Phone []:
        Other []:
Is the information correct? [Y/n] Y
```

By default, this will create a home directory for the user in the */home* directory (in this case */home/john*). To specify a different home directory, use the --home command-line option when creating the account:

```
# adduser --home /users/johnsmith john
```

Once the account has been created, the password can be changed at any time using the passwd tool:

```
# passwd john
Changing password for user john.
New password:
Retype new password:
passwd: all authentication tokens updated successfully.
```

An existing user may be deleted via the command-line using the *deluser* utility. While this will delete the account, the users files and data will remain intact on the system:

```
# deluser john
```

It is also possible to remove the user's home directory and mail spool as part of the deletion process:

```
# deluser --remove-home john
```

All users on an Ubuntu system are members of one or more groups. By default, new users are added to a private group with the same name as the user (in the above example, the account created for user john was a member of a private group also named john). As an administrator, it makes sense to organize users into more logical groups. For example all sales people might belong to a sales group, while accounting staff might belong to the accounts group and so on. New groups are added from the command-line using the *addgroup* command-line tool, for example:

```
# addgroup accounts
```

Use the *adduser* tool to add an existing user to an existing group from the command-line:

```
# adduser john accounts
```

To remove a user from a group, use the *deluser* command as follows:

```
# deluser john accounts
```

An existing group may be deleted from a system using the *delgroup* utility:

```
# delgroup accounts
```

Note that if the group to be deleted is the primary or initial group for any user it cannot be deleted. The user must first be deleted, or assigned a new primary group using the *usermod* command before the group can be removed. A user can be assigned to a new primary group using the *usermod* -g option:

```
# usermod -g sales john
# delgroup accounts
```

To find out the groups to which a user belongs, simply run the *groups* command. For example:

```
$ groups john
john : accounts support
```

By default, only the first user account created on an Ubuntu system has the ability to use the sudo command to perform privileged tasks. If a newly added user attempts to use sudo, a message similar to the following will be displayed:

```
john is not in the sudoers file.  This incident will be reported.
```

To add the user to the sudoers file, simply add the user to the sudo group:

```
# adduser john sudo
```

10.2 User Management with Cockpit

If the Cockpit web interface is installed and enabled on the system (a topic covered in the chapter entitled *"An Overview of the Ubuntu Cockpit Web Interface"*), a number of user management tasks can be performed within the Accounts screen shown in Figure 10-1 below:

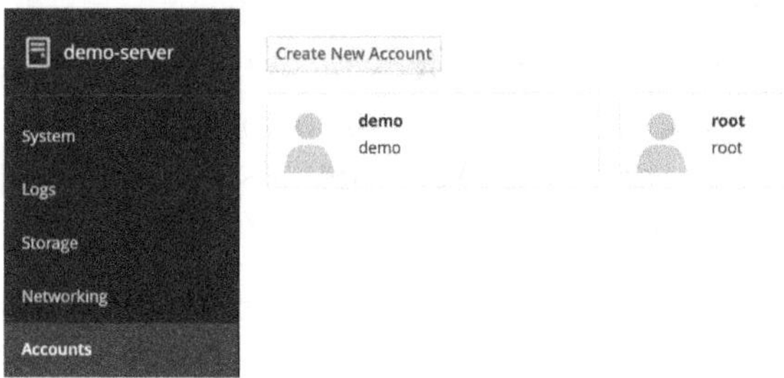

Figure 10-1

The screen will display any existing user accounts on the system and provides a button to add additional accounts. To create a new account, click on the *Create New Account* button and enter the requested information in the resulting dialog (Figure 10-2). Note that the option is also available to create the account but to lock it until later:

Create New Account

Full Name: John Smith
User Name: john
Password: •••••••••••••
Confirm: •••••••••••••
Access: Lock Account

Cancel | Create

Figure 10-2

To modify a user account, select it from the main screen and make any modifications to the account details:

John Smith | Terminate Session | Delete

Full Name: John Smith

User Name: John

Roles: Server Administrator

Last Login: Never

Access: Lock Account — Never lock account

Password: Set Password | Force Change — Never expire password

Authorized Public SSH Keys

There are no authorized public keys for this account.

Figure 10-3

This screen allows a variety of tasks to be performed including locking or unlocking the account, changing the password or forcing the user to configure a new password. If the Server Administrator option is selected, the user will be added to the sudo group and permitted to use sudo to perform administrative tasks. A button is also provided to delete the user from the system.

If the user will be accessing the system remotely using an SSH connection with key encryption, the user's public key may be added within this screen. SSH access and authentication will be covered later in *"Configuring SSH Key-based Authentication on Ubuntu"*.

10.3 User Management using the Settings App

A third user account management option is available via the GNOME desktop settings app. This app is accessed by clicking on the down arrow located in the top right-hand corner of the GNOME desktop and selecting the button displaying the tools icon as shown in Figure 10-4:

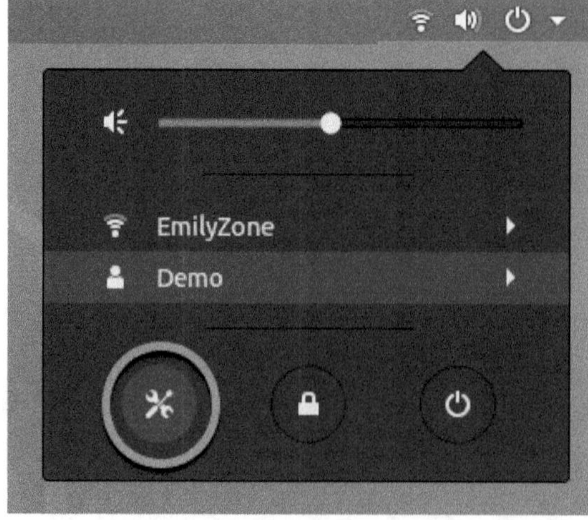

Figure 10-4

When the main settings screen appears, click on the *Details* option in the left-hand navigation panel and choose the *Users* option in the resulting screen. By default, the settings will be locked and it will not be possible to make any changes to the user accounts on the system. To unlock the settings app, click on the *Unlock* button shown in Figure 10-5 below and enter your password. Note that it will only be possible to unlock the settings if you are logged in as a user with sudo privileges:

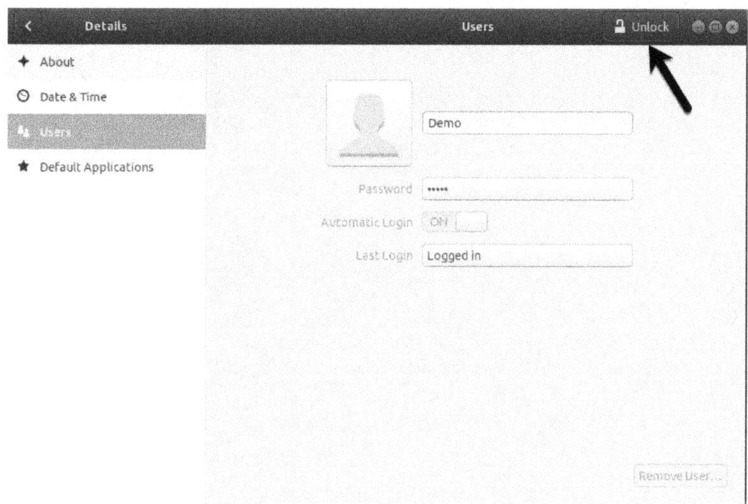

Figure 10-5

Once the app has been unlocked, the *Unlock* button will change to a green button labeled *Add User....* Click this button to display the dialog shown in Figure 10-6 below:

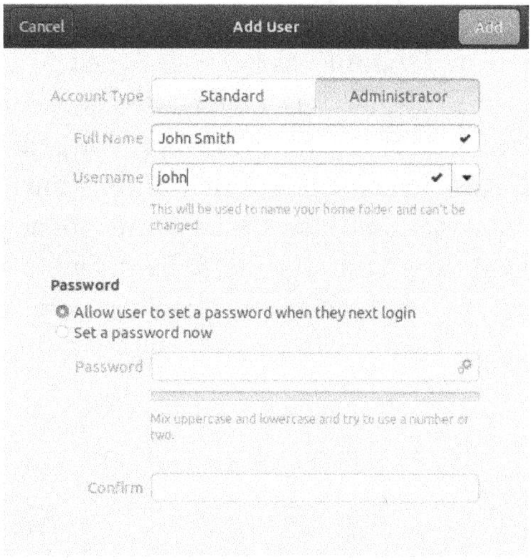

Figure 10-6

To assign sudo access to the new user, select the Administrator account, otherwise leave Standard selected. Enter the user's full name and username and either assign a password now, or allow the user to set up the password when they first log into their account. Once the information as been entered, click on the Add button to create the account.

The settings for an existing user can be viewed, modified or the account deleted at any time by selecting the corresponding icon within the Users screen as shown in Figure 10-7. The option is also available to view the user's login activity. Note that it will be necessary to unlock the Settings app again before any changes can be made to an account:

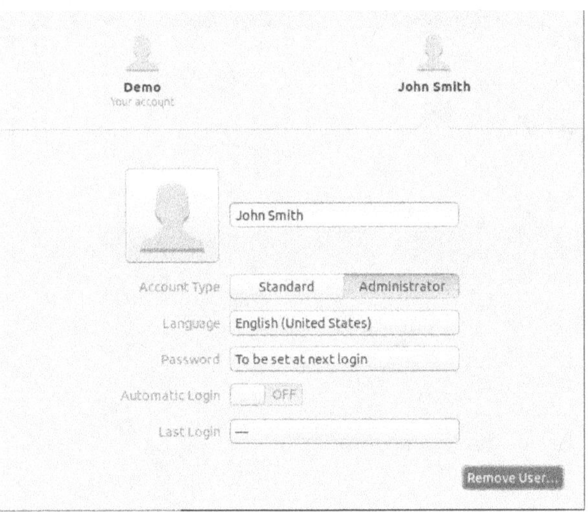

Figure 10-7

10.4 Summary

As a multi-user operating system, Ubuntu has been designed to support controlled access for multiple users. During installation, a single user account was created. Additional user accounts may be added to the system using a set of command-line tools, via the Cockpit web interface or using the GNOME settings app. In addition to user accounts, Linux also implements the concept of groups. New groups can be added and users assigned to those groups using command-line tools and each user must belong to at least one group. By default a standard, non-root user does not have permission to perform privileged tasks. Users that are members of the special sudo group, however, may perform privileged tasks by making use of the *sudo* command.

Chapter 11

11. Ubuntu Software Package Management and Updates

It is highly unlikely that a newly installed Ubuntu system will contain all of the software packages necessary to perform the tasks for which it is intended. Even once all the required software has been installed, it is almost certain that newer versions of many of those packages will be released during the lifespan of the system. In some cases, you will need to ensure that these latest package releases are installed on the system so that bugs and security vulnerabilities are fixed.

This chapter introduces the basic concepts of software management on Ubuntu, explains how these issues are addressed, introduces the concepts of repositories and software packages while exploring how to list, install and remove the software packages that make up a functioning Ubuntu system.

11.1 Repositories

Linux is essentially comprised of a set of base packages that provide the core functionality of the operating system together with a range of other packages and modules that add functionality and features on top of the base operating system.

When Ubuntu is first installed, a number of different packages will be installed depending on the software options selected during the installation phase. Once the system is up and running, however, additional software can be installed as needed. Typically, all software that is part of Ubuntu (in other words software that is not provided by a third party vendor) is downloaded and installed on the system using the Advanced Package Tool (*apt*) command. As we have seen in earlier chapters, this typically consists of a command similar to the following being issued at the command prompt:

```
# apt install apache2
```

When such a command is issued, the requested software is downloaded from a remote *repository* and installed on the local system. By default, Ubuntu is configured to download software from a number of different repositories:

- **main** - Contains the core set of packages that are officially supported, tested and updated by Ubuntu.
- **restricted** - Proprietary drivers for hardware devices for which no open source equivalent exists.
- **universe** - Contains packages that are not officially supported by the Ubuntu team at Canonical. These packages are, however, maintained by the Ubuntu community and include packages not available within the main repository.

- **multiverse** - Packages that may not conform to the open source licensing terms under which Ubuntu is released due to copyright or other legal issues.

The list of currently enabled repositories on an Ubuntu system is contained within the */etc/apt/sources.list* file which can be loaded into an editor to be viewed and modified. The file may be manually loaded into an editor, or edited using a choice of available editors using the following command:

```
# apt edit-sources
```

The first few lines of this file usually reference the main and restricted repositories, for example:

```
deb http://us.archive.ubuntu.com/ubuntu/ bionic main restricted
```

In the above example the list is configured to allow packages to be downloaded from the main and restricted repositories. Entries for the universe and multiverse repositories will also be included in the file:

```
## N.B. software from this repository may not have been tested as
## extensively as that contained in the main release, although it includes
## newer versions of some applications which may provide useful features.
## Also, please note that software in backports WILL NOT receive any review
## or updates from the Ubuntu security team.
deb http://us.archive.ubuntu.com/ubuntu/ bionic-backports main restricted
universe multiverse
```

To disable a repository so that it will no longer be used to download packages, simply comment out the line by prefixing it with a '#' character:

```
# deb http://us.archive.ubuntu.com/ubuntu/ bionic-backports main restricted
universe multiverse
```

In addition to the standard repositories there are also many third-party repositories. In the event that you need to use one of these, simply add an entry for it to the *sources.list* file.

One such example is the partners repository which is included in the *sources.list* file but commented out by default:

```
# deb http://archive.canonical.com/ubuntu bionic partner
```

To enable this repository, simply remove the '#' comment character and save the file.

11.2 Managing Repositories with Software & Updates

As an alternative to using the command-line, repositories may be configured from within the GNOME desktop environment using the *Software & Updates* app. To launch this app, press the *special key* on the keyboard (on Windows keyboards this is the Windows key, on macOS the Command key and on Chromebooks the key displaying a magnifying glass) and enter Software & Updates into the search bar. In the results panel click on the corresponding icon to launch the app. Alternatively, open a terminal window and run the following command:

```
# update-manager
```

When the app loads, click on the Settings button as shown in Figure 11-1:

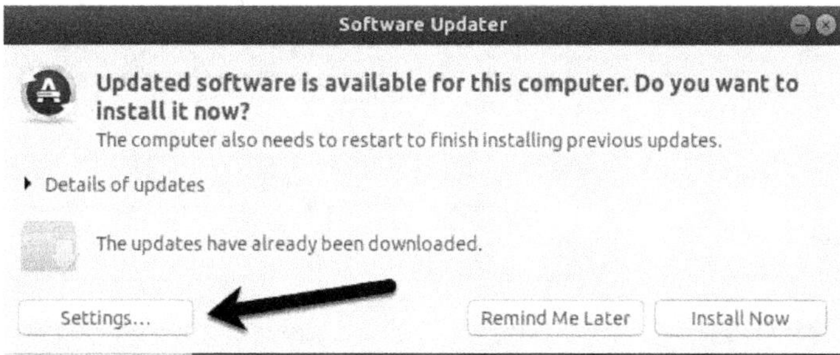

Figure 11-1

From the settings screen, enable or disable the required repositories listed under the *Downloadable from the Internet* heading:

Figure 11-2

To enable partner repositories, select the Other Software tab as shown in Figure 11-3:

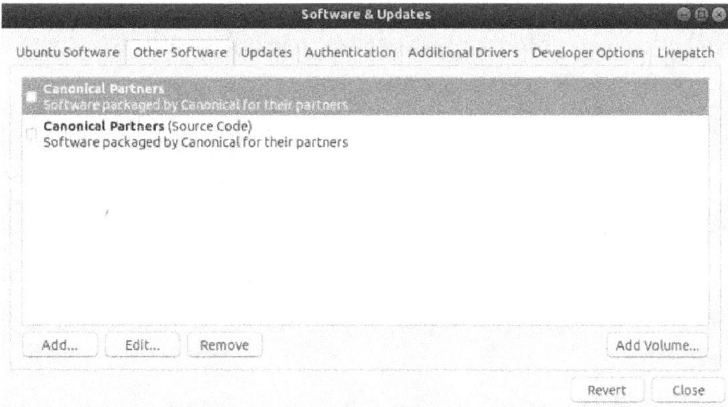

Figure 11-3

To add other third-party repositories, click on the *Add...* button and enter the repository information in the resulting dialog:

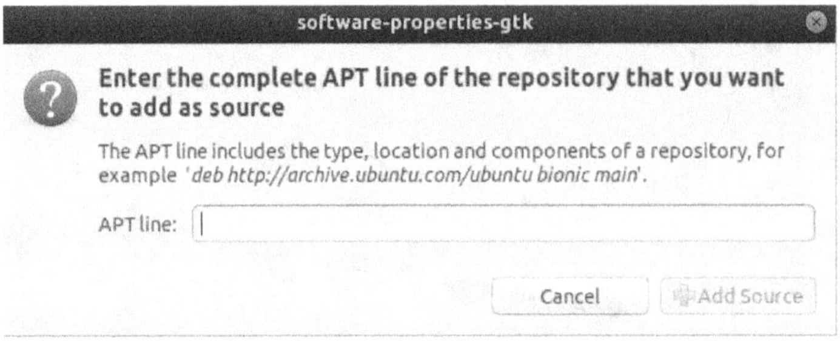

software-properties-gtk

Enter the complete APT line of the repository that you want to add as source

The APT line includes the type, location and components of a repository, for example *'deb http://archive.ubuntu.com/ubuntu bionic main'*.

APT line:

Cancel | Add Source

Figure 11-4

11.3 Managing Packages with APT

The apt tool provides a way to perform most package management tasks directly from the command line. In this section we will explore some of the more frequently used *apt* command-line options.

An Ubuntu system keeps a local copy of the latest package information and, as such, it is recommended that this list be updated before performing any other apt operations as follows:

```
# apt update
```

One of the most common apt activities is to perform a package installation:

```
# apt install package_name
```

Similarly, an installed package may be removed from the system using the remove option:

```
# apt remove package_name
```

When a package is removed this way, configuration files associated with the package will remain on the system. This allows the package to be reinstalled later without losing any custom configuration settings. To remove these files either during the deletion, or even after the deletion as been performed, use the purge option:

```
# apt purge package_name
```

To obtain a list of packages available for installation, use apt as follows:

```
# apt list
```

Alternatively, to list only those packages which are already installed, use the list option with the --installed flag:

```
# apt list --installed
```

To check whether a specific package is already installed on the system, combine the list option with the package name:

```
# apt list package_name
```

Use the search option to list all packages that match certain criteria. For example to list all packages that relate to the Apache web server:

```
# apt search apache
```

To find which package contains a specific file, use the *apt-file* command. For example, to list the name of the packages which contain a file named gimp:

```
# apt-file --package-only list  gimp
```

To view details about a package, run apt with the show option:

```
# apt show apache2
```

Typical output from running the above command might read as follows:

```
Package: apache2
Version: 2.4.29-1ubuntu4.13
Priority: optional
Section: web
Origin: Ubuntu
Maintainer: Ubuntu Developers <ubuntu-devel-discuss@lists.ubuntu.com>
Original-Maintainer: Debian Apache Maintainers <debian-apache@lists.debian.org>
Bugs: https://bugs.launchpad.net/ubuntu/+filebug
Installed-Size: 535 kB
Provides: httpd, httpd-cgi
Pre-Depends: dpkg (>= 1.17.14)
Depends: lsb-base, procps, perl, mime-support, apache2-bin (=
2.4.29-1ubuntu4.13), apache2-utils (= 2.4.29-1ubuntu4.13), apache2-data (=
2.4.29-1ubuntu4.13), perl:any
Recommends: ssl-cert
Suggests: www-browser, apache2-doc, apache2-suexec-pristine | apache2-suexec-
custom, ufw
Conflicts: apache2.2-bin, apache2.2-common
Replaces: apache2.2-bin, apache2.2-common
Homepage: http://httpd.apache.org/
Task: lamp-server
Supported: 5y
Download-Size: 95.1 kB
APT-Sources: http://us.archive.ubuntu.com/ubuntu bionic-updates/main amd64
Packages
Description: Apache HTTP Server
 The Apache HTTP Server Project's goal is to build a secure, efficient and
 extensible HTTP server as standards-compliant open source software. The
 result has long been the number one web server on the Internet.
 .
 Installing this package results in a full installation, including the
 configuration files, init scripts and support scripts.
```

11.4 Performing Updates

Over the lifetime of both the base operating system and the installed software packages, multiple updates will be issued to resolve problems and add functionality. To manually download and install any pending updates from the command-line, the first step is to update the package information stored on the local system using apt with the update option:

```
# apt update
```

Once the package information has been updated, the upgrade can be performed. This will download any updates for currently installed packages from the repositories configured in the *sources.list* file and install them on the system:

```
# apt upgrade
```

As an alternative to the command-line, the system may be updated using the Software & Updates GNOME desktop app. If updates are available the dialog shown in Figure 11-5 will appear providing the option to view information about the available updates and to perform the upgrade:

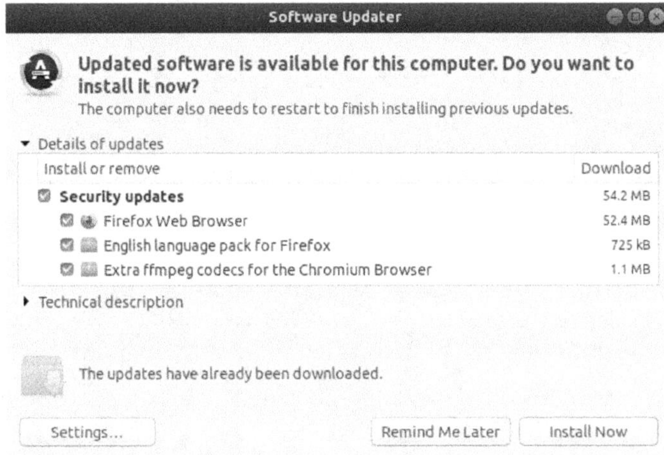

Figure 11-5

11.5 Enabling Automatic Updates

The previous section looked at how to manually install package upgrades. Ubuntu systems may also be configured to install upgrades automatically. This can be configured either from the command-line or from within the Software & Updates tool.

From within the Software and Updates tool, open the Settings screen as outlined previously and click on the Updates tab to display the screen shown in Figure 11-6:

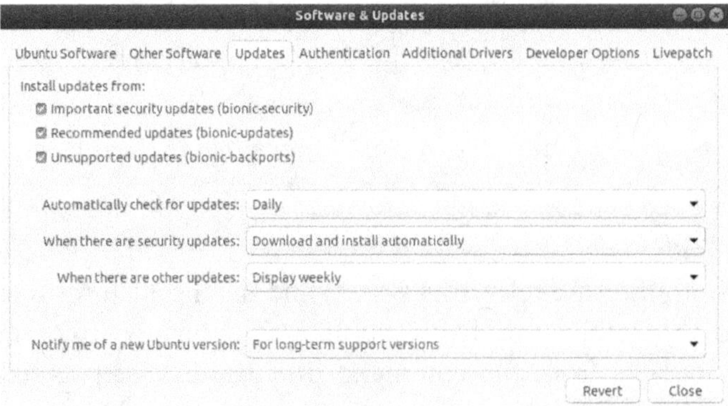

Figure 11-6

Select the repositories from which updates are to be performed before selecting how often the system should check for updates (daily, every other day, weekly, etc.). Next choose what is to be done when updates are available (download only, download and install, or display a notification on the desktop). You can also configure the updater to let you know when new versions of Ubuntu are available.

To configure automatic updates from the command-line, follow these steps:

1. Install the unattended-upgrades package:

```
# apt install unattended-upgrades
```

2. Edit the */etc/apt/apt.conf.d/50unattended-upgrades* file and locate the following lines:

```
        "${distro_id}ESMApps:${distro_codename}-apps-security";
        "${distro_id}ESM:${distro_codename}-infra-security";
//      "${distro_id}:${distro_codename}-updates";
//      "${distro_id}:${distro_codename}-proposed";
//      "${distro_id}:${distro_codename}-backports";
```

3. Remove the // comment markers from the repository types for which updates are to be automatically installed.

4. Edit the */etc/apt/apt.conf.d/20auto-upgrades* file and declare the frequency (in days) with which the system is to check to for updates:

```
APT::Periodic::Update-Package-Lists "1";
APT::Periodic::Download-Upgradeable-Packages "1";
APT::Periodic::AutocleanInterval "0";
APT::Periodic::Unattended-Upgrade "1";
4. Perform a dry run update to make sure the settings are valid:
# unattended-upgrades --dry-run --debug
```

A few days after configuring automatic updates, check the log files to confirm that the updates are occurring as planned:

```
# cat /var/log/unattended-upgrades/unattended-upgrades.log
```

11.6 Enabling Livepatch

The chapter entitled *"A Brief History of Linux"* explained how the kernel provides the foundation on which the Linux operating system is built, managing the system's resources and handling communication between the hardware and the applications.

As with any software, the kernel is subject to updates to fix bugs and address potential security vulnerabilities. Although most software packages can be updated without the need to reboot the operating system, the same has not historically been true of the kernel. With the introduction of the Livepatch, this is no longer the case for Ubuntu.

Livepatch is a subscription service offered by Canonical that allows the kernel of running Ubuntu systems to be patched while the system is running without the interruption of a system reboot.

The service is available for personal use free of charge on up to three systems and for larger numbers of systems with a paid Ubuntu Advantage subscription.

The first step in configuring Livepatch is to create an Ubuntu One account at the following URL if you do not have one already:

https://login.ubuntu.com/

Once an account has been created, remain in the browser window and navigate to the following URL:

https://auth.livepatch.canonical.com/

When the page has loaded, select the type of user you are (if you are not a paid Ubuntu customer simply select the Ubuntu User option):

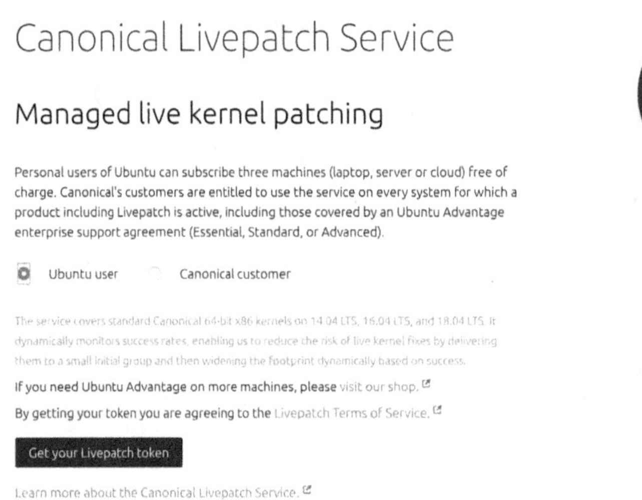

Figure 11-7

Next, click on the *Get your Livepatch token* button. On the subsequent screen, sign in using your Ubuntu One credentials.

A page will now appear containing your Livepatch key and a list of commands to be run on your Ubuntu system. Copy the commands, open a terminal window and run them:

```
# snap install canonical-livepatch
# canonical-livepatch enable your_key_here
```

To check Livepatch status, simply run the following command:

```
# canonical-livepatch status
last check: 2 minutes ago
kernel: 5.3.0-46.38~18.04.1-generic
server check-in: succeeded
patch state: no livepatches needed for this kernel yet
```

11.7 Summary

The Ubuntu operating system is comprised of thousands of software packages that are downloaded and installed from the main, restricted, universe, multiverse, partner and third-party repositories.

Software packages are installed using the Advanced Package Tool (apt) or one of a number of graphical desktop tools and downloaded from the repositories defined within the *sources.list* file.

In addition to installing and removing software packages, apt may also be used to upgrade those packages with the latest updates. These software upgrades can be performed manually, or configured to automatically update.

In the past, updates to the operating system kernel required a system reboot. With the introduction of Livepatch, the Ubuntu Linux kernel can now be updated dynamically without system interruption.

Chapter 12

12. Configuring Ubuntu systemd Units

In order to gain proficiency in Ubuntu system administration it is important to understand the concepts of systemd units with a particular emphasis on two specific types known as targets and services. The goal of this chapter, therefore, is to provide a basic overview of the different systemd units supported by Ubuntu combined with an overview of how to configure the many services that run in the background of a running Linux system.

12.1 Understanding Ubuntu systemd Targets

Ubuntu can be configured to boot into one of a number of states (referred to as *targets*), each of which is designed to provide a specific level of operating system functionality. The target to which a system will boot by default is configured by the system administrator based on the purpose for which the system is being used. A desktop system, for example, will most likely be configured to boot using the graphical user interface target, while a cloud-based server system would be more likely to boot to the multi-user target level.

During the boot sequence, a process named *systemd* looks in the */etc/systemd/system* folder to find the default target setting. Having identified the default target, it proceeds to start the systemd units associated with that target so that the system boots with all the necessary processes running.

For those familiar with previous Ubuntu versions, systemd targets are the replacement for the older *runlevel* system.

12.2 Understanding Ubuntu systemd Services

A service is essentially a process, typically running in the background, that provides specific functionality. The sshd service, for example, is the background process (also referred to as a daemon) that provides secure shell access to the system. Different systemd targets are configured to automatically launch different collections of services, depending on the functionality that is to be provided by that target.

Targets and services are types of *systemd unit*, a topic which will be covered later in this chapter.

12.3 Ubuntu systemd Target Descriptions

As previously outlined, Ubuntu can be booted into one of a number of target levels. The default target to which the system is configured to boot will, in turn, dictate which systemd units are started. The targets that relate specifically to system startup and shutdown can be summarized as follows:

- **poweroff.target** - This is the target in which the system shuts down. For obvious reasons it is unlikely you would want this as your default target.

• **rescue.target** – Causes the system to start up in a single user mode under which only the root user can log in. In this mode the system does not start any networking, graphical user interface or multi-user services. This run level is ideal for system administrators to perform system maintenance or repair activities.

• **multi-user.target** - Boots the system into a multi-user mode with text based console login capability.

• **graphical.target** - Boots the system into a networked, multi-user state with X Window System capability. By default the graphical desktop environment will start at the end of the boot process. This is the most common run level for desktop or workstation use.

• **reboot.target** - Reboots the system. Another target that, for obvious reasons, you are unlikely to want as your default.

In addition to the above targets, the system also includes about 70 other targets, many of which are essentially sub-targets used by the above main targets. Behind the scenes, for example, *multi-user.target* will also start a target named *basic.target* which will, in turn, start the *sockets.target* unit which is required for communication between different processes. This ensures that all of the services on which the multi-user target is dependent are also started during the boot process.

A list of the targets and services on which a specified target is dependent can be viewed by running the following command in a terminal window:

```
# systemctl list-dependencies <target>
```

Figure 12-1, for example, shows a partial listing of the systemd unit dependencies for the multi-user target (the full listing contains over 120 targets and services required for a fully functional multi-user system):

```
root@demo-server:~# systemctl list-dependencies multi-user.target
multi-user.target
● ├─anacron.service
● ├─apport.service
● ├─avahi-daemon.service
● ├─console-setup.service
● ├─cron.service
● ├─cups-browsed.service
● ├─cups.path
● ├─dbus.service
● ├─dns-clean.service
● ├─grub-common.service
● ├─irqbalance.service
● ├─kerneloops.service
● ├─ModemManager.service
● ├─networkd-dispatcher.service
● ├─networking.service
● ├─NetworkManager.service
```

Figure 12-1

The listing is presented as a hierarchical tree illustrating how some dependencies have sub-dependencies of their own. Scrolling to the bottom of the list, for example, would reveal that the multi-user target depends on the local-fs.target with its own service and target sub-dependencies:

```
● │ │ ├─local-fs.target
● │ │ │ ├─-.mount
● │ │ │ ├─systemd-fsck-root.service
● │ │ │ └─systemd-remount-fs.service
● │ │ └─swap.target
● │ │   └─swapfile.swap
```

Figure 12-2

The colored dots to the left of each entry in the list indicate the current status of that service or target as follows:

- **Green** - The service or target is active and running.
- **White** - The service or target is inactive (dead). Typically because the service or target has not yet been enabled, has been stopped for some reason, or a condition on which the service or target depends has not been met.
- **Red** - The service or target failed to start due to a fatal error.

To find out more details about the status of a systemd unit, use the *systemctl status* command followed by the unit name as follows:

```
# systemctl status systemd-machine-id-commit.service
○ systemd-machine-id-commit.service - Commit a transient machine-id on disk
   Loaded: loaded (/usr/lib/systemd/system/systemd-machine-id-commit.service;
static; vendor preset: disabled)
   Active: inactive (dead)
Condition: start condition failed at Thu 2019-02-14 15:27:47 EST; 1h 14min ago
           ConditionPathIsMountPoint=/etc/machine-id was not met
     Docs: man:systemd-machine-id-commit.service(8)
```

12.4 Identifying and Configuring the Default Target

The current default target for an Ubuntu system can be identified using the *systemctl* command as follows:

```
# systemctl get-default
multi-user.target
```

In the above case, the system is configured to boot using the multi-user target by default. The default setting can be changed at any time using the *systemctl* command with the *set-default* option. The following example changes the default target to start the graphical user interface the next time the system boots:

```
# systemctl set-default graphical.target
Removed /etc/systemd/system/default.target.
```

```
Created symlink /etc/systemd/system/default.target → /usr/lib/systemd/system/graphical.target.
```

The output from the default change operation reveals the steps performed in the background by the *systemctl* command to implement the change. The current default is configured by establishing a symbolic link from the *default.target* file located in */etc/systemd/system* to point to the corresponding target file located in the */usr/lib/systemd/system* folder (in this case the *graphical.target* file).

12.5 Understanding systemd Units and Unit Types

As previously mentioned, targets and services are both types of *systemd unit.* All of the files within the */usr/lib/systemd/system* folder are referred to as *systemd unit configuration files*, each of which represents a systemd unit. Each unit is, in turn, categorized as being of a particular *unit type.* Ubuntu supports 12 different unit types including the target and service unit types already covered in this chapter.

The type of a unit file is represented by the filename extension as outlined in Table 12-1 below:

Unit Type	Filename Extension	Type Description
Service	.service	System service.
Target	.target	Group of systemd units.
Automount	.automount	File system auto-mount point.
Device	.device	Device file recognized by the kernel.
Mount	.mount	File system mount point.
Path	.path	File or directory in a file system.
Scope	.scope	Externally created process.
Slice	.slice	Group of hierarchically organized units that manage system processes.
Snapshot	.snapshot	Saved state of the systemd manager.
Socket	.socket	Inter-process communication socket.
Swap	.swap	Swap device or a swap file.
Timer	.timer	Systemd timer.

Table 12-1

Note that the target unit type differs from other types in that it is essentially comprised of a group of systemd units such as services or other targets.

12.6 Dynamically Changing the Current Target

The *systemctl set-default* command outlined previously specifies the target that will be used the next time the system starts, but does not change the state of the currently running system. To change to a different target dynamically, use the *systemctl* command once again, this time using the *isolate* option followed by the destination target. To switch the current system to the graphical target without rebooting, for example, the following command would be used:

```
# systemctl isolate graphical.target
```

Once executed, the system will start the graphical desktop environment.

12.7 Enabling, Disabling and Masking systemd Units

A newly installed Ubuntu system will include the base systemd service units but is unlikely to include all of the services that will eventually be needed by the system once it goes into a production environment. A basic Ubuntu installation, for example, will typically not include the packages necessary to run an Apache web server, a key element of which is the *apache2.service* unit.

The system administrator will resolve this problem by installing the necessary Apache packages using the following command:

```
# apt install apache2
```

Having configured the web server, the next task will be to check the status of the apache2service unit to identify whether it was activated as part of the installation process:

```
# systemctl status apache2.service
● apache2.service - The Apache HTTP Server
   Loaded: loaded (/lib/systemd/system/apache2.service; enabled; vendor preset: enabled)
  Drop-In: /lib/systemd/system/apache2.service.d
           └─apache2-systemd.conf
   Active: active (running) since Wed 2020-04-08 14:34:54 EDT; 34s ago
 Main PID: 3513 (apache2)
    Tasks: 55 (limit: 4915)
   CGroup: /system.slice/apache2.service
           ├─3513 /usr/sbin/apache2 -k start
           ├─3515 /usr/sbin/apache2 -k start
           └─3516 /usr/sbin/apache2 -k start
```

As we can see from the above output, the apache2 service is already loaded and active without having to be manually started. This is because the vendor preset is set to enable to ensure the service starts after installation is complete.

A currently running service may be stopped at any time as follows:

```
# systemctl stop apache2.service
```

Because the service is listed as enabled in the status output, the next time the system reboots to the current target, the apache2 service will start automatically. Assuming, for example, that the service was enabled while the system was running the multi-user target, the apache2 service will have been added as another dependency to the *multi-user.target* systemd unit.

Behind the scenes, *systemctl* adds dependencies to targets by creating symbolic links in the *.wants* folder for the target within the */etc/systemd/system* folder. The *multi-user.target* unit, for example, has a folder named *multi-user.target.wants* in */etc/systemd/system* containing symbolic links to all of the systemd units located in */usr/lib/systemd/system* on which it is dependent. A review of this folder will show a correlation with the dependencies listed by the *systemctl list-dependencies* command outlined earlier in the chapter.

To disable a service so that it no longer starts automatically as a target dependency, simply disable it as follows:

```
# systemctl disable apache2.service
```

This command will remove the symbolic link to the *apache2.service* unit file from the *.wants* directory so that it is no longer a dependency and, as such, will not be started the next time the system boots.

The *.wants* folder contains dependencies which, if not available, will not prevent the unit from starting and functioning. Mandatory dependencies (in other words dependencies that will cause the unit to fail if not available) should be placed in the *.requires* folder (for example *multi-user.target.requires*).

In addition to enabling and disabling, it is also possible to mask a systemd unit as follows:

```
# systemctl mask apache2.service
```

A masked systemd unit cannot be enabled, disabled or started under any circumstances even if it is listed as a dependency for another unit. In fact, as far as the system is concerned, it is as though a masked systemd unit no longer exists. This can be useful for ensuring that a unit is never started regardless of the system conditions. The only way to regain access to the service is to unmask it:

```
# systemctl unmask apache2.service
```

12.8 Working with systemd Units in Cockpit

In addition to the command-line techniques outlined so far in this chapter, it is also possible to review and manage systemd units from within the Cockpit web-based interface. Assuming that Cockpit has been installed and set up as outlined in the chapter entitled *"An Overview of the Cockpit Web Interface"*, access to the list of systemd units on the system can be accessed by logging into Cockpit and selecting the Services option in the left-hand navigation panel marked A in Figure 12-3:

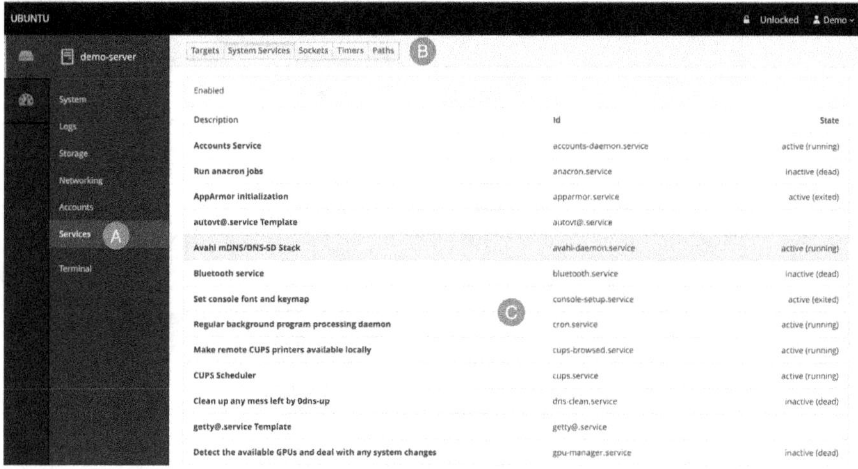

Figure 12-3

The button marked B displays units of specific types in the main area marked C where the current status of each unit is listed in the State column.

Selecting a unit from the list will display detailed information. Figure 12-4, for example, shows the detail screen for an *apache2.service* instance including service logs (A) and menu options (B) for performing tasks such as starting, stopping, enabling/disabling and masking/unmasking the unit.

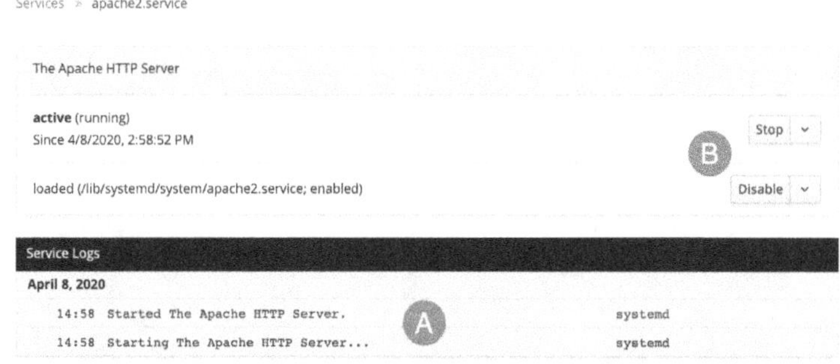

Figure 12-4

12.9 Summary

A newly installed Ubuntu system includes a base set of systemd units many of which run in the background to provide much of the functionality of the system. These units are categorized by type, the most common of which being targets and services. A target unit is simply a group of other units that are to be started collectively. The system has a default target unit which defines the other units which are to be started up each time the system boots. The most common targets are those which boot the system to either multi-user or graphical mode. The *systemctl* command-line tool provides a range of options for performing systemd unit configuration tasks, many of which are also available through the Cockpit web-based interface.

Chapter 13

13. Ubuntu Network Management

It is difficult to envisage an Ubuntu system that does not have at least one network connection, and harder still to imagine how such an isolated system could be of much practical use. The simple fact is that Ubuntu is designed to provide enterprise level services over network and internet connections. A key part of learning how to administer an Ubuntu system involves learning how to configure and manage the network interfaces installed on the system.

This chapter is intended to provide an overview of network management on Ubuntu including the NetworkManager service and tools together with some other useful utilities.

13.1 An Introduction to NetworkManager

NetworkManager is a service and set of tools designed specifically to make it easier to manage the networking configuration on Linux systems and is the default network management service on Ubuntu.

In addition to a service that runs in the background, NetworkManager also includes the following tools:

- **nmcli** - A tool for working with NetworkManager via the command-line. This tool is useful when access to a graphical environment is not available and can also be used within scripts to make network configuration changes.
- **nmtui** - A basic text-based user interface for managing NetworkManager. This tool can be run within any terminal window and allows changes to be made by making menu selections and entering data. While useful for performing basic tasks, *nmtui* lacks many of the features provided by the *nmcli* tool.
- **nm-connection-editor** - A full graphical management tool providing access to most of the NetworkManager configuration options.
- **GNOME Settings** - The Network screen of the GNOME desktop Settings application allows basic network management tasks to be performed.
- **Cockpit Network Settings** - The Network screen of the Cockpit web interface allows a range of network management tasks to be performed.

Although there are a number of different ways to manage the network environment on an Ubuntu system, for the purposes of this chapter we will focus on the *nmcli* command. While the graphical tools are certainly useful when you have access to a desktop environment or Cockpit has been enabled, understanding the command-line interface is essential for situations where a command prompt is all that is available. Also, the graphical tools (Cockpit included) do not include all of the capabilities of the *nmcli* tool. Finally, once you have gained some familiarity with NetworkManager and *nmcli*, those skills will translate easily when using the more intuitive tool options. The same cannot be said of the graphical tool options. It is harder to use *nmcli* if, for example, you have only ever used *nm-connection-editor.*

13.2 Installing and Enabling NetworkManager

NetworkManager should be installed by default for most Ubuntu installations if the Desktop installation image was used. Use the *apt* command to find out if it needs to be installed:

```
# apt -qq list network-manager
network-manager/bionic-updates,now 1.10.6-2ubuntu1.4 amd64 [installed,automatic]
```

If necessary, install the package as follows:

```
# apt install network-manager
```

Once the package is installed, the NetworkManager daemon will need to be enabled so that it starts each time the system boots:

```
# systemctl status network-manager
```

Finally, start the service running and check the status to verify that the launch was successful:

```
# systemctl status network-manager
● NetworkManager.service - Network Manager
   Loaded: loaded (/lib/systemd/system/NetworkManager.service; enabled; vendor
preset: enabled)
   Active: active (running) since Wed 2020-04-08 14:31:58 EDT; 19h ago
     Docs: man:NetworkManager(8)
 Main PID: 704 (NetworkManager)
    Tasks: 4 (limit: 4915)
   CGroup: /system.slice/NetworkManager.service
           ├─704 /usr/sbin/NetworkManager --no-daemon
.
.
```

13.3 Basic nmcli Commands

The *nmcli* tool will have been installed as part of the NetworkManager package and can be executed from the command-line using the following syntax:

```
# nmcli [Options] Object {Command | help}
```

In the above syntax, *Object* will be one of *general*, *networking*, *radio*, *connection*, *monitor*, *device* or *agent*, all of which can be abbreviated to a few letters of the word (for example *con*, or even just the letter *c*, for *connection*). For example, all of the following commands will output help information relating to the *device* object:

```
# nmcli device help
# nmcli dev help
# nmcli d help
```

To check the overall status of NetworkManager on the system, use the following command:

```
# nmcli general status
```

```
STATE      CONNECTIVITY  WIFI-HW  WIFI     WWAN-HW  WWAN
connected  full          enabled  enabled  enabled  enabled
```

To check the status of the devices installed on a system, the following command can be used:

```
# nmcli dev status
DEVICE           TYPE      STATE      CONNECTION
eno1             ethernet  connected  Wired connection 1
wlxc83a35cad517  wifi      connected  zoneone
virbr0           bridge    connected  virbr0
lo               loopback  unmanaged  --
virbr0-nic       tun       unmanaged  --
```

The output may also be modified by using the -p (pretty) option to make the output more human friendly:

```
# nmcli -p dev status
=====================
  Status of devices
=====================
DEVICE           TYPE      STATE      CONNECTION
--------------------------------------------------------------------------------
eno1             ethernet  connected  Wired connection 1
wlxc83a35cad517  wifi      connected  zoneone
virbr0           bridge    connected  virbr0
lo               loopback  unmanaged  --
virbr0-nic       tun       unmanaged  --
```

Conversely, the -t option may be used to make the output more terse and suitable for automated processing:

```
# nmcli -t dev status
eno1:ethernet:connected:Wired connection 1
wlxc83a35cad517:wifi:connected:EmilyZone
virbr0:bridge:connected:virbr0
lo:loopback:unmanaged:
virbr0-nic:tun:unmanaged:
```

From the status output, we can see that the system has two physical devices installed, one Ethernet and the other a WiFi device.

The bridge (virbr) entries are virtual devices used to provide networking for virtual machines (the topic of virtualization will be covered starting with the chapter entitled *"An Overview of Virtualization Techniques"*). The loopback interface is a special virtual device that allows the system to communicate with itself and is typically used to perform network diagnostics.

When working with NetworkManager, it is important to understand the difference between a device and a connection. As described above, a device is either a physical or virtual network device while a connection is a network configuration that the device connects to.

The following command displays information about the connections configured on the system:

```
# nmcli con show
NAME                UUID                                  TYPE      DEVICE
zoneone             bbd6e294-5d0c-4eac-b3c2-4dfd44becc9c  wifi      wlxc83a35cad517
Wired connection 1  56f32c14-a4d2-32c8-9391-f51967efa173  ethernet  eno1
virbr0              f2d3494f-6ea4-4c90-936c-5eda9ac96a85  bridge    virbr0
zonetwo             f2a20df5-aa5e-4576-8379-579d154c3e0d  wifi      --
zonethree           45beac50-8741-41a6-abff-415640e24071  wifi      --
```

From the above output, we can see that the WiFi device (*wlxc83a35cad517*) is connected to a wireless network named *zoneone* while the Ethernet device (*eno1*) is connected to a connection named *Wired connection 1*. In addition to zoneone, NetworkManager has also listed two other WiFi connections named *zonetwo* and *zonethree*, neither of which currently have a device connected.

To find out the IP address allocated to a connection, the *ip* tool can be used with the *address* option:

```
# ip address
```

This can also be abbreviated:

```
# ip a
.
.
3: wlxc83a35cad517: <BROADCAST,MULTICAST,UP,LOWER_UP> mtu 1500 qdisc mq state UP
group default qlen 1000
    link/ether c8:3a:35:ca:d5:17 brd ff:ff:ff:ff:ff:ff
    inet 192.168.1.121/24 brd 192.168.86.255 scope global dynamic noprefixroute
wlxc83a35cad517
       valid_lft 86076sec preferred_lft 86076sec
.
.
```

The ip command will output information for all of the devices detected on the system. The above output shows that the WiFi device has been assigned an IP address of 192.168.1.121.

If we only wanted to list active connections, the *nmcli* command could have been used with the -a option:

```
# nmcli con show -a
NAME                UUID                                  TYPE      DEVICE
zoneone             bbd6e294-5d0c-4eac-b3c2-4dfd44becc9c  wifi      wlxc83a35cad517
Wired connection 1  56f32c14-a4d2-32c8-9391-f51967efa173  ethernet  eno1
virbr0              f2d3494f-6ea4-4c90-936c-5eda9ac96a85  bridge    virbr0
```

To switch the WiFi device connection from zoneone to zonetwo, we can run the following command:

```
# nmcli device wifi connect zonetwo -ask
```

```
Password:
```

The *-ask* flag causes *nmcli* to prompt the user to enter the password for the WiFi network. To include the WiFi password on the command-line (particularly useful if the command is being executed in a script), use the *password* option:

```
# nmcli device wifi connect zonetwo password <password here>
```

The *nmcli* tool may also be used to scan for available WiFi networks as follows:

```
# nmcli device wifi list
IN-USE  SSID         MODE   CHAN  RATE          SIGNAL  BARS  SECURITY
        zoneone      Infra  6     195 Mbit/s    80            WPA2
*       zonetwo      Infra  11    130 Mbit/s    74            WPA1 WPA2
```

A currently active connection can be deactivated as follows:

```
# nmcli con down <connection name>
```

Similarly, an inactive connection can be brought back up at any time:

```
# nmcli con up <connection name>
```

When a connection is brought down, NetworkManager automatically searches for another connection, activates it and assigns it to the device to which the previous connection was established. To prevent a connection from being used in this situation, disable the autoconnect option as follows:

```
# nmcli con mod <connection name> connection.autoconnect no
```

The following command may be used to obtain additional information about a specific connection. This includes the current values for all the connection properties:

```
# nmcli con show "Wired connection 1"
connection.id:                          Wired connection 1
connection.uuid:                        56f32c14-a4d2-32c8-9391-f51967efa173
connection.stable-id:                   --
connection.type:                        802-3-ethernet
connection.interface-name:              --
connection.autoconnect:                 yes
connection.autoconnect-priority:        -999
connection.autoconnect-retries:         -1 (default)
connection.auth-retries:                -1
connection.timestamp:                   1586442354
connection.read-only:                   no
connection.permissions:                 --
connection.zone:                        --
connection.master:                      --
connection.slave-type:                  --
connection.autoconnect-slaves:          -1 (default)
.
.
```

All of these properties can be modified using *nmcli* with the modify option using the following syntax:

```
# nmcli con mod <connection name> connection.<property name> <setting>
```

13.4 Working with Connection Profiles

So far we have explored the use of connections without explaining how a connection is configured. The configuration of a connection is referred to as a *connection profile* and is stored in a file located in the */etc/NetworkManager/system-connections* directory, the contents of which might read as follows:

```
# ls /etc/NetworkManager/system-connections
 zoneone   zonetwo  zonethree
```

Each of the files is an interface configuration file containing the connection profile for the corresponding connection.

Consider, for example, the contents of our hypothetical *zoneone* connection:

```
[connection]
id=zoneone
uuid=2842f180-1969-4dda-b473-6c641c25308d
type=wifi
permissions=

[wifi]
mac-address=C8:3A:35:CA:D5:17
mac-address-blacklist=
mode=infrastructure
ssid=zoneone

[wifi-security]
auth-alg=open
key-mgmt=wpa-psk
psk=MyPassword

[ipv4]
dns-search=
method=auto

[ipv6]
addr-gen-mode=stable-privacy
dns-search=
method=auto
```

The file contains basic information about the connection, including the type (wifi), and the SSID and WPA password key for the WiFi network. For both IPV4 and IPV6 the method property is set to auto (in other words the IP address for the connection will be obtained dynamically using DHCP). Changes to the connection profile can be implemented by modifying this file and instructing *nmcli* to reload the connection configuration files:

```
# nmcli con reload
```

New connection profiles can also be created manually or generated automatically by *nmcli*. As an example, assume that a new network device has been installed on the system. When this happens, the NetworkManager service will detect the new hardware and create a device for it. In the example below, the new device has been assigned the name *enp0s8*:

```
# nmcli dev status
DEVICE  TYPE      STATE      CONNECTION
enp0s3  ethernet  connected  Wired connection 1
enp0s8  ethernet  connected  Wired connection 2
```

NetworkManager automatically detected the device, activated it and assigned it to a connection named "Wired connection 2". This is a default connection over which we have no configuration control because there is no interface configuration file for it in */etc/NetworkManager/system-connections*. The next steps are to delete the "Wired connection 2" connection and use *nmcli* to create a new connection and assign it to the device. The command to delete a connection is as follows:

```
# nmcli con delete "Wired connection 2"
```

Next, *nmcli* can be used to create a new connection profile configured either with a static IP address, or a dynamic IP address obtained from a DHCP server. To create a dynamic connection profile named *dyn_ip*, the following command would be used:

```
# nmcli connection add type ethernet con-name dyn_ip ifname enp0s8
Connection 'dyn_ip' (160d9e10-bbc8-439a-9c47-a2ec52990472) successfully added.
```

After the connection has been created, a file named *dyn_ip* will have been added to the */etc/NetworkManager/system-connections* directory and will read as follows:

```
[connection]
id=dyn_ip
uuid=3dc0bb6b-33dc-4cf8-b5da-5b9fd560342a
type=ethernet
interface-name=enp0s8
permissions=

[ethernet]
mac-address-blacklist=

[ipv4]
dns-search=
method=auto

[ipv6]
addr-gen-mode=stable-privacy
```

```
dns-search=
method=auto
```

Checking the device status should now verify that the enp0s8 is now using the dyn_ip connection profile:

```
# nmcli dev status
DEVICE  TYPE      STATE      CONNECTION
enp0s8  ethernet  connected  dyn_ip
enp0s3  ethernet  connected  Wired connection 1
```

At this point it is worth pointing out that the enp0s3 device is also using a default connection profile for which there is no interface file through which to modify the connection settings. The same steps used to create the dyn_ip profile can also be used for the enp0s3 device. For example, to create a connection named *static_ip* assigned a static IP address (in this case 192.168.1.200) assigned to the enp0s3 device, the following command would be used (keeping in mind that if you are connected remotely to the system via the Wired connection 1 interface you will lose the connection):

```
# nmcli con delete "Wired connection 1"
# nmcli con add type ethernet con-name static_ip ifname enp0s3 ip4
192.168.1.200/24 gw4 192.168.1.1
Connection 'static_ip' (3fccafb3-e761-4271-b310-ad0f28ee8606) successfully added.
# nmcli reload
```

The corresponding *static_ip* file will read as follows:

```
[connection]
id=static_ip
uuid=6e03666b-26a1-476e-b5b2-77c8eac6006c
type=ethernet
interface-name=enp0s3
permissions=

[ethernet]
mac-address-blacklist=

[ipv4]
address1=192.168.1.200/24,192.168.1.1
dns-search=
method=manual

[ipv6]
addr-gen-mode=stable-privacy
dns-search=
method=auto
```

The command to add a new connection may be altered slightly to also assign both IPv4 and IPv6 static addresses:

```
# nmcli con add type ethernet con-name static_ip ifname enp0s3 ip4
192.168.1.200/24 gw4 192.168.1.1  gw4 192.168.1.1 ip6 cabf::4532 gw6 2010:dfa::1
```

13.5 Interactive Editing

In addition to using *nmcli* with command-line options, the tool also includes an interactive mode that can be used to create and modify connection profiles. The following transcript, for example, shows interactive mode being used to create a new Ethernet connection named *demo_con*:

```
# nmcli con edit
Valid connection types: 6lowpan, 802-11-olpc-mesh (olpc-mesh), 802-11-wireless
(wifi), 802-3-ethernet (ethernet), adsl, bluetooth, bond, bridge, cdma, dummy,
generic, gsm, infiniband, ip-tunnel, macsec, macvlan, ovs-bridge, ovs-interface,
ovs-port, pppoe, team, tun, vlan, vpn, vxlan, wimax, wpan, bond-slave, bridge-
slave, team-slave
Enter connection type: ethernet

===| nmcli interactive connection editor |===

Adding a new '802-3-ethernet' connection

Type 'help' or '?' for available commands.
Type 'print' to show all the connection properties.
Type 'describe [<setting>.<prop>]' for detailed property description.

You may edit the following settings: connection, 802-3-ethernet (ethernet), 802-
1x, dcb, sriov, ethtool, match, ipv4, ipv6, tc, proxy
nmcli> set connection.id demo_con
nmcli> set connection.interface enp0s8
nmcli> set connection.autoconnect yes
nmcli> set ipv4.method auto
nmcli> set 802-3-ethernet.mtu auto
nmcli> set ipv6.method auto
nmcli> save
Saving the connection with 'autoconnect=yes'. That might result in an immediate
activation of the connection.
Do you still want to save? (yes/no) [yes] yes
Connection 'demo_con' (cb837408-6c6f-4572-9548-4932f88b9275) successfully saved.
nmcli> quit
```

The following transcript, on the other hand, modifies the previously created *static_ip* connection profile to use a different static IP address to the one originally specified:

```
# nmcli con edit static_ip

===| nmcli interactive connection editor |===
```

```
Editing existing '802-3-ethernet' connection: 'static_ip'

Type 'help' or '?' for available commands.
Type 'print' to show all the connection properties.
Type 'describe [<setting>.<prop>]' for detailed property description.

You may edit the following settings: connection, 802-3-ethernet (ethernet), 802-1x, dcb, sriov, ethtool, match, ipv4, ipv6, tc, proxy
nmcli> print ipv4.addresses
ipv4.addresses: 192.168.1.200/24
nmcli> set ipv4.addresses 192.168.1.201/24
nmcli> save
Connection 'static_ip' (3fccafb3-e761-4271-b310-ad0f28ee8606) successfully updated.
nmcli> quit
```

After modifying an existing connection, remember to instruct NetworkManager to reload the configuration profiles:

```
# nmcli con reload
```

When using interactive mode, it is useful to know that there is an extensive built-in help system available to learn how to use the tool. The help topics can be accessed by typing *help* or *?* at the *nmcli* > prompt:

```
nmcli> ?
------------------------------------------------------------------------------
---[ Main menu ]---
goto      [<setting> | <prop>]         :: go to a setting or property
remove    <setting>[.<prop>] | <prop>  :: remove setting or reset property value
set       [<setting>.<prop> <value>]   :: set property value
describe  [<setting>.<prop>]           :: describe property
print     [all | <setting>[.<prop>]]   :: print the connection
verify    [all | fix]                  :: verify the connection
save      [persistent|temporary]       :: save the connection
activate  [<ifname>] [/<ap>|<nsp>]     :: activate the connection
back                                   :: go one level up (back)
help/?    [<command>]                  :: print this help
nmcli     <conf-option> <value>        :: nmcli configuration
quit                                   :: exit nmcli
------------------------------------------------------------------------------
```

13.6 Configuring NetworkManager Permissions

In addition to making it easier to manage networks on Ubuntu, NetworkManager also allows permissions to be specified for connections. The following command, for example, restricts a connection profile to root and user accounts named john and caitlyn:

```
# nmcli con mod static_ip connection.permissions user:root,john,caitlyn
```

Once the connection profiles have been reloaded by NetworkManager, the *static_ip* connection will only be active and accessible to other users when at least one of the designated users is logged in to an active session on the system. As soon as the last of these users logs out, the connection will go down and remain inactive until one of the users signs back in.

In addition, only users with permission are able to make changes to the connection status or configuration.

13.7 Summary

Network management on Ubuntu is handled by the NetworkManager service. NetworkManager views a network as consisting of network interface devices and connections. A network device can be a physical Ethernet or WiFi device or a virtual device used by a virtual machine guest. Connections represent the network to which the devices connect and are configured by connection profiles. A configuration profile will, among other settings, define whether the connection has a static or dynamic IP address, the IP address of any gateway used by the network and whether or not the connection should be established automatically each time the system starts up.

NetworkManager can be administered using a number of different tools including the *nmcli* and *nmtui* command-line tools, the *nm-connection-editor* graphical tool and the network settings section of the Cockpit web interface. In general, the *nmcli* command-line tool provides the most features and flexibility.

Chapter 14

14. Ubuntu Firewall Basics

A firewall is a vital component in protecting an individual computer system or network of computers from external attack (typically from an internet connection). Any computer connected directly to an internet connection should ideally run a firewall to protect against malicious activity. Similarly, any internal network must have some form of firewall between it and an external internet connection.

Ubuntu is supplied with powerful firewall technology known as iptables built-in. Entire books can, and indeed have, been written about configuring iptables. If you would like to learn about iptables we recommend:

https://www.linuxtopia.org/Linux_Firewall_iptables/index.html

The goal of this chapter is to cover some of the basic concepts of firewalls, TCP/IP ports and services. The configuration of a firewall on an Ubuntu system will be covered in *"Using gufw and ufw to Configure an Ubuntu Firewall"*. For more complex firewall requirements, a detailed overview of the firewalld firewall will be covered in the chapter entitled *"Basic Ubuntu Firewall Configuration with firewalld"*.

14.1 Understanding Ports and Services

The predominant network communications protocol in use these days is TCP/IP. It is the protocol used by the internet and as such has swept away most of the formerly popular protocols used for local area networks (LANs).

TCP/IP defines a total of 65,535 ports of which 1023 are considered to be well known ports. It is important to understand that these are not physical ports into which network cables are connected, but rather virtual ports on each network connection which can be used by applications and services to communicate over a TCP/IP network connection. In reality the number of ports that are used by popular network clients and services comprises an even smaller subset of the well known group of ports.

There are a number of different TCP/IP services that can be provided by an operating system. A comprehensive list of such services is provided in the table at the end of this chapter, but such services include HTTPS for running a secure web server, FTP for allowing file transfers, SSH for providing secure remote login access and file transfer and SMTP for the transport of email messages. Each service is, in turn, assigned to a standard TCP/IP port. For example, HTTPS is assigned to port 443 while SSH communication takes place on port 22.

14.2 Securing Ports and Services

A large part of securing servers involves defining roles, and based on the roles, defining which services and ports should be enabled. For example, a server that is to act solely as a web server should only run the HTTPS service (in addition to perhaps SSH for remote administration access). All other services should be disabled and, ideally, removed entirely from the operating system (thereby making it harder for an intruder to re-enable the service).

Securing a system involves both removing any unnecessary services from the operating system and ensuring that the ports associated with the non-essential services are blocked using a firewall. The rules that define which ports are accessible and under what circumstances are defined using iptables.

Many operating systems are installed with a number of services installed and activated by default. Before installing a new operating system it is essential that the installation be carefully planned. This involves deciding which services are not required and identifying which services have been installed and enabled by default. Deployment of new operating system installations should never be rushed. The fewer services and open ports available on a system the smaller the surface area and opportunities for attackers.

14.3 Ubuntu Services and iptables Rules

By default, a newly installed Ubuntu system does not have any iptables rules defined to restrict access to ports. To view the current iptables settings, the following command may be executed in a terminal window:

```
# iptables -L
Chain INPUT (policy ACCEPT)
target     prot opt source               destination

Chain FORWARD (policy ACCEPT)
target     prot opt source               destination

Chain OUTPUT (policy ACCEPT)
target     prot opt source               destination
```

As illustrated in the above output, no rules are currently defined. Whilst this may appear to be an unsafe configuration it is important to keep in mind that a newly installed Ubuntu system also has few services running by default, making the ports essentially useless to a potential attacker. It is not possible, for example, to remotely log into a newly installed Ubuntu system or access a web server for the simple reason that neither the ssh nor web server services are installed or running by default. Once services begin to be activated on the system, however, it will be important to begin to establish a firewall strategy by defining iptables rules.

A number of methods are available for defining iptables rules, including the use of command line tools and configuration files. For example, to block access to port 25 (used by the SMTP mail transfer protocol) from IP address 192.168.2.76, the following command could be issued in a terminal window:

```
# iptables -A INPUT -s 192.168.2.76 -p tcp --destination-port 25 -j DROP
```

If we now check the current rules, we will see that this one is now listed:

```
# iptables -L
Chain INPUT (policy ACCEPT)
target     prot opt source               destination
DROP       tcp  --  192.168.2.76         anywhere             tcp dpt:smtp

Chain FORWARD (policy ACCEPT)
target     prot opt source               destination

Chain OUTPUT (policy ACCEPT)
target     prot opt source               destination
```

The rule may subsequently be removed as follows:

```
# iptables -D INPUT -s 192.168.2.76 -p tcp --destination-port 25 -j DROP
```

Given the complexity of iptables it is not surprising that a number of user friendly graphical configuration tools have been created to ease the rule creation process. One such tool is the Uncomplicated Firewall with its *ufw* command-line tool and graphical equivalent (*gufw*) which will be covered in the chapter entitled *"Using gufw and ufw to Configure an Ubuntu Firewall"*. For more advanced firewall configurations, firewalld will be covered in *"Basic Ubuntu Firewall Configuration with firewalld"*.

14.4 Well Known Ports and Services

Before moving on to cover more complex firewall rules, it is first worth taking time to outline some of the key services that can be provided by an Ubuntu system, together with the corresponding port numbers:

Port	Assignment	Description
20	FTP	**File Transfer Protocol (Data)** - The File Transfer protocol provides a mechanism for transferring specific files between network connected computer systems. Transfer is typically performed using the ftp client. Most modern web browsers also have the ability to browse and download files located on a remote FTP server. FTP uses TCP (rather than UDP) to transfer files so is considered to be a highly reliable transport mechanism. FTP does not encrypt data and is not considered to be a secure file transfer protocol. The use of Secure Copy Protocol (SCP) and Secure File Transfer Protocol (SFTP) is strongly recommended in place of FTP.

21	FTP	**File Transfer (Control)** - Traditionally FTP has two ports assigned (port 20 and port 21). Port 20 was originally considered the data transfer port, while port 21 was assigned to communicate control information. In modern implementations port 20 is now rarely used, with all communication taking place on port 21.
22	SSH	**Secure Shell** - The Secure Shell is used to provide a secure, encrypted, remote logon session to a remote host over a TCP/IP network. The original mechanism for remote access was the Telnet protocol. Because Telnet transmits data in plain text its use is now strongly discouraged in favor of the secure shell, which encrypts all communications, including log-in and password credentials. SSH also provides the mechanism by which files can be securely transferred using the Secure Copy Protocol (SCP), and is also the basis for the Secure File Transfer Protocol (SFTP). SSH also replaces both the rsh and rlogin clients.
23	Telnet	**Telnet** - Telnet is a terminal emulation protocol that provides the ability to log into a remote system over a TCP/IP connection. The access is text based allowing the user to type into a command prompt on the remote host and text displayed by the remote host is displayed on the local Telnet client. Telnet encrypts neither the password nor the text communicated between the client and server. As such, the use of telnet is strongly discouraged. Most modern systems will have port 23 closed and the telnet service disabled to prevent its use. SSH should be used in place of Telnet.

25	SMTP	**Simple Mail Transfer Protocol** - SMTP defines the mechanism by which email messages are sent from one network host to another. SMTP is a very simple protocol and requires that the mail service always be available at the receiving host. Typically the receiving host will store incoming messages in a spool for subsequent access by the recipient using the POP3 or IMAP protocols. SMTP uses the TCP transport protocol to ensure error free message delivery.
53	DNS	**Domain Name Server** - The service used by TCP/IP networks to translate host names and Fully Qualified Domain Names (FQDN) to IP addresses.
69	TFTP	**Trivial File Transfer Protocol** - TFTP is a stripped down version of the File Transfer Protocol (FTP). It has a reduced command-set and lacks authentication. The most significant feature of TFTP is that it uses UDP to transfer data. This results in extremely fast transfer speeds but, consequently, lacks data reliability. TFTP is typically used in network based booting for diskless workstations.
80	HTTP	**Hypertext Text Transfer Protocol** - HTTP is the protocol used to download text, graphics and multimedia from a web server and to a web browser. Essentially it defines the command and control mechanism between the browser and server defining client requests and server responses. HTTP is based on the TCP transport protocol and, as such, is a connection-oriented protocol.

110	POP3	**Post Office Protocol** - The POP3 protocol is a mechanism for storage and retrieval of incoming email messages from a server. In most corporate environments incoming email is stored on an email server and then downloaded to an email client running on the user's desktop or laptop when the user checks email. POP3 downloads all new messages to the client, and does not provide the user the option of choosing which messages to download, view headers, or download only parts of messages. It is for this reason the IMAP protocol is increasingly being used in place of POP3.
119	NNTP	**Network News Transfer Protocol** - The protocol responsible for posting and retrieving messages to and from Usenet News Servers (i.e. newsgroups and discussion forums hosted on remote servers). NNTP operates at the Application layer of the OSI stack and uses TCP to ensure error free message retrieval and transmission.
123	NTP	**Network Time Protocol** - A protocol designed to synchronize computer clocks with an external time source. Using this protocol an operating system or application can request the current time from a remote NTP server. The remote NTP server is usually based on the time provided by a nuclear clock. NTP is useful for ensuring that all systems in a network are set to the same, accurate time of day. This is of particular importance in security situations when, for example, the time a file was accessed or modified on a client or server is in question.

143	IMAP4	**Internet Message Access Protocol, Version 4** - IMAP4 is an advanced and secure email retrieval protocol. IMAP is similar to POP3 in that it provides a mechanism for users to access email messages stored on an email server, although IMAP includes many additional features such as the ability to selectively download messages, view message headers, search messages and download part of a message. IMAP4 uses authentication and fully supports Kerberos authentication.
161	SNMP	**Simple Network Management Protocol** - Provides a mechanism whereby network administrators are able to collect information about the devices (such as hubs, bridges, routers and switches) on a network. The SNMP protocol enables agents running on network devices to communicate their status to a central manager and, in turn, enables the manager to send new configuration parameters to the device agent. The agents can further be configured to notify the manager when certain events, known as traps, occur. SNMP uses UDP to send and receive data.
443	HTTPS	**Hypertext Transfer Protocol Secure** - The standard HTTP (non-secure) protocol transfers data in clear text (i.e. with no encryption and visible to anyone who might intercept the traffic). Whilst this is acceptable for most web browsing purposes it poses a serious security risk when confidential information such as credit card details need to be transmitted from the browser to the web server. HTTPS addresses this by using the Secure Sockets Layer (SSL) to send encrypted data between the client and server.

2049	NFS	**Network File System** - Originally developed by Sun Microsystems and subsequently widely adopted throughout the industry, NFS allows a file system on a remote system to be accessed over the network by another system as if the file system were on a local disk drive. NFS is widely used on UNIX and LINUX based systems. Later versions of Microsoft Windows possess the ability to also access NFS shared file systems on UNIX and LINUX based systems.

14.5 Summary

A newly install Ubuntu system is generally considered to be secure due to the absence of any services running on the system ports. Once the system begins to be configured for use, however, it is important to ensure that it is protected from attack through the implementation of a firewall. When configuring firewalls, it is important to have an understanding of the various ports and the corresponding services.

A number of firewall options are available, the most basic being command-line configuration of the iptables firewall interface. More intuitive and advanced options are available via the Uncomplicated Firewall (ufw) and firewalld, both of which will be covered in the chapters that follow.

Chapter 15

15. Using gufw and ufw to Configure an Ubuntu Firewall

In the previous chapter we looked at ports and services on an Ubuntu system. We also briefly looked at iptables firewall rules on Ubuntu including the creation of a few very simple rules from the command line. In this chapter we will look at a more user friendly approach to iptables configuration using two tools named gufw and ufw. As we will see, gufw and ufw provide a high level of control over both inbound and outbound network traffic and connections without the need to understand the lower level iptables syntax.

15.1 An Overview of gufw and ufw

Included with Ubuntu is a package called ufw which is an acronym for Uncomplicated Firewall. This package provides a command line interface for managing and configuring rules for the Netfilter iptables based firewall. The gufw tool provides a user friendly graphical interface to ufw designed to make firewall management possible without the need to issue ufw commands at the command line.

15.2 Installing gufw on Ubuntu

Whilst ufw is installed on Ubuntu by default, the gufw package is not. To install gufw, therefore, open a Terminal window (Ctrl-Alt-T) and enter the following command at the resulting prompt:

```
# apt install gufw
```

15.3 Running and Enabling gufw

Once installed, launch *gufw* by pressing Alt-F2 within the GNOME desktop and entering *gufw* into the Run a command text box. When invoked for the first time it is likely that the firewall will be disabled as illustrated in Figure 15-1.

To enabled the firewall, move the Status switch (A) to the on position. By default, the main panel (D) will be displaying the gufw home page containing some basic information about the tool. Selecting options from the row of buttons (C) will change the information displayed in the panel. For example, select the Rules button to add, remove and view rules.

The gufw tool is provided with a small set of pre-configured profiles for work, home and public environments. To change the profile and view the settings simply select the profile from the menu (B). To modify an existing profile, select it from the menu and use the Incoming and Outgoing menus to change the selections. To configure specific rules, display the Rules screen and add, remove and modify rules as required. These will then be applied to the currently selected profile.

Figure 15-1

The currently selected profile dictates how the firewall handles traffic in the absence of any specific policy rules. By default the Home profile, for example, is configured to deny all incoming traffic and allow all outgoing traffic. These default policy settings are changed using the Incoming: and Outgoing: menus (E).

Exceptions to the default policy are defined through the creation of additional rules. With the Home profile denying incoming traffic, for example, rules would need to be added to enable certain acceptable types of incoming connections. Such rules are referred to in the security community as a whitelist.

If, on the other hand, the incoming policy was changed to Allow all traffic then all incoming traffic would be permitted unless rules were created for specific types of connections that must be blocked. These rules, unsurprisingly, are referred to as a blacklist. The blacklist/whitelist approach applies equally to incoming and outgoing connections.

15.4 Creating a New Profile

While it is possible to modify the pre-defined profiles, it will typically make more sense to create one or more profiles to configure the firewall for your specific needs. New profiles are created by selecting the *Edit -> Preferences...* menu option to display the dialog shown in Figure 15-2:

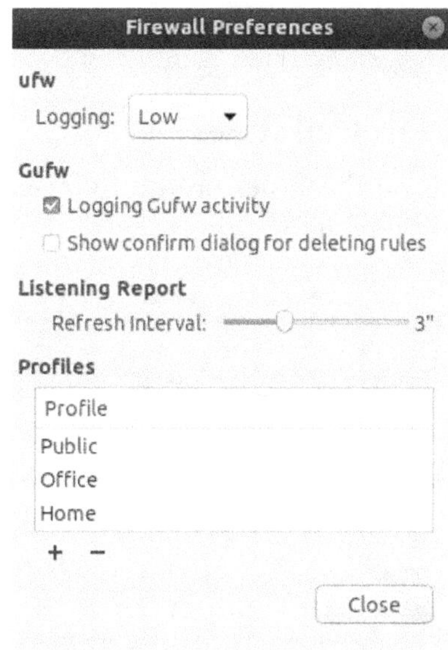

Figure 15-2

To add a new profile, click on the '+' button located beneath the list of profiles. A new profile named Profile 1 will appear in the list. To give the profile a more descriptive name, double-click on the entry to enter edit mode and enter a new name:

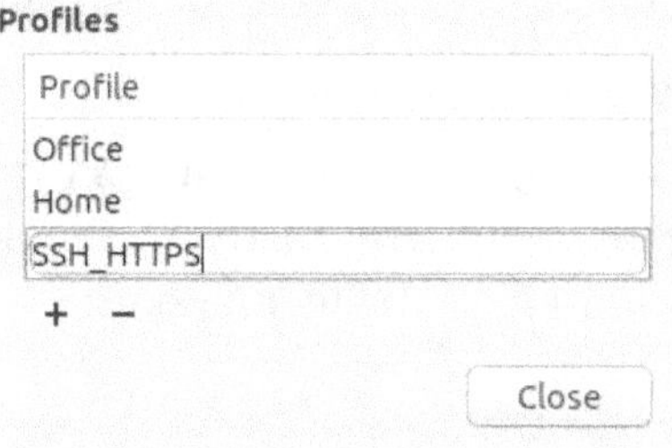

Figure 15-3

Once the profile has been created and named, click on the Close button to return to the main screen and select it from the Profile menu:

Figure 15-4

With the custom profile selected, it is ready to set up some custom rules that override the default incoming and outgoing settings.

15.5 Adding Preconfigured Firewall Rules

New rules are created by clicking on the Rules button followed by the + button located at the bottom of the rules panel as highlighted in Figure 15-5:

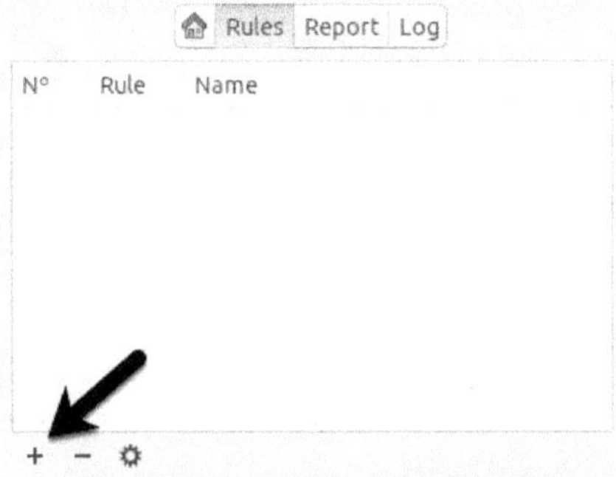

Figure 15-5

Once selected the dialog shown in Figure 15-6 will appear with the Preconfigured tab selected. The Preconfigured panel allows rules to be selected that match specific applications and services. For example traffic from such tools as Skype, and BitTorrent may be enabled by selecting the entry from the Application menu and the Policy and Direction menus accordingly to restrict or allow traffic.

To help find a specific application or service, use the Category and Subcategory menus to filter the items that appear in the Application menu. Alternatively, simply enter the application or service name in the Application Filter field to filter the menu items:

Figure 15-6

The Policy menu provides the following options for controlling traffic for the selected application or service:

- **Allow** – Traffic is permitted on the port.
- **Deny** – Traffic is not permitted on the port. The requesting system is not notified of the denial. The data packet is simply dropped.

• **Reject** - Traffic is not permitted on the port. The data packet is dropped and the requesting system is notified of the rejection.

• **Limit** - Connections are denied if the same IP address has attempted to establish 6 or more connections over a 30 seconds time frame.

Once a rule has been defined, clicking the Add button will implement the rule, dismiss the Add Rule dialog and the new rule will be listed in the main screen of the gufw tool (with rules for both IPv4 and IPv6 protocols):

Figure 15-7

To delete a rule, select it within the list and click on the '-' button located at the bottom of the dialog. Similarly, edit and existing rule by selecting it and clicking on the gear button to the right of the '-' button.

15.6 Adding Simple Firewall Rules

Whereas preconfigured rules allow the firewall to be configured based on well known services and applications, the Simple tab of the Add Rule dialog allows incoming and outgoing rules to be defined simply by referencing the corresponding TCP/IP port. The ports used by known applications and services represent only a small subset of the ports available for use by applications and for which firewall rules may need to be defined. A third party application might for example use port 5700 to communicate with a remote server. That being the case, it may be necessary to allow traffic on this specific port using the Simple panel:

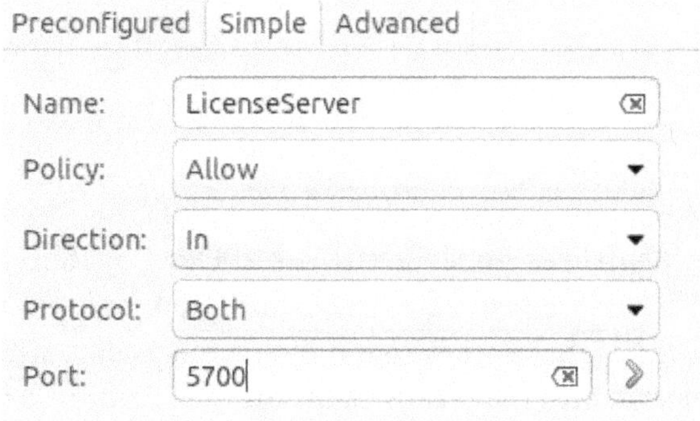

Figure 15-8

The rule may be configured to filter either TCP, UDP or both traffic types. In addition the port may be specified as a single port number or as a range of ports with the start and end ports separated by a colon (1000:1500, for example, would apply the rule to all ports between 1000 and 1500). Alternatively, enter the name of the service associated with the port (for example https or ssh)

15.7 Adding Advanced Rules

So far we have looked at rules to control only the type of traffic to block (incoming traffic on port 22 for example) regardless of the source or destination of the traffic. It is often the case, however, that rules will need to be defined to allow or deny traffic based on an IP address or range of IP addresses.

For the purposes of an example, assume that the local system has an IP address of 192.168.0.102. The firewall may be configured to only allow access on port 22 from a system with the IP address of, for example, 192.168.0.105. To achieve this, the From: field of the Advanced settings panel should be set to the IP address of the system from which the connection request is originating (in this case 192.168.0.105).

The To: fields provide the option to specify the IP address and port of the system to which the connection is being made. In this example this would be port 22 on the local system (192.168.0.102). The To: IP address is actually optional and may be left blank:

Figure 15-9

Assuming that the incoming default policy is still set to Deny or Reject on the main screen, the above rule will allow SSH access via port 22 to the local system only from the remote system with the IP address of 192.168.0.105. SSH access attempts from systems with other IP addresses will fail. Note that if the target system is the local system the To: IP address field may be left blank.

The Insert field in the above dialog allows the new rule to be inserted at the specified position in the list of existing rules, thereby allowing you to control the order in which the rules are applied within the firewall.

It is also possible to specify a range of addresses by using the IP address bitmask. For example, to create a rule for a range of IP addresses from 192.168.0.1 to 192.168.0.255 the IP address should be entered into the From: field as 192.168.0.0/24.

Similarly, to specify a rule covering IP address range 192.168.0.1 to 192.168.0.30, a bitmask of 27 would be used, i.e. 192.168.0.0/27.

A useful calculator for identifying the address range covered by each bit mask value is available online at *http://subnet-calculator.com*.

15.8 Configuring the Firewall from the Command Line using ufw

All of the firewall configuration options available through the graphical gufw tool are also available from the underlying command line using *ufw* command.

To enable or disable the firewall:

```
# ufw enable
# ufw disable
```

The current status of the firewall may be obtained using the *status* option:

```
# ufw status
Status: active

To                         Action      From
--                         ------      ----
22                         ALLOW       192.168.86.30
```

For more details status information, combine the above command with the verbose option:

```
# ufw status verbose
Status: active
Logging: on (full)
Default: deny (incoming), allow (outgoing), deny (routed)
New profiles: skip

To                         Action      From
--                         ------      ----
22                         ALLOW IN    192.168.86.30
```

The output in the above example shows that the default policy for the firewall is to deny all incoming and routed connections while allowing all outgoing connections. To change any of these default settings, use the ufw command with the default option using the following syntax:

```
# ufw default <policy> <direction>
```

For example, to enable all incoming connections by default:

```
# ufw default allow incoming
```

To allow or block traffic on a specific port use the following syntax:

```
# ufw <policy> <port number>/<optional protocol>
```

For example, to allow both TCP and UDP incoming traffic on port 30:

```
# ufw allow 30
```

Similarly, to deny incoming TCP traffic on port 5700

```
# ufw deny 5700/tcp
```

Rules may also be declared by referencing the name of the service corresponding to the port. For example to enable SSH access on port 22:

```
# ufw allow ssh
```

As with the gufw tool, ufw also allows access to be controlled from specific external IP addresses. For example, to allow all incoming traffic from IP address 192.168.0.20:

```
# ufw allow from 192.168.0.20
```

To specifically deny traffic from an IP address:

```
# ufw deny 192.168.0.20
```

To limit access for IP address 192.168.0.20 to only port 22:

```
# ufw allow from 192.168.0.22 to any port 22
```

To further restrict access for the IP address to only TCP packets, use the following syntax:

```
# ufw allow from 192.168.0.20 to any port 22 proto tcp
```

The position of a new rule within the list of existing rules may be declared using the insert option. For example to create a new rule and insert it at position 3 in the rules list:

```
# ufw insert 3 allow from 192.168.0.123 to any port 2
```

To display the list of rules with associated numbers:

```
# ufw status numbered
Status: active

     To                         Action      From
     --                         ------      ----
[ 1] 22                         ALLOW IN    192.168.86.30
[ 2] 30                         ALLOW IN    Anywhere
[ 3] 22                         ALLOW IN    192.168.0.123
[ 4] 5700/tcp                   DENY IN     Anywhere
[ 5] 22/tcp                     ALLOW IN    Anywhere
[ 6] Anywhere                   ALLOW IN    192.168.0.20
[ 7] 22                         ALLOW IN    192.168.0.4
[ 8] 30 (v6)                    ALLOW IN    Anywhere (v6)
[ 9] 5700/tcp (v6)              DENY IN     Anywhere (v6)
[10] 22/tcp (v6)                ALLOW IN    Anywhere (v6)
```

Having identified the number assigned to a rule, that number may be used to remove the rule from the firewall:

```
# ufw delete 4
```

To obtain a full listing of the capabilities of the ufw tool run the command with the –help argument:

```
# ufw help
```

Logging of firewall activity can be enabled and disabled using the logging command-line option:

```
# ufw logging on
# ufw logging off
```

The amount of logging performed by ufw may also be declared including a low, medium, high or full setting when turning on logging, for example:

```
# ufw logging on low
```

The ufw log file can be found at:

```
/var/log/ufw.log
```

Use the reload option to restart the firewall and reload all current settings:

```
# ufw reload
```

Finally, to reset the firewall to the default settings (thereby removing all existing rules and settings):

```
# ufw reset
```

15.9 Summary

Any computer system that is connected to other systems, either via an internal network or through an internet connection should implement some form of firewall to mitigate the risk of attack. The Uncomplicated Firewall provided with Ubuntu provides a simple yet effective firewall that allows basic rules to be defined either using the command-line or the graphical gufw tool. This chapter has outlined the basics of enabling the firewall and configuring firewall rules.

Chapter 16

16. Basic Ubuntu Firewall Configuration with firewalld

All Linux distributions are provided with a firewall solution of some form. In the case of Ubuntu this takes the form of the Uncomplicated Firewall outlined in the previous chapter. This chapter will introduce a more advanced firewall solution available for Ubuntu in the form of firewalld.

16.1 An Introduction to firewalld

Originally developed for Red Hat-based Linux distributions, the firewalld service uses a set of rules to control incoming network traffic and define which traffic is to be blocked and which is to be allowed to pass through to the system and is built on top of a more complex firewall tool named *iptables*.

The firewalld system provides a flexible way to manage incoming traffic. The firewall could, for example, be configured to block traffic arriving from a specific external IP address, or to prevent all traffic arriving on a particular TCP/IP port. Rules may also be defined to forward incoming traffic to different systems or to act as an internet gateway to protect other computers on a network.

In keeping with common security practices, a default firewalld installation is configured to block all access with the exception of SSH remote login and the DHCP service used by the system to obtain a dynamic IP address (both of which are essential if the system administrator is to be able to gain access to the system after completing the installation).

The key elements of firewall configuration on Ubuntu are *zones*, *interfaces*, *services* and *ports*.

16.1.1 Zones

By default, firewalld is installed with a range of pre-configured *zones*. A zone is a preconfigured set of rules which can be applied to the system at any time to quickly implement firewall configurations for specific scenarios. The *block* zone, for example, blocks all incoming traffic, while the *home* zone imposes less strict rules on the assumption that the system is running in a safer environment where a greater level of trust is expected. New zones may be added to the system, and existing zones modified to add or remove rules. Zones may also be deleted entirely from the system. Table 16-1 lists the set of zones available by default on an Ubuntu system:

Zone	Description
drop	The most secure zone. Only outgoing connections are permitted and all incoming connections are dropped without any notification to the connecting client.

Zone	Description
block	Similar to the drop zone with the exception that incoming connections are rejected with an icmp-host-prohibited or icmp6-adm-prohibited notification.
public	Intended for use when connected to public networks or the internet where other computers are not known to be trustworthy. Allows select incoming connections.
external	When a system is acting as the internet gateway for a network of computers, the external zone is applied to the interface that is connected to the internet. This zone is used in conjunction with the *internal* zone when implementing masquerading or network address translation (NAT) as outlined later in this chapter. Allows select incoming connections
internal	Used with the *external* zone and applied to the interface that is connected to the internal network. Assumes that the computers on the internal network are trusted. Allows select incoming connections.
dmz	For use when the system is running in the demilitarized zone (DMZ). These are generally computers that are publicly accessible but isolated from other parts of your internal network. Allows select incoming connections.
work	For use when running a system on a network in a work environment where other computers are trusted. Allows select incoming connections.
home	For use when running a system on a home network where other computers are trusted. Allows select incoming connections.
trusted	The least secure zone. All incoming connections are accepted.

Table 16-1

To review specific settings for a zone, refer to the corresponding XML configuration file located on the system in the */usr/lib/firewalld/zones* directory. The following, for example, lists the content of the *public.xml* zone configuration file:

```
<?xml version="1.0" encoding="utf-8"?>
<zone>
  <short>Public</short>
  <description>For use in public areas. You do not trust the other computers
on networks to not harm your computer. Only selected incoming connections are
accepted.</description>
  <service name="ssh"/>
  <service name="mdns"/>
  <service name="dhcpv6-client"/>
</zone>
```

16.1.2 Interfaces

Any Ubuntu system connected to the internet or a network (or both) will contain at least one *interface* in the form of either a physical or virtual network device. When firewalld is active, each of these interfaces is assigned to a zone allowing different levels of firewall security to be assigned to different interfaces. Consider a server containing two interfaces, one connected externally to the internet and the other to an internal network. In such a scenario, the external facing interface would most likely be assigned to the more restrictive *external* zone while the internal interface might use the *internal* zone.

16.1.3 Services

TCP/IP defines a set of services that communicate on standard ports. Secure HTTPS web connections, for example, use port 443, while the SMTP email service uses port 25. To selectively enable incoming traffic for specific services, firewalld rules can be added to zones. The *home* zone, for example, does not permit incoming HTTPS connections by default. This traffic can be enabled by adding rules to a zone to allow incoming HTTPS connections without having to reference the specific port number.

16.1.4 Ports

Although common TCP/IP services can be referenced when adding firewalld rules, situations will arise where incoming connections need to be allowed on a specific port that is not allocated to a service. This can be achieved by adding rules that reference specific ports instead of services.

16.2 Checking firewalld Status

The firewalld service is not usually installed and enabled by default on all Ubuntu installations. The status of the service can be checked via the following command:

```
# systemctl status firewalld
● firewalld.service - firewalld - dynamic firewall daemon
   Loaded: loaded (/lib/systemd/system/firewalld.service; enabled; vendor preset: enabled)
   Active: active (running) since Fri 2020-04-10 10:17:54 EDT; 20s ago
     Docs: man:firewalld(1)
 Main PID: 4488 (firewalld)
    Tasks: 2 (limit: 4915)
   CGroup: /system.slice/firewalld.service
           └─4488 /usr/bin/python3 -Es /usr/sbin/firewalld --nofork --nopid

Apr 10 10:17:54 demo-server systemd[1]: Starting firewalld - dynamic firewall daemon...
Apr 10 10:17:54 demo-server systemd[1]: Started firewalld - dynamic firewall daemon.
```

If necessary, the firewalld service may be installed as follows:

```
# apt install firewalld
```

The firewalld service is enabled by default so will start automatically both after installation is complete and each time the system boots.

16.3 Configuring Firewall Rules with firewall-cmd

The *firewall-cmd* command-line utility allows information about the firewalld configuration to be viewed and changes to be made to zones and rules from within a terminal window.

When making changes to the firewall settings, it is important to be aware of the concepts of *runtime* and *permanent* configurations. By default, any rule changes are considered to be runtime configuration changes. This means that while the changes will take effect immediately, they will be lost next time the system restarts or the firewalld service reloads, for example by issuing the following command:

```
# firewall-cmd --reload
```

To make a change permanent, the *--permanent* command-line option must be used. Permanent changes do not take effect until the firewalld service reloads but will remain in place until manually changed.

16.3.1 Identifying and Changing the Default Zone

To identify the default zone (in other words the zone to which all interfaces will be assigned unless a different zone is specifically selected) use the *firewall-cmd* tool as follows:

```
# firewall-cmd --get-default-zone
public
```

To change the default to a different zone:

```
# firewall-cmd --set-default-zone=home
success
```

16.3.2 Displaying Zone Information

To list all of the zones available on the system:

```
# firewall-cmd --get-zones
block dmz drop external home internal public trusted work
```

Obtain a list of zones currently active together with the interfaces to which they are assigned as follows:

```
# firewall-cmd --get-active-zones
external
  interfaces: eth0
internal
 interfaces: eth1
```

All of the rules currently configured for a specific zone may be listed as follows:

```
# firewall-cmd --zone=home --list-all
home (active)
  target: default
  icmp-block-inversion: no
  interfaces: eth0
```

```
  sources:
  services: cockpit dhcpv6-client http mdns samba-client ssh
  ports:
  protocols:
  masquerade: no
  forward-ports:
  source-ports:
  icmp-blocks:
  rich rules:
```

Use the following command to list the services currently available for inclusion in a firewalld rule:

```
# firewall-cmd --get-services
RH-Satellite-6 amanda-client amanda-k5-client amqp amqps apcupsd audit bacula
bacula-client bgp bitcoin bitcoin-rpc bitcoin-testnet bitcoin-testnet-rpc ceph
ceph-mon cfengine cockpit ...
```

To list the services currently enabled for a zone:

```
# firewall-cmd --zone=public --list-services
cockpit dhcpv6-client ssh
```

A list of port rules can be obtained as follows:

```
# firewall-cmd --zone=public --list-ports
9090/tcp
```

16.3.3 Adding and Removing Zone Services

To add a service to a zone, in this case adding HTTPS to the public zone, the following command would be used:

```
# firewall-cmd --zone=public --add-service=https
success
```

By default this is a *runtime* change, so the added rule will be lost after a system reboot. To add a service permanently so that it remains in effect next time the system restarts, use the *--permanent* flag:

```
# firewall-cmd --zone=public --permanent --add-service=https
success
```

To verify that a service has been added permanently, be sure to include the *--permanent* flag when requesting the service list:

```
# firewall-cmd --zone=public --permanent --list-services
cockpit dhcpv6-client http https ssh
```

Note that as a permanent change, this new rule will not take effect until the system restarts or firewalld reloads:

```
# firewall-cmd --reload
```

Remove a service from a zone using the *--remove-service* option. Since this is a runtime change, the rule will be re-instated the next time the system restarts:

```
# firewall-cmd --zone=public --remove-service=https
```

To remove a service permanently use the *--permanent* flag, remembering to reload firewalld if the change is required to take immediate effect:

```
# firewall-cmd --zone=public --permanent --remove-service=https
```

16.3.4 Working with Port-based Rules

To enable a specific port, use the *--add-port* option. Note that when manually defining the port, both the port number and protocol (TCP or UDP) will need to be provided:

```
# firewall-cmd --zone=public --permanent --add-port=5000/tcp
```

It is also possible to specify a range of ports when adding a rule to a zone:

```
# firewall-cmd --zone=public --permanent --add-port=5900-5999/udp
```

16.3.5 Creating a New Zone

An entirely new zone may be created by running the following command. Once created, the zone may be managed in the same way as any of the predefined zones:

```
# firewall-cmd --permanent --new-zone=myoffice
success
```

After adding a new zone, firewalld will need to be restarted before the zone becomes available:

```
# firewall-cmd --reload
success
```

16.3.6 Changing Zone/Interface Assignments

As previously discussed, each interface on the system must be assigned to a zone. The zone to which an interface is assigned can also be changed using the *firewall-cmd* tool. In the following example, the eth0 interface is assigned to the *public* zone:

```
# firewall-cmd --zone=public --change-interface=eth0
success
```

16.3.7 Masquerading

Masquerading is better known in networking administration circles as Network Address Translation (NAT). When using an Ubuntu system as a gateway to the internet for a network of computers, masquerading allows all of the internal systems to use the IP address of that Ubuntu system when communicating over the internet. This has the advantage of hiding the internal IP addresses of any systems from malicious external entities and also avoids the necessity to allocate a public IP address to every computer on the network.

Use the following command to check whether masquerading is already enabled on the firewall:

```
# firewall-cmd --zone=external --query-masquerade
```

Use the following command to enable masquerading (remembering to use the *--permanent* flag if the change is to be permanent):

```
# firewall-cmd --zone=external --add-masquerade
```

16.3.8 Adding ICMP Rules

The Internet Control Message Protocol (ICMP) is used by client systems on networks to send information such as error messages to each other. It is also the foundation of the *ping* command which is used by network administrators and users alike to detect whether a particular client is alive on a network. The ICMP category allows for the blocking of specific ICMP message types. For example, an administrator might choose to block incoming ping (Echo Request) ICMP messages to prevent the possibility of a ping based denial of service (DoS) attack (where a server is maliciously bombarded with so many ping messages that it becomes unable to respond to legitimate requests).

To view the ICMP types available for inclusion in firewalld rules, run the following command:

```
# firewall-cmd --get-icmptypes
address-unreachable bad-header beyond-scope communication-prohibited destination-
unreachable echo-reply ...
```

The following command, for example, permanently adds a rule to block echo-reply (ping request) messages for the public zone:

```
# firewall-cmd --zone=public --permanent --add-icmp-block=echo-reply
```

16.3.9 Implementing Port Forwarding

Port forwarding is used in conjunction with masquerading when the Ubuntu system is acting as a gateway to the internet for an internal network of computer systems. Port forwarding allows traffic arriving at the firewall via the internet on a specific port to be forwarded to a particular system on the internal network. This is perhaps best described by way of an example.

Suppose that an Ubuntu system is acting as the firewall for an internal network of computers and one of the systems on the network is configured as a web server. Let's assume the web server system has an IP address of 192.168.2.20. The domain record for the web site hosted on this system is configured with the public IP address behind which the Ubuntu firewall system sits. When an HTTP web page request arrives on port 80 the Ubuntu system acting as the firewall needs to know what to do with it. By configuring port forwarding it is possible to direct all web traffic to the internal system hosting the web server (in this case, IP address 192.168.2.20), either continuing to use port 80 or diverting the traffic to a different port on the destination server. In fact, port forwarding can even be configured to forward the traffic to a different port on the same system as the firewall (a concept known as local forwarding).

To use port forwarding, begin by enabling masquerading as follows (in this case the assumption is made that the interface connected to the internet has been assigned to the *external* zone):

```
# firewall-cmd --zone=external --add-masquerade
```

To forward from a port to a different local port, a command similar to the following would be used:

```
# firewall-cmd --zone=external --add-forward-port=port=22:proto=tcp:toport=2750
```

In the above example, any TCP traffic arriving on port 22 will be forwarded to port 2750 on the local system. The following command, on the other hand, forwards port 20 on the local system to port 22 on the system with the IP address of 192.168.0.19:

```
# firewall-cmd --zone=external \
         --add-forward-port=port=20:proto=tcp:toport=22:toaddr=192.168.0.19
```

Similarly, the following command forwards local port 20 to port 2750 on the system with IP address 192.168.0.18:

```
# firewall-cmd --zone=external --add-forward-port=port=20:proto=tcp:toport=2750:to
addr=192.168.0.18
```

16.4 Managing firewalld using firewall-config

If you have access to the graphical desktop environment, the firewall may also be configured using the *firewall-config* tool. Though not installed by default, *firewall-config* may be installed as follows:

```
# apt install firewall-config
```

When launched, the main *firewall-config* screen appears as illustrated in Figure 16-1:

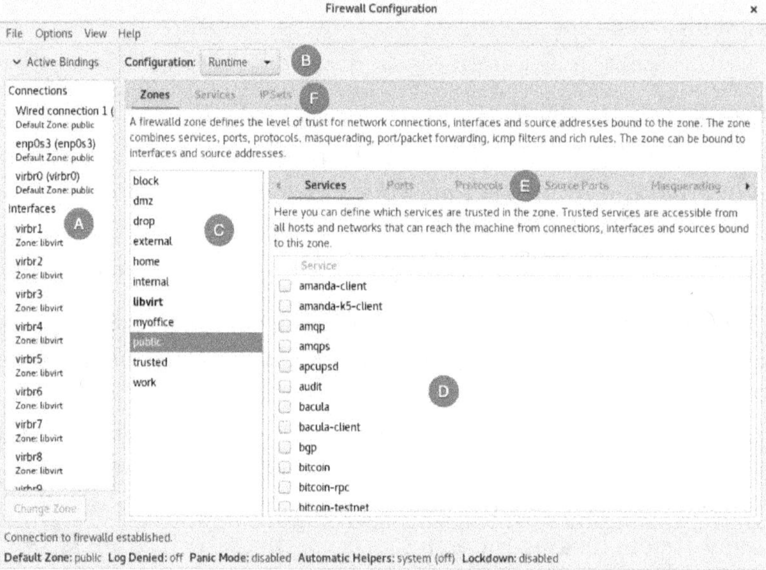

Figure 16-1

The key areas of the tool can be summarized as follows:

A - Displays all of the currently active interfaces and the zones to which they are assigned. To assign an interface to a different zone, select it from this panel, click on the *Change Zone* button and select the required zone from the resulting dialog.

B - Controls whether the information displayed and any changes made within the tool apply to the runtime or permanent rules.

C - The list of zones, services or IPSets configured on the system. The information listed in this panel depends on the selection made from toolbar F. Selecting an item from the list in this panel updates the main panel marked D.

D - The main panel containing information about the current category selection in toolbar E. In this example, the panel is displaying services for the *public* zone. The checkboxes next to each service control whether the service is enabled or not within the firewall. It is within these category panels that new rules can be added or existing rules configured or removed.

E - Controls the content displayed in panel D. Selecting items from this bar displays the current rule for the chosen category.

F - Controls the list displayed in panel C.

The *firewall-config* tool is straightforward and intuitive to use and allows many of the tasks available with *firewall-cmd* to be performed in a visual environment.

16.5 Summary

A carefully planned and implemented firewall is a vital component of any secure system. In the case of Ubuntu, the firewalld service provides a firewall system that is both flexible and easy to administer.

The firewalld service uses the concept of zones to group together sets of firewall rules and includes a suite of pre-defined zones designed to meet a range of firewall protection requirements. These zones may be modified to add or remove rules, or entirely new zones created and configured. The network devices on the system that connect to networks or the internet are referred to as interfaces. Each interface, in turn, is assigned to a zone. The primary tools for working with firewalld are the *firewall-cmd* command-line tool and the *firewall-config* graphical utility.

Chapter 17

17. Configuring SSH Key-based Authentication on Ubuntu

When an Ubuntu system is first installed, it is not configured by default to allow remote command-line access via Secure Shell (SSH) connections. When installed, SSH provides password protected and encrypted access to the system for the root account and any other users added during the installation phase. This level of security is far from adequate and should be upgraded to SSH key-based authentication as soon as possible.

This chapter will outline the steps to increase the security of an Ubuntu system by implementing key-based SSH authentication.

17.1 An Overview of Secure Shell (SSH)

SSH is designed to allow secure remote access to systems for the purposes of gaining shell access and transferring files and data. As will be covered in *"Ubuntu Remote Desktop Access with Vino"*, SSH can also be used to provide a secure *tunnel* through which remote access to the GNOME desktop can be achieved over a network connection.

A basic SSH configuration consists of a client (used on the computer establishing the connection) and a server (running on the system to which the connection is to be established). A user might, for example, use an SSH client running on a Linux, Windows or macOS system to connect to the SSH server running on an Ubuntu system to gain access to a shell command-line prompt or to perform file transfers. All of the communications between client and server, including the password entered to gain access, are encrypted to prevent outside parties from intercepting the data.

The inherent weakness in a basic SSH implementation is that it depends entirely on the strength of the passwords assigned to the accounts on the system. If a malicious party is able to identify the password for an account (either through guess work, subterfuge or a brute force attack) the system becomes vulnerable. This weakness can be addressed by implementing SSH key-based authentication.

17.2 SSH Key-based Authentication

SSH key-based authentication makes use of asymmetric *public key encryption* to add an extra layer of security to remote system access. The concept of public key encryption was devised in 1975 by Whitfield Diffie and Martin Hellman and is based on the concept of using a pair of keys, one private and one public.

In a public key encryption system, the public key is used to encrypt data that can only be decrypted by the owner of the private key.

In the case of SSH key-based authentication, the private key is held by the host on which the SSH client is located while the corresponding public key resides on the system on which the SSH server is running. It is important to protect the private key, since ownership of the key will allow anyone to log into the remote system. As an added layer of protection, therefore, the private key may also be encrypted and protected by a password which must be entered each time a connection is established to the server.

17.3 Setting Up Key-based Authentication

There are four steps to setting up key-based SSH authentication which can be summarized as follows:

1. Generate the public and private keys.

2. Install the public key on the server.

3. Test authentication.

4. Disable password-based authentication on the server.

The remainder of this chapter will outline these steps in greater detail for Linux, macOS and Windows-based client operating systems.

17.4 Installing and Starting the SSH Service

If the SSH server is not already installed and running on the system, it can be added using the following commands:

```
# apt install openssh-server
# systemctl start sshd.service
# systemctl enable sshd.service
```

17.5 SSH Key-based Authentication from Linux and macOS Clients

The first step in setting up SSH key-based authentication is to generate the key pairs on the client system. If the client system is running Linux or macOS, this is achieved using the *ssh-keygen* utility:

```
# ssh-keygen
```

This will result in output similar to the following:

```
Generating public/private rsa key pair.
Enter file in which to save the key (/home/<username>/.ssh/id_rsa):
```

Press the Enter key to accept the default location for the key files. This will place two files in the *.ssh* sub-directory of the current user's home directory. The private key will be stored in a file named *id_rsa* while the public key will reside in the file named *id_rsa.pub*.

Next, *ssh-keygen* will prompt for a passphrase with which to protect the private key. If a passphrase is provided, the private key will be encrypted on the local disk and the passphrase required in order to gain access to the remote system. For better security, use of a passphrase is recommended.

```
Enter passphrase (empty for no passphrase):
```

Finally, the *ssh-keygen* tool will generate the following output indicating that the keys have been generated:

```
Your identification has been saved in /home/neil/.ssh/id_rsa.
Your public key has been saved in /home/neil/.ssh/id_rsa.pub.
The key fingerprint is:
SHA256:FOLGWEEGFIjWnCT5wtTOv5VK4hdimzWghZizUEMYbfo <username>@<hostname>
The key's randomart image is:
+---[RSA 2048]----+
|.BB+=+*..        |
|o+B= * . .       |
|===.. + .        |
|*+ * . .         |
|.++ o   S        |
|..E+ * o         |
|  o B *          |
|   + +           |
|    .            |
+----[SHA256]-----+
```

The next step is to install the public key onto the remote server system. This can be achieved using the *ssh-copy-id* utility as follows:

```
$ ssh-copy-id username@remote_hostname
```

For example:

```
$ ssh-copy-id neil@192.168.1.100
/usr/bin/ssh-copy-id: INFO: Source of key(s) to be installed: "/home/neil/.ssh/
id_rsa.pub"
/usr/bin/ssh-copy-id: INFO: attempting to log in with the new key(s), to filter
out any that are already installed
/usr/bin/ssh-copy-id: INFO: 1 key(s) remain to be installed -- if you are
prompted now it is to install the new keys
neil@192.168.1.100's password:

Number of key(s) added: 1

Now try logging into the machine, with:   "ssh 'neil@192.168.1.100'"
and check to make sure that only the key(s) you wanted were added.
```

Once the key is installed, test that the authentication works by attempting a remote login using the *ssh* client:

```
$ ssh -l <username> <hostname>
```

If the private key is encrypted and protected with a passphrase, enter the phrase when prompted to complete the authentication and establish remote access to the Ubuntu system:

```
Enter passphrase for key '/home/neil/.ssh/id_rsa':
Last login: Thu Feb 21 13:41:23 2019 from 192.168.1.101
[neil@demosystem02 ~]$
```

Repeat these steps for any other accounts on the server for which remote access is required. If access is also required from other client systems, simply copy the *id_rsa* private key file to the *.ssh* sub-directory of your home folder of the other systems.

As currently configured, access to the remote system can still be achieved using the less secure password authentication. Once you have verified that key-based authentication works, log into the remote system, edit the */etc/ssh/ssh_config* file and change the *PasswordAuthentication* setting to *no*:

```
PasswordAuthentication no
```

Save the file and restart the *sshd* service to implement the change:

```
# systemctl restart sshd.service
```

From this point on, it will only be possible to remotely access the system using SSH key-based authentication.

17.6 Managing Multiple Keys

It is not uncommon for multiple private keys to reside on a client system, each providing access to a different server. There are a number of options for selecting a specific key when establishing a connection. It is possible, for example, to specify the private key file to be used when launching the *ssh* client as follows:

```
$ ssh -l neilsmyth -i ~/.ssh/id_work 35.194.18.119
```

Alternatively, the SSH client user configuration file may be used to associate key files with servers. The configuration file is named *config*, must reside in the *.ssh* directory of the user's home directory and can be used to configure a wide range of options including the private key file, the default port to use when connecting, the default user name, and an abbreviated nickname via which to reference the server. The following example *config* file defines different key files for two servers and allows them to be referenced by the nicknames *home* and *work*. In the case of the work system, the file also specifies the user name to be used when authenticating:

```
Host work
  HostName 35.194.18.119
  IdentityFile ~/.ssh/id_work
  User neilsmyth

Host home
  HostName 192.168.0.21
  IdentityFile ~/.ssh/id_home
```

Prior to setting up the configuration file, the user would have used the following command to connect to the work system:

```
$ ssh -l neilsmyth -i ~/.ssh/id_work 35.194.18.119
```

Now, however, the command can be shortened as follows:

```
$ ssh work
```

A full listing of configuration file options can be found by running the following command:

```
$ man ssh_config
```

17.7 SSH Key-based Authentication from Windows 10 Clients

Recent releases of Windows 10 include a subset of the OpenSSH implementation that is used by most Linux and macOS systems as part of Windows PowerShell. This allows SSH key-based authentication to be set up from a Windows 10 client using similar steps to those outlined above for Linux and macOS.

To open Windows PowerShell on a Windows 10 system press the Win+X keyboard combination and select it from the menu, or locate and select it from the Start menu. Once running, the PowerShell window will appear as shown in Figure 17-1:

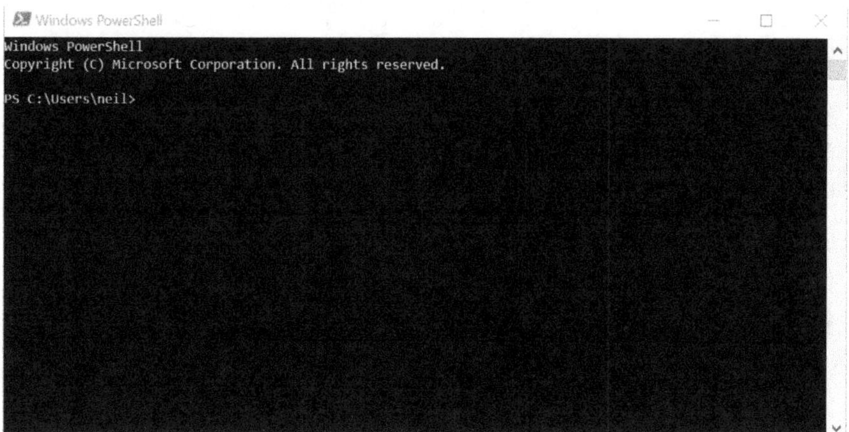

Figure 17-1

If you already have a private key from another client system, simply copy the *id_rsa* file to a folder named *.ssh* on the Windows 10 system. Once the file is in place, test the authentication within the PowerShell window as follows:

```
$ ssh -l <username>@<hostname>
```

For example:

```
PS C:\Users\neil> ssh -l neil 192.168.1.101
Enter passphrase for key 'C:\Users\neil/.ssh/id_rsa':
```

Enter the passphrase when prompted and complete the authentication process.

If an existing private key does not yet exist, generate a new private and public key pair within the PowerShell window using the *ssh-keygen* utility using the same steps as those outlined for Linux and macOS. Once the keys have been generated, they will once again be located in the *.ssh* directory of the current user's home folder, and the public key file *id_rsa.pub* will need to be installed on the remote Ubuntu system. Unfortunately, Windows PowerShell does not include the *ssh-copy-id* utility, so this task will need to be performed manually.

Within the PowerShell window, change directory into the *.ssh* sub-directory and display the content of the public key *id_rsa.pub* file:

```
PS C:\Users\neil> cd .ssh
PS C:\Users\neil\.ssh> type id_rsa.pub
ssh-rsa AAAAB3NzaC1yc2EAAAADAQABAAABAQDFgx1vzu59lll6/uQw7FbmKVsQ3fzLz9MW1fgo4sdsx
Xp81wCHNAlqcjx1Pgr9BJPXWUMInQOi7BQ5I+vc2xQ2AS0kMq3ZH9ybWuQe/U2GjueXZd0FKrEXrT55wM
36Rm6Ii3roUCoGCzGR8mn95JvRB3VtCyDdzTWSi8JBpK5gV5oOxNTNPsewlLzouBlCT1qW3CKwEiIwu8S
9MTL7m3nrcaNeLewTTHevvHw4QDwzFQ+B0PDg96fzsYoTXVhzyHSWyo6H0gqrft7aK+gILBtEIhWTkSVE
MAzy1piKtCrlIYTmVK6engv0aoGtMUq6FnOeGp5FjvKkF4aQkh1QR28r neil@DESKTOP-S8P8D3N
```

Highlight the content of the file and copy it using the Ctrl-C keyboard shortcut.

Remaining within the PowerShell window, log into the remote system using password authentication:

```
PS C:\Users\neil\.ssh> ssh -l <username> <hostname>
```

Once signed in, check if the *.ssh* sub-directory exists. If it does not, create it as follows:

```
$ mkdir .ssh
```

Change directory into *.ssh* and check whether a file named *authorized_keys* already exists. If it does not, create it and paste the content of the public key file from the Windows 10 system into it.

If the *authorized_keys* file already exists it most likely already contains other keys. If this is the case, edit the file and paste the new public key at the end of the file. The following file, for example, contains two keys:

```
ssh-rsa AAAAB3NzaC1yc2EAAAADAQABAAABAQCzRWH27Xs8ZA5rIbZXKgxFY5XXauMv+6F5PljBLJ6j
+9nkmykVe3GjZTp3oD+KMRbT2kTEPbDpFD67DNL0eiX2ZuEEiYsxZfGCRCPBGYmQttFRHEAFnlS1Jx/
G4W5UNKvhAXWyMwDEKiWvqTVy6syB2Ritoak+D/Sc8nJflQ6dtw0jBs+S7Aim8TPfgpi4p5XJGruXNRS
camk68NgnPfTL3vT726EuABCk6C934KARd+/AXa8/5rNOh4ETPstjBRfFJ0tpmsWWhhNEnwJRqS2LD0
ug7E3yFI2qsNKGEzvAYUC8Up45MRP7liR3aMlCBil1tsy9R+IB7oMEycZAe/qj neil@localhost.
localdomain
ssh-rsa AAAAB3NzaC1yc2EAAAADAQABAAABAQDFgx1vzu59lll6/uQw7FbmKVsQ3fzLz9MW1fgo4sdsx
Xp81wCHNAlqcjx1Pgr9BJPXWUMInQOi7BQ5I+vc2xQ2AS0kMq3ZH9ybWuQe/U2GjueXZd0FKrEXrT55wM
36Rm6Ii3roUCoGCzGR8mn95JvRB3VtCyDdzTWSi8JBpK5gV5oOxNTNPsewlLzouBlCT1qW3CKwEiIwu8S
9MTL7m3nrcaNeLewTTHevvHw4QDwzFQ+B0PDg96fzsYoTXVhzyHSWyo6H0gqrft7aK+gILBtEIhWTkSVE
MAzy1piKtCrlIYTmVK6engv0aoGtMUq6FnOeGp5FjvKkF4aQkh1QR28r neil@DESKTOP-S8P8D3N
```

Once the public key is installed on the server, test the authentication by logging in to the server from within the Windows 10 PowerShell window, for example:

```
PS C:\Users\neil\.ssh> ssh -l neil 192.168.1.100
Enter passphrase for key 'C:\Users\neil/.ssh/id_rsa':
```

When key-based authentication has been set up for all the accounts and verified, disable password authentication on the Ubuntu system as outlined at the end of the previous section.

17.8 SSH Key-based Authentication using PuTTY

For Windows systems that do not have OpenSSH available, or as a more flexible alternative to using PowerShell, the PuTTY tool is a widely used alternative. The first step in using PuTTY is to download and install it on any Windows systems that need an SSH client. PuTTY is a free utility and can be downloaded using the following link:

https://www.chiark.greenend.org.uk/~sgtatham/putty/latest.html

Download the Windows installer executable that matches your Windows system (32-bit and 64-bit versions are available) then execute the installer to complete installation.

If a private key already exists on another system, create the *.ssh* folder in the home folder of the current user and copy the private *id_rsa key* into it.

Next, the private key file needs to be converted to a PuTTY private key format file using the *PuTTYgen* tool. Locate this utility in the Windows Start menu and launch it:

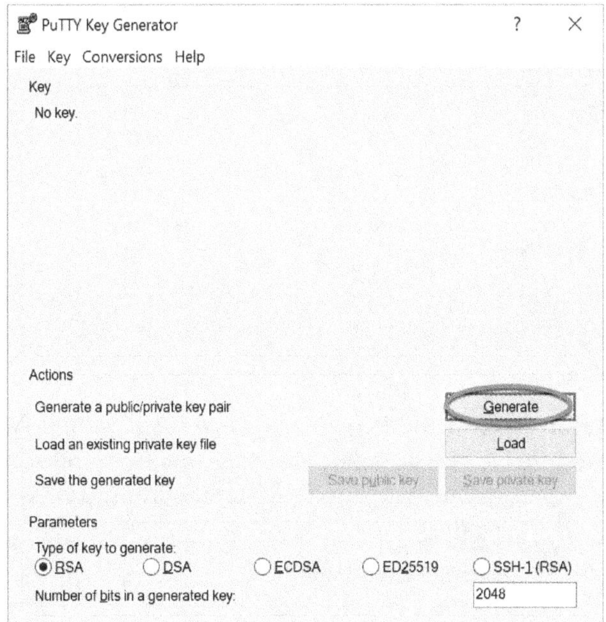

Figure 17-2

Once launched, click on the *Load* button located in the *Actions* section and navigate to the private key file previously copied to the *.ssh* folder (note that it may be necessary to change the file type filter to *All Files (*.*)* in order for the key file to be visible). Once located, select the file and load it into *PuttyGen*. When prompted, enter the passphrase originally used to encrypt the file. Once the private key has been imported, save it as a PuTTY key file by clicking on the *Save Private Key* button. For consistency, save the key file to the *.ssh* folder but give it a different name to differentiate it from the original key file.

Launch PuTTY from the Start menu and enter the IP address or host name of the remote server into the main screen before selecting the *Connection -> SSH -> Auth* category in the left-hand panel as highlighted in Figure 17-3:

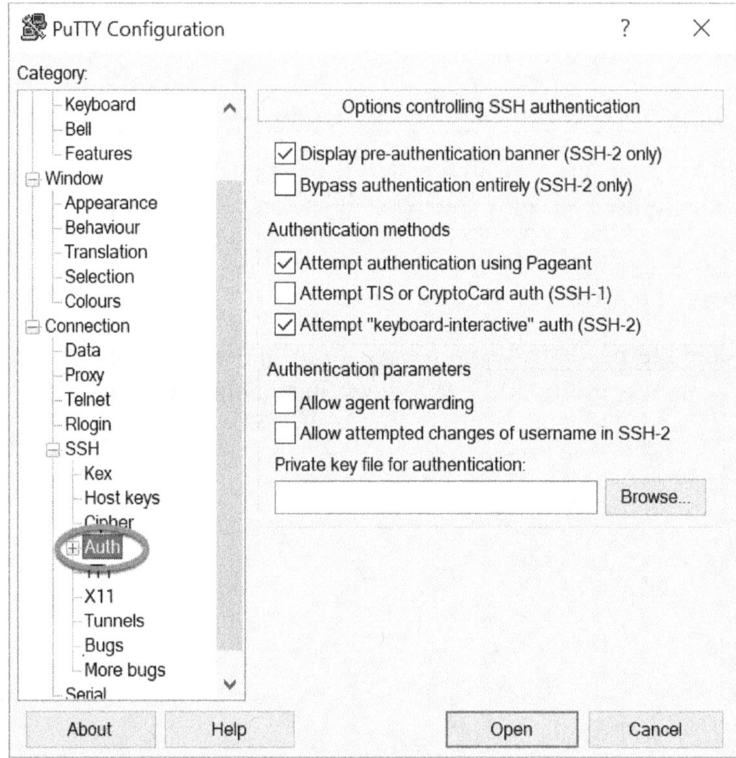

Figure 17-3

Click on the Browse button next to the *Private key for authentication* field and navigate to and select the previously saved PuTTY private key file. Optionally, scroll to the top of the left-hand panel, select the *Session* entry and enter a name for the session in the *Saved Sessions* field before clicking on the *Save* button. This will save the session configuration so that it can be used in future without having to re-enter the settings each time.

Finally, click on the *Open* button to establish the connection to the remote server, entering the user name and passphrase when prompted to do so to complete the authentication.

17.9 Generating a Private Key with PuTTYgen

The previous section explored the use of existing private and public keys when working with PuTTY. If keys do not already exist, they can be created using the *PuTTYgen* tool which is included with the main PuTTY installation.

To create new keys, launch *PuttyGen* and click on the *Generate* button highlighted in Figure 17-4:

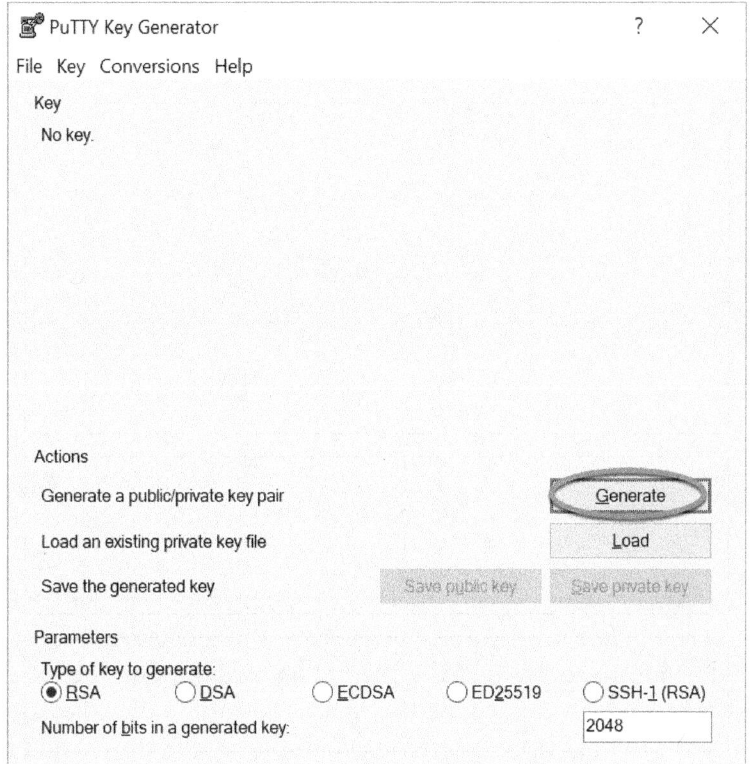

Figure 17-4

Move the mouse pointer around to generate random data as instructed, then enter an optional passphrase with which to encrypt the private key. Once the keys have been generated, save the files to suitable locations using the *Save public key* and *Save private key* buttons. The private key can be used with PuTTY as outlined in the previous section. To install the public key on the remote server use the steps covered in the earlier section on using SSH within PowerShell on Windows 10.

17.10 Installing the Public Key for a Google Cloud Instance

If your Ubuntu system is hosted by Google Cloud, for example as a Compute Engine instance, there are a number of different ways to gain SSH access to the server using key-based authentication. Perhaps the most straightforward is to add your public key to the metadata for your Google Cloud account. This will make the public key available for all Virtual Machine instances that you create within Google Cloud. To add the public key, log into the Google Cloud Platform console, select the *Metadata* option from the left-hand navigation panel as highlighted in Figure 17-5 followed by the *SSH keys* tab:

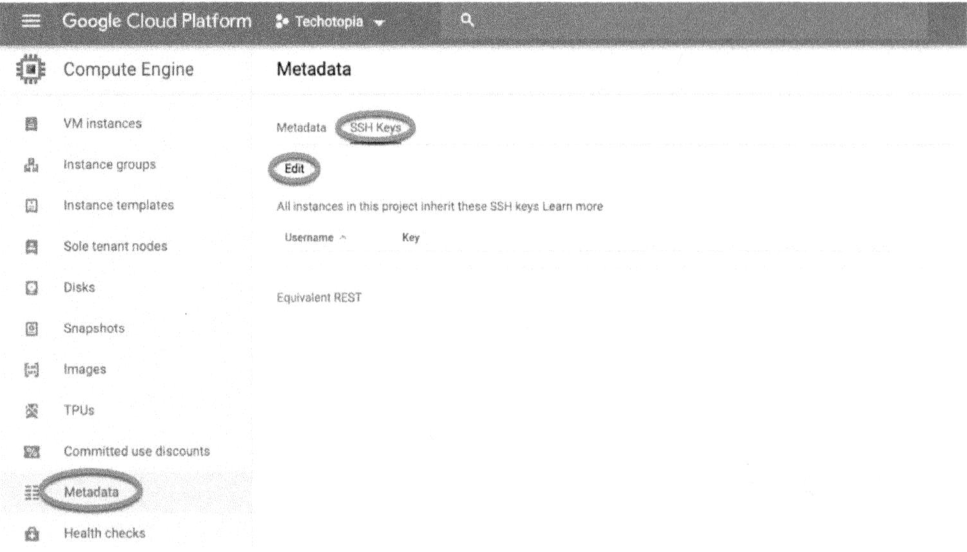

Figure 17-5

On the SSH Keys screen, click on the *Edit* button (also highlighted in Figure 17-5) to edit the list of keys. Scroll down to the bottom of the current list and click on the + *Add Item* button. A new field will appear into which you will need to paste the entire public key as it appears in your *id_rsa.pub* file. Once the key has been entered, click on the *Save* button to add the key.

The public key will now appear in the list of SSH Keys. Note that the key entry also includes the username which must be used when logging into any Google Cloud instances:

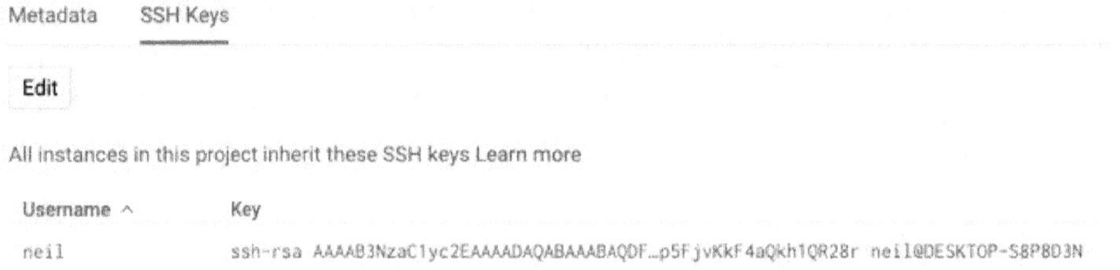

Figure 17-6

With the public key added to the metadata it should be possible to access any virtual machine instance from any client on which the corresponding private key has been installed and on which the user has an account. In fact, behind the scenes, all Google Cloud has done to enable this is add the public key to the *.ssh/authorized_keys* file in the user's home directory on any virtual machines on which the account exists.

17.11 Summary

It is important that any remote access to an Ubuntu system be implemented in a way that provides a high level of security. By default, SSH allows remote system access using password-based authentication. This leaves the system vulnerable to anyone who can either guess a password, or find out the password through other means. For this reason, the use of key-based authentication is recommended to protect system access. Key-based authentication uses the concept of public key encryption involving public and private keys. When implemented, users are only able to connect to a server if they are using a client which has a private key that matches a public key on the server. As an added layer of security, the private key may also be encrypted and password protected. Once key-based encryption has been implemented, the server system is then configured to disable support for the less secure password-based authentication.

This chapter has provided an overview of SSH key-based authentication and outlined the steps involved in generating keys and configuring clients on macOS, Linux and Windows, in addition to the installation and management of public keys on an Ubuntu server.

Chapter 18

18. Ubuntu Remote Desktop Access with Vino

Ubuntu can be configured to provide remote access to the graphical desktop environment over a network or internet connection. Although not enabled by default, it is relatively straightforward to display and access an Ubuntu desktop from a system anywhere else on a network or the internet. This can be achieved regardless of whether that system is running Linux, Windows or macOS. In fact, there are even apps available for Android and iOS that will allow you to access your Ubuntu desktop from just about anywhere that a data signal is available.

Remote desktop access can be useful in a number of scenarios. It enables you or another person, for example, to view and interact with your Ubuntu desktop environment from another computer system either on the same network or over the internet. This is useful if you need to work on your computer when you are away from your desk such as while traveling. It is also useful in situations where a co-worker or IT support technician needs access to your desktop to resolve a problem.

The Ubuntu remote desktop functionality is based on technology known as Virtual Network Computing (VNC) and in this and the next chapter we will cover the key aspects of configuring and using remote desktops within Ubuntu.

18.1 Remote Desktop Access Types

Before starting it is important to understand that there are essentially two types of remote desktop access. The approach covered in this chapter is useful if you primarily use Ubuntu as a desktop operating system and require remote access to your usual desktop session. When configured, you will take over your desktop session and view and control it remotely.

The second option, covered in the next chapter entitled *"Ubuntu Remote Desktop Access with VNC"*, is intended for situations where you need to start and access one or more remote desktop sessions on a remote server-based system, regardless of whether the remote system has a graphical console attached. This allows you to launch multiple desktop sessions in the background on the remote system and view and control those desktops over a network or internet connection.

18.2 Secure and Insecure Remote Desktop Access

In this chapter we will cover both secure and insecure remote desktop access methods. Assuming that you are accessing one system from another within the context of a secure internal network then it is generally safe to use the insecure access method. If, on the other hand, you plan to access your desktop remotely over any kind of public network you must use the secure method of access to avoid your system and data being compromised.

18.3 Enabling Remote Desktop Access on Ubuntu

Remote desktop access on Ubuntu is provided by the Vino package. Vino is a VNC server that was developed specifically for use with the GNOME desktop.

The first step in enabling remote access is to install this package:

```
# apt install vino
```

Once Vino has been installed, the next step is to enable remote desktop access from within GNOME. Begin by opening the settings app as shown in Figure 18-1:

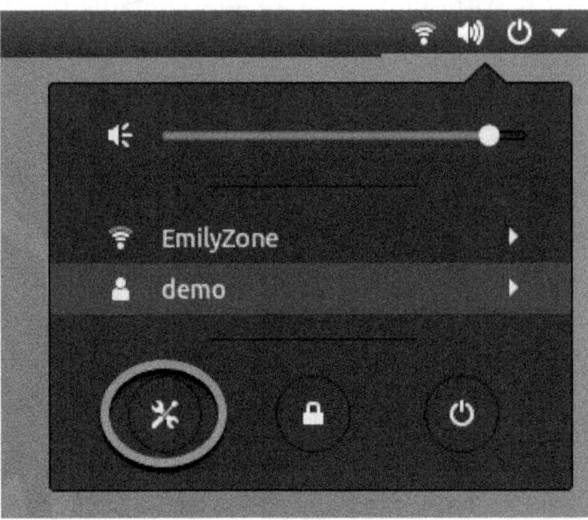

Figure 18-1

From within the Settings application, select the Sharing option (marked A in Figure 18-2):

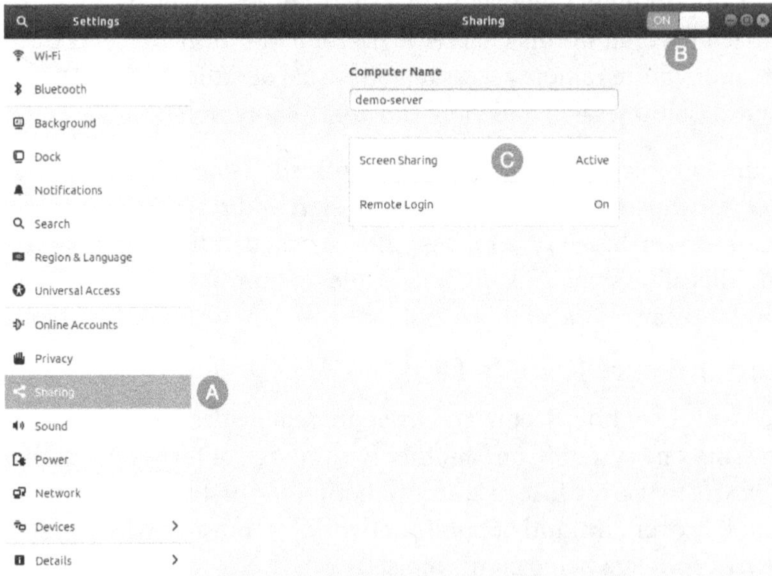

Figure 18-2

Turn on the Sharing switch (B) and click on the Screen Sharing option (C) to display the dialog shown in Figure 18-3 below:

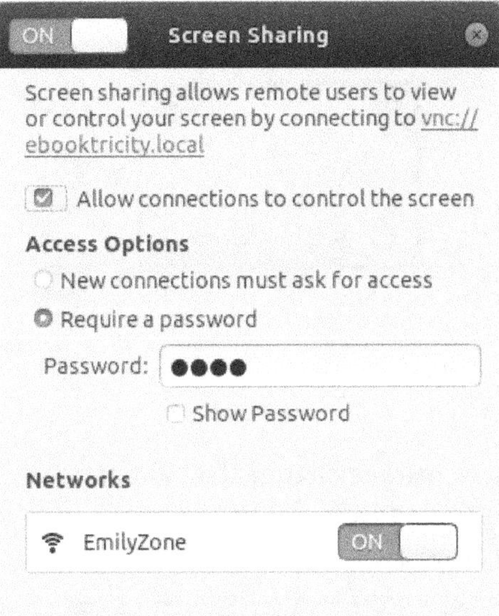

Figure 18-3

The Screen Sharing dialog provides the following configuration options to manage remote desktop access:

- **Allows connections to control the screen** - If enabled, the remote session will be able to use the mouse and keyboard to interact with the desktop environment. If disabled the remote session will only allow the desktop to be viewed.
- **New connections must ask for access** - When selected, a prompt will appear on the host screen asking to give permission to the remote user to access the desktop. Do not select this option if you plan to access your screen remotely and nobody will be at the host system to accept the connection request.
- **Require a password** - Requires the user to enter the specified password prior to gaining access to the desktop.
- **Networks** - The network connections on the host system via which remote access is to be permitted.

After configuring the settings, close both the Screen Settings and Settings dialogs.

18.4 Connecting to the Shared Desktop

Although VNC viewer implementations are available for a wide range of operating systems a tool such as the Remmina Desktop Client is recommended when connecting from Ubuntu or other Linux-based systems. Remmina is a user friendly tool with a graphical interface that supports the encryption used by Vino to ensure a secure remote connection.

To install this tool, open the Ubuntu Software application and search for and install Remmina:

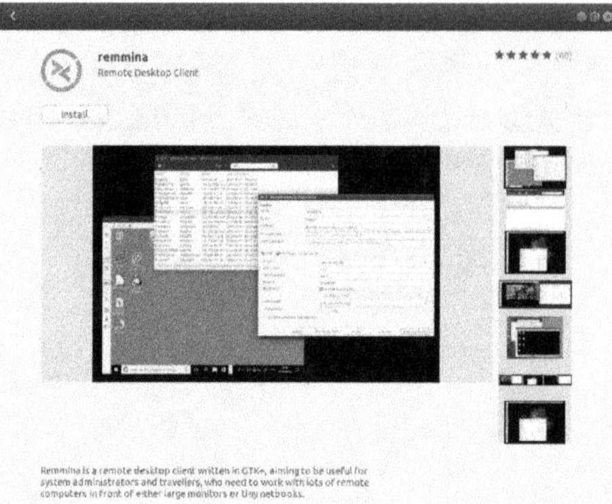

Figure 18-4

After installing and launching Remmina change the connection type menu (marked A in Figure 18-5) to VNC and enter into the address field (B) the IP address or hostname of the remote system to which you wish to connect:

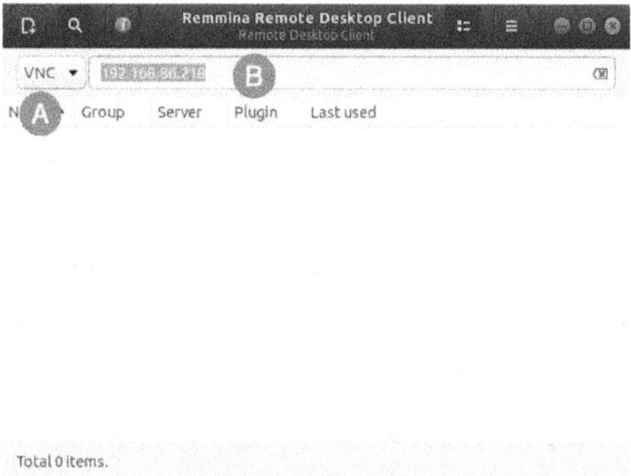

Figure 18-5

To establish the connection, tap the keyboard Enter key to begin the connection process. After a short delay, a second screen will appear requesting the desktop access password (if one was entered when screen sharing was enabled earlier in the chapter):

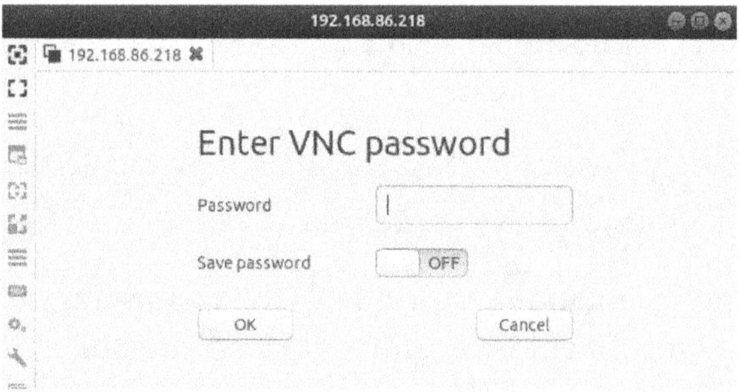

Figure 18-6

After entering the password, click on OK to access the remote screen:

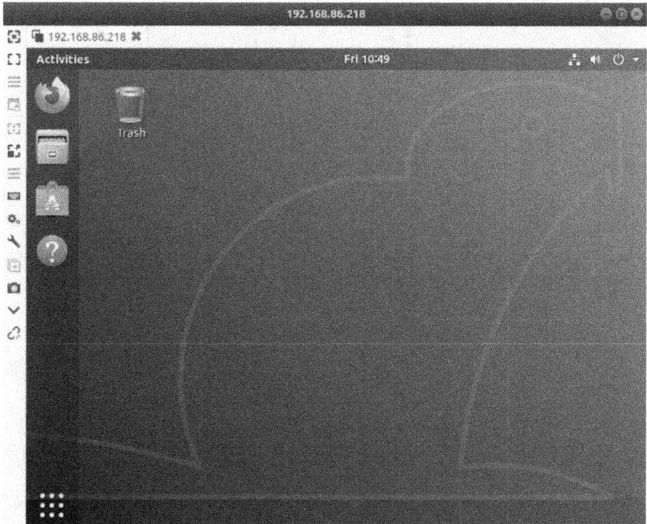

Figure 18-7

The default settings for Remmina prioritize speed over image quality. If you find that the quality of the desktop rendering is unacceptably poor, click on the settings button (Figure 18-8) in the left-hand toolbar within the remote viewer window and experiment with different settings until you find the ideal balance of performance and image quality:

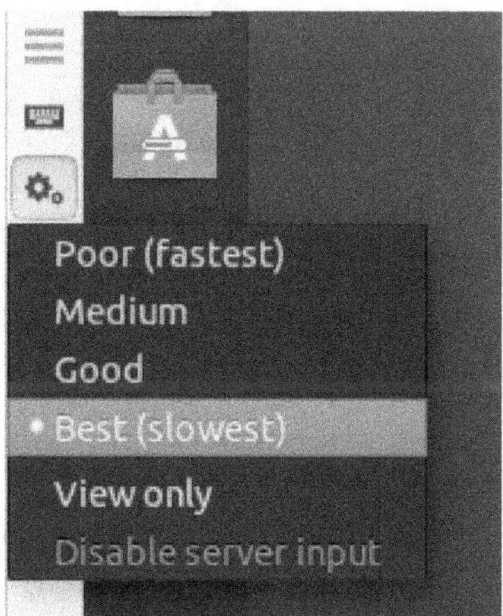

Figure 18-8

18.5 Connecting from Non-Linux Clients

The previous section assumed that the remote desktop was being accessed from a Linux or UNIX system. It is important to understand that Vino, by default, requires that the remote connection be encrypted to ensure security. One of the reasons for using Remmina is that it fully supports the encryption used by Vino.

If you need to connect from a non-Linux system such as Windows or macOS you will need to install a third-party VNC viewer such as TightVNC, TigerVNC or RealVNC. Unfortunately, these viewers do not support the encryption that Vino uses by default. To experience this in action, download the RealVNC viewer for your macOS or Windows system from the following URL:

https://www.realvnc.com/en/connect/download/viewer/

Once installed, launch the viewer and enter the hostname or IP address of your remote Ubuntu system. On attempting to connect, a failure dialog will appear similar to the one shown in Figure 18-9:

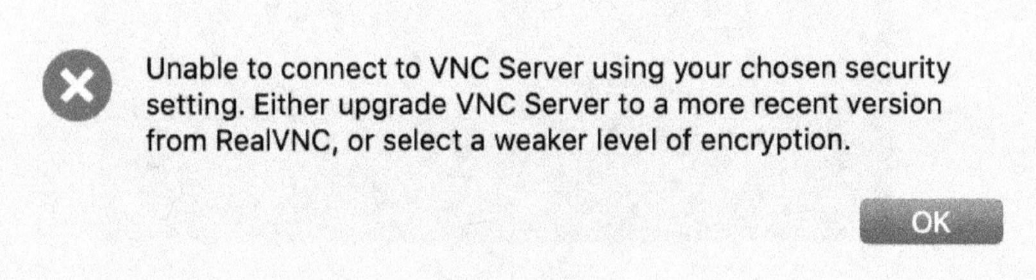

Figure 18-9

To allow a connection to be established from a non-Linux system it is necessary to turn off the encryption requirement for the remote desktop connection. To do this, open a terminal window on the Ubuntu system and run the following command (using your account and without sudo privileges):

```
$ gsettings set org.gnome.Vino require-encryption false
```

After disabling the Vino encryption requirement, attempt to connect from the RealVNC viewer once again. This time a warning will appear indicating that the connection is not encrypted:

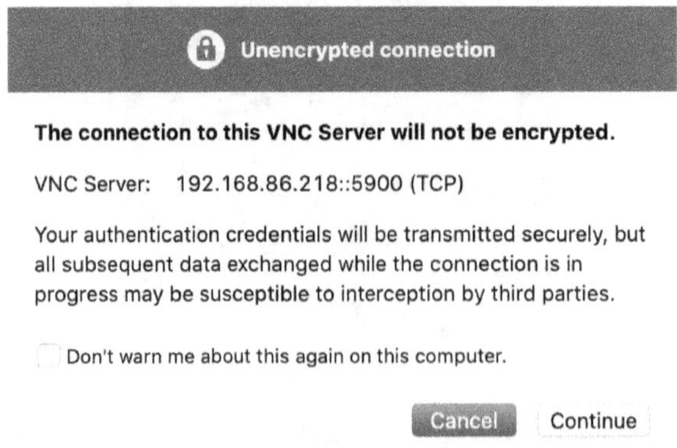

Figure 18-10

Clicking the Continue button will dismiss the warning dialog and establish the remote connection.

Clearly, connecting to a remote VNC server using the steps in this section results in an insecure, unencrypted connection between the client and server. This means that the data transmitted during the remote session is vulnerable to interception. To establish a secure and encrypted connection from an Ubuntu system to a non-Linux client a few extra steps are necessary.

18.6 Establishing a Secure Remote Desktop Session

The remote desktop connection from macOS and Windows in the previous section is considered to be insecure because no encryption is used. This is acceptable when the remote connection does not extend outside of an internal network protected by a firewall. When a remote session is required over an internet connection, however, a more secure option is needed. This is achieved by tunneling the remote desktop through a secure shell (SSH) connection. This section will cover how to do this on Linux, UNIX and macOS client systems.

When a remote desktop session is invoked on an Ubuntu system a connection is made using TCP/IP network port 5900. To prove this, establish a connection to your remote Ubuntu system referencing port 5900 after the hostname or IP address, for example, and note that the connection is still established:

```
192.168.86.218:5900
```

To implement an encrypted remote desktop session for non-Linux system the session needs to be *tunneled* though a secure SSH connection.

If the SSH server has not yet been installed on your Ubuntu system, refer to the chapter entitled *"Configuring SSH Key-based Authentication on Ubuntu"*.

Assuming the SSH server is installed and active it is time to move to the other system. At the other system, log in to the remote system using the following command, which will establish the secure tunnel between the two systems. This assumes the client system is running macOS, Linux or UNIX (instructions for Windows systems are covered in the next section):

```
$ ssh -l <username> -L 5900:localhost:5900 <remotehost>
```

In the above example, <username> references the user account on the remote system for which VNC access has been configured, and *<remotehost>* is either the host name or IP address of the remote system, for example:

```
$ ssh -l demo -L 5900:localhost:5900 192.168.86.218
```

When prompted, log in using the account password. With the secure connection established it is time to launch vncviewer so that it uses the secure tunnel. Leaving the SSH session running in the terminal window, launch the VNC viewer and enter the following into the address field:

```
localhost:5900
```

The vncviewer session will prompt for a password if one is required, and then launch the VNC viewer providing secure access to your desktop environment.

Although the connection is now secure and encrypted, the VNC viewer will most likely still report that the connection is insecure. Unfortunately, although the connection is now secure, the VNC viewer software has no way of knowing this and consequently continues to issue warnings.

Rest assured that as long as the SSH tunnel is being used, the connection is indeed secure.

In the above example we left the SSH tunnel session running in a terminal window. If you would prefer to run the session in the background, this can be achieved by using the –f and –N flags when initiating the connection:

```
$ ssh -l <username> -f -N -L 5900:localhost:5900 <remotehost>
```

The above command will prompt for a password for the remote server and then establish the connection in the background, leaving the terminal window available for other tasks.

If you are connecting to the remote desktop from outside the firewall keep in mind that the IP address for the SSH connection will be the external IP address provided by your ISP or cloud hosting provider, not the LAN IP address of the remote system (since this IP address is not visible to those outside the firewall). You will also need to configure your firewall to forward port 22 (for the SSH connection) to the IP address of the system running the desktop. It is not necessary to forward port 5900. Steps to perform port forwarding differ between firewalls, so refer to the documentation for your firewall, router or wireless base station for details specific to your configuration.

18.7 Establishing a Secure Tunnel on Windows using PuTTY

A similar approach is taken to establishing a secure desktop session from a Windows system to an Ubuntu server. Assuming that you already have a VNC client such as TightVNC installed, the one remaining requirement is a Windows SSH client (in this case PuTTY).

Once PuTTY is downloaded and installed, the first step is to establish a secure connection between the Windows system and the remote system with appropriate tunneling configured. When launched, PuTTY displays the following screen:

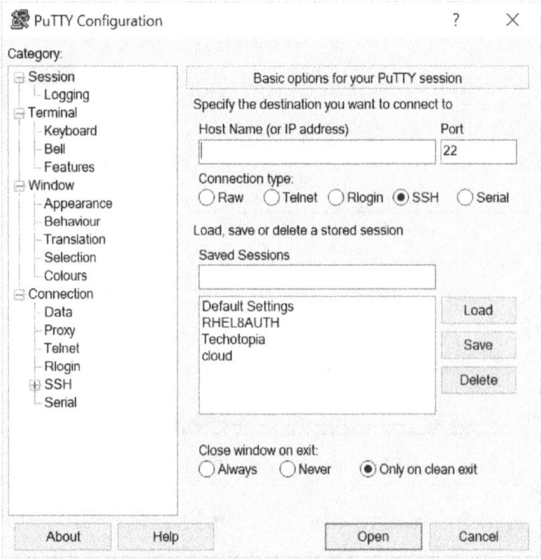

Figure 18-11

Enter the IP address or host name of the remote host (or the external IP address of the gateway if you are connecting from outside the firewall). The next step is to set up the tunnel. Click on the + next to SSH in the Category tree on the left-hand side of the dialog and click on Tunnels. The screen should subsequently appear as follows:

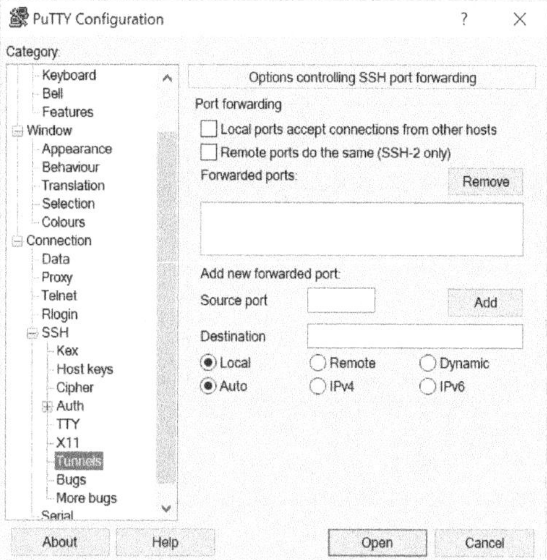

Figure 18-12

Enter 5900 as the Source port and localhost:5900 as the Destination and click on the *Add* button. Finally return to the main screen by clicking on the *Session* category. Enter a name for the session in the Saved Sessions text field and press *Save*. Click on *Open* to establish the connection. A terminal window will appear with the login prompt from the remote system. Enter the appropriate user login and password credentials.

The SSH connection is now established. Launch the VNC viewer, enter localhost:5900 in the VNC Server text field and click on *Connect*. The viewer will establish the connection, prompt for the password and then display the desktop. You are now accessing the remote desktop of a Linux system from Windows over a secure SSH tunnel connection.

18.8 Summary

Remote access to the GNOME desktop environment of an Ubuntu system can be enabled by making use of Virtual Network Computing (VNC). Comprising the VNC server running on the remote server and a corresponding client on the local host, VNC allows remote access to multiple desktop instances running on the server.

The standard remote server solution for the GNOME desktop is Vino. Once installed, remote desktop sessions can be established from other Linux systems using a remote desktop viewer such as Remmina.

When connecting from non-Linux systems such as Windows or macOS, it is necessary to disable Vino's encryption requirements. Once disabled, connections from client systems should be established using SSH tunneling,

When the VNC connection is being used over a public connection with Vino encryption disabled, the use of SSH tunneling is recommended when connecting to ensure that the communication between client and server is encrypted and secure.

Chapter 19

19. Ubuntu Remote Desktop Access with VNC

The chapter entitled *"Ubuntu Remote Desktop Access with Vino"* explored remote access to the Ubuntu GNOME desktop using the Vino server, an approach that is intended solely for situations where the remote system is already running a GNOME desktop session. In this chapter we will cover launching and accessing GNOME desktop sessions that run in the background, allowing multiple desktop sessions to be accessed remotely, including on server based system that do not have a graphical console attached.

19.1 Installing the GNOME Desktop Environment

It is, of course, only possible to access the desktop environment if the desktop itself has been installed. If, for example, the system was initially configured as a server it is unlikely that the desktop packages were installed. The easiest way to install the packages necessary to run the GNOME desktop is via the *apt* command as follows:

```
# apt install ubuntu-gnome-desktop
```

To prevent the desktop from attempting to launch automatically each time the system reboots, change the default systemd target back to multi-user:

```
# systemctl set-default multi-user.target
```

If the system has a graphical display attached, the desktop can be launched using the following command:

```
$ startx
```

If, on the other hand, the system is a server with no directly connected display, the only way to run and access the desktop will be to configure VNC support on the system.

19.2 Installing VNC on Ubuntu

Access to a remote desktop requires a VNC server installed on the remote system, a VNC viewer on the system from which access is being established and, optionally, a secure SSH connection. While a number of VNC server and viewer implementations are available, this chapter will make use of TigerVNC which provides both server and viewer components for Linux-based operating systems. VNC viewer clients for non-Linux platforms include RealVNC and TightVNC.

To install the TigerVNC server package on Ubuntu, simply run the following command:

```
# apt install tigervnc-standalone-server
```

If required, the TigerVNC viewer may also be installed as follows:

```
# apt install tigervnc-viewer
```

Once the server has been installed the system will need to be configured to run one or more VNC services and to open the appropriate ports on the firewall.

19.3 Configuring the VNC Server

With the VNC server packages installed, the next step is to configure the server. The first step is to specify a password for the user that will be accessing the remote desktop environment. While logged in as root (or with superuser privileges), execute the *vncpasswd* command (where the user name is assumed to be demo):

```
# su - demo
demo@demoserver:~$ vncpasswd
Password:
Verify:
Would you like to enter a view-only password (y/n)? n
A view-only password is not used
```

The above command will create a file named *passwd* in the *.vnc* directory of the user's home directory. Next, change directory to the *.vnc* directory and create a new file named *xstartup* containing the following:

```
#!/bin/sh
# Start Gnome 3 Desktop
[ -x /etc/vnc/xstartup ] && exec /etc/vnc/xstartup
[ -r $HOME/.Xresources ] && xrdb $HOME/.Xresources
vncconfig -iconic &
dbus-launch --exit-with-session gnome-session &
```

These are the commands that will be executed to start the GNOME desktop when the VNC server is launched.

19.4 Starting the VNC Server

With the necessary packages installed and configured for the user's account, the VNC server can be started as follows (making sure to run the command as the user and without superuser privileges):

```
$ vncserver
```

This will start the first desktop session running on the system. Since this is the first session, it will be configured to use port 5901 (which may be abbreviated to :1). Running the command a second time while the first session is running will create a VNC server listening on port 5902 (:2) and so on. The following command may be used to obtain a list of desktop sessions currently running:

```
$ vncserver -list
TigerVNC server sessions:

X DISPLAY #   PROCESS ID
:1            1607
:2            4726
```

To terminate a session, use the vncserver command with the -kill option referencing the corresponding port. For example:

```
$ vncserver -kill :2
Killing Xtigervnc process ID 4726... success!
```

Alternatively, use the following command to kill all currently running VNC server sessions:

```
$ vncserver -kill :*
Killing Xtigervnc process ID 1607... success!
Killing Xtigervnc process ID 5287... success!
```

To manually specify the port to be used by the VNC server session, include the number in the command-line as follows:

```
$ vncserver :5
```

In the above example, the session will listen for a remote connection on port 5905.

19.5 Connecting to a VNC Server

For details on remotely connecting to a desktop session from another system, follow the steps outlined in the sections titled *"Establishing a Secure Remote Desktop Session"* and *"Establishing a Secure Tunnel on Windows using PuTTY"* in the previous chapter.

19.6 Summary

In this and the preceding chapter we have explored two different ways to remotely access the GNOME desktop environment of an Ubuntu system. While the previous chapter explored access to an existing desktop session, this chapter has focused on launching GNOME desktop sessions as background processes, thereby allowing remote access to multiple desktop sessions, This is a particularly useful technique for running and remotely accessing desktop sessions on "headless" server-based systems.

Chapter 20

20. Displaying Ubuntu Applications Remotely (X11 Forwarding)

In the previous chapter we looked at how to display the entire Ubuntu desktop on a remote computer. While this works well if you actually need to remotely display the entire desktop, it could be considered overkill if all you want to do is display a single application. In this chapter, therefore, we will look at displaying individual applications on a remote system.

20.1 Requirements for Remotely Displaying Ubuntu Applications

In order to run an application on one Ubuntu system and have it display on another system there are a couple of prerequisites. First, the system on which the application is to be displayed must be running an X server. If the system is a Linux or UNIX-based system with a desktop environment running then this is no problem. If the system is running Windows or macOS, however, then you must install an X server on it before you can display applications from a remote system. A number of commercial and free Windows based X servers are available for this purpose and a web search should provide you with a list of options.

Second, the system on which the application is being run (as opposed to the system on which the application is to be displayed) must be configured to allow SSH access. Details on configuring SSH on an Ubuntu system can be found in the chapter entitled *"Configuring SSH Key-based Authentication on Ubuntu"*. This system must also be running the X Window system from X.org instead of Wayland. To find out which system is being used, open a terminal window and run the following command:

```
# echo $XDG_SESSION_TYPE
x11
```

If the above command outputs "wayland" instead of "x11", edit the */etc/gdm3/custom.conf* file and uncomment the *WaylandEnable* line as follows and restart the system:

```
# Uncomment the line below to force the login screen to use Xorg
WaylandEnable=false
```

Finally, SSH must be configured to allow X11 forwarding. This is achieved by adding the following directive to the SSH configuration on the system from which forwarding is to occur. Edit the */etc/ssh/ssh_config* file and uncomment the ForwardX11 entry (in other words remove the '#' at the beginning of the line) and change the value to *yes* entry as follows:

```
.
.
Host *
#   ForwardAgent no
    ForwardX11 yes
```

.

.

After making the change, save the file and restart the SSH service:

```
# systemctl restart sshd
```

Once the above requirements are met it should be possible to remotely display an X-based desktop application.

20.2 Remotely Displaying an Ubuntu Application

The first step in remotely displaying an application is to move to the system where the application is to be displayed. At this system, establish an SSH connection to the remote system so that you have a command prompt. This can be achieved using the *ssh* command. When using the *ssh* command we need to use the -X flag to tell it that we plan to tunnel X11 traffic through the connection:

```
$ ssh -X user@hostname
```

In the above example *user* is the user name to use to log into the remote system and *hostname* is the hostname or IP address of the remote system. Enter your password at the login prompt and, once logged in, run the following command to see the DISPLAY setting:

```
$ echo $DISPLAY
```

The command should output something similar to the following:

```
localhost:10.0
```

To display an application simply run it from the command prompt. For example:

```
$ gedit
```

When executed, the above command should run the *gedit* tool on the remote system, but display the user interface on the local system.

20.3 Trusted X11 Forwarding

If the */etc/ssh/ssh_config* file on the remote system contains the following line, then it is possible to use trusted X11 forwarding:

```
ForwardX11Trusted yes
```

Trusted X11 forwarding is slightly faster than untrusted forwarding but is less secure since it does not engage the X11 security controls. The -Y flag is needed when using trusted X11 forwarding:

```
$ ssh -Y user@hostname
```

20.4 Compressed X11 Forwarding

When using slower connections the X11 data can be compressed using the -C flag to improve performance:

```
$ ssh -X -C user@hostname
```

20.5 Displaying Remote Ubuntu Apps on Windows

To display Ubuntu based apps on Windows an SSH client and an X server will need to be installed on the Windows system. The subject of installing and using the PuTTY client on Windows was covered earlier in the book in the *"Configuring SSH Key-based Authentication on Ubuntu"* chapter. Refer to this chapter if you have not already installed PuTTY on your Windows system.

In terms of the X server, a number of options are available, though a popular choice appears to be VcXsrv which is available for free from the following URL:

https://sourceforge.net/projects/vcxsrv/

Once the VcXsrv X server has been installed, an application named *XLaunch* will appear on the desktop and in the start menu. Start XLaunch and select a display option (the most flexible being the *Multiple windows* option which allows each client app to appear in its own window):

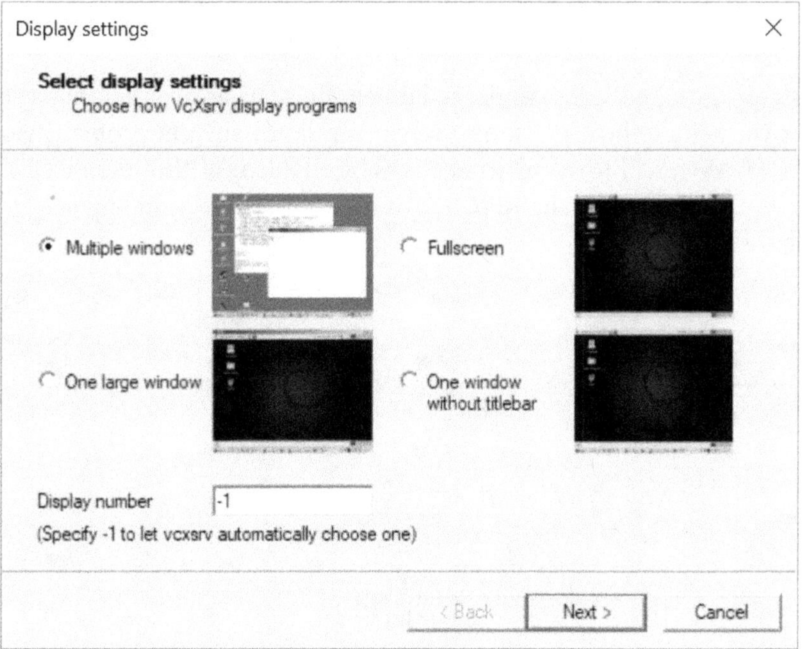

Figure 20-1

Click the *Next* button to proceed through the remaining screens, accepting the default configuration settings. On the final screen, click on the *Finish* button to start the X server. If the Windows Defender dialog appears click on the button to allow access to your chosen networks.

Once running, XLaunch will appear in the taskbar and can be exited by right-clicking on the icon and selecting the *Exit...* menu option:

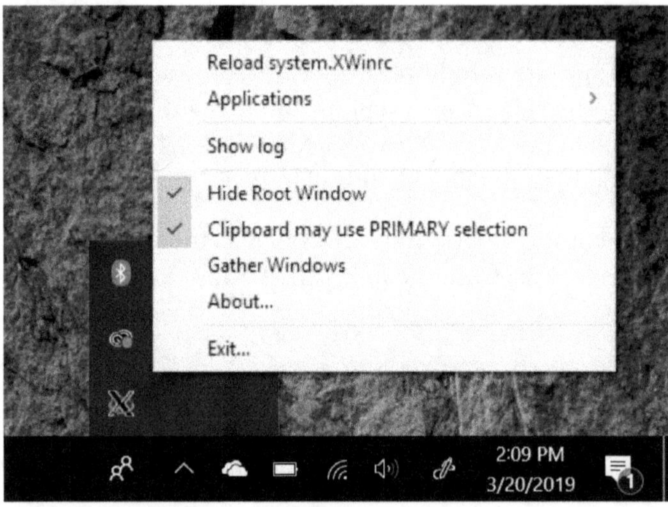

Figure 20-2

With the X server installed and running, launch PuTTY and either enter the connection information for the remote host or load a previously saved session profile. Before establishing the connection, however, X11 forwarding needs to be enabled. Within the PuTTY main window, scroll down the options in the left-hand panel, unfold the SSH section and select the X11 option as shown in Figure 20-3:

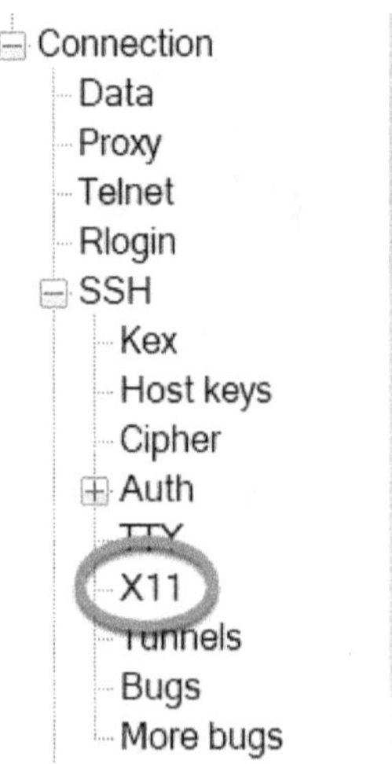

Figure 20-3

Turn on the *Enable X11 forwarding* checkbox highlighted in Figure 20-4, return to the sessions screen and open the connection (saving the session beforehand if you plan to use it again).

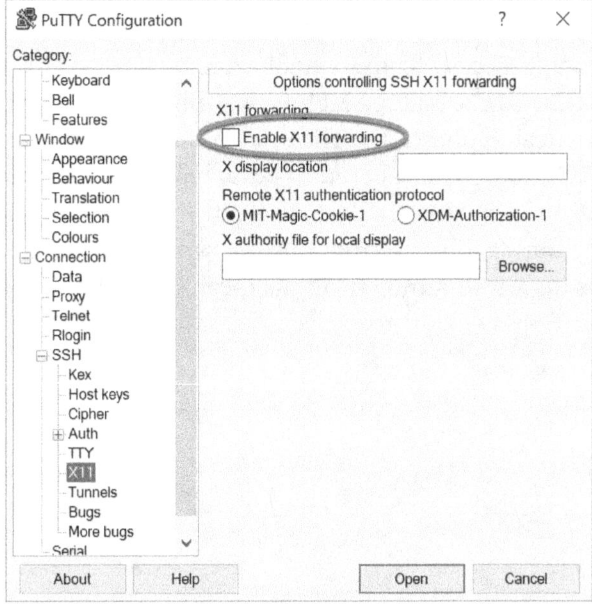

Figure 20-4

Log into the Ubuntu system within the PuTTY session window and run a desktop app. After a short delay, the app will appear in the Windows desktop in its own window. Any dialogs that are opened by the app will also appear in separate windows, just as they would on the Ubuntu GNOME desktop. Figure 20-5, for example, shows the Ubuntu *nm-connection-editor* tool displayed on a Windows 10 system:

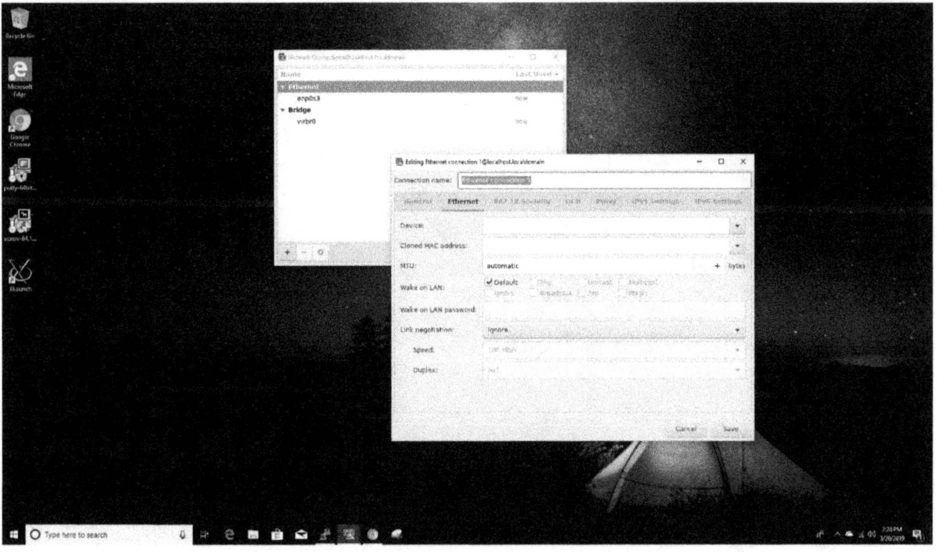

Figure 20-5

20.6 Summary

For situations where remote access to individual Ubuntu desktop applications is required as opposed to the entire GNOME desktop, X11 forwarding provides a lightweight solution to remotely displaying graphical applications. The system on which the applications are to appear must be running an X Window System based desktop environment (such as GNOME) or have an X server installed and running. Once X11 forwarding has been enabled on the remote server and a secure SSH connection established from the local system using the X11 forwarding option, most applications can be displayed remotely on the local X server.

Chapter 21

21. Using NFS to Share Ubuntu Files with Remote Systems

Ubuntu provides two mechanisms for sharing files and folders with other systems on a network. One approach is to use technology called Samba. Samba is based on Microsoft Windows Folder Sharing and allows Linux systems to make folders accessible to Windows systems, and also to access Windows based folder shares from Linux. This approach can also be used to share folders between other Linux and UNIX based systems as long as they too have Samba support installed and configured. This is by far the most popular approach to sharing folders in heterogeneous network environments. The topic of folder sharing using Samba is covered in *"Sharing Files between Ubuntu and Windows Systems with Samba"*.

Another option, which is targeted specifically at sharing folders between Linux and UNIX based systems, uses technology called Network File System (NFS). NFS allows the file system on one Linux computer to be accessed over a network connection by another Linux or UNIX system. NFS was originally developed by Sun Microsystems (now part of Oracle Corporation) in the 1980s and remains the standard mechanism for sharing of remote Linux/UNIX file systems to this day.

NFS is very different to the Windows SMB resource sharing technology used by Samba. In this chapter we will be looking at network based sharing of folders between Ubuntu and other UNIX/ Linux based systems using NFS.

21.1 Ensuring NFS Services are running on Ubuntu

The first task is to verify that the NFS services are installed and running on your Ubuntu system. This can be achieved either from the command-line, or using the Cockpit interface.

Begin by installing the NFS service by running the following command from a terminal window:

```
# apt install nfs-kernel-server
```

Next, configure the service to automatically start at boot time:

```
# systemctl enable nfs-kernel-server
```

Once the service has been enabled, start it as follows:

```
# systemctl start nfs-kernel-server
```

21.2 Configuring the Ubuntu Firewall to Allow NFS Traffic

Next, the firewall needs to be configured to allow NFS traffic.

If the Uncomplicated Firewall is enabled, run the following command to add a rule to allow NFS traffic:

```
# ufw allow nfs
```

If, on the other hand, you are using firewalld, run the following *firewall-cmd* commands where <zone> is replaced by the appropriate zone for your firewall and system configuration:

```
# firewall-cmd --zone=<zone> --permanent --add-service=mountd
# firewall-cmd --zone=<zone> --permanent --add-service=nfs
# firewall-cmd --zone=<zone> --permanent --add-service=rpc-bind
# firewall-cmd --reload
```

21.3 Specifying the Folders to be Shared

Now that NFS is running and the firewall has been configured, we need to specify which parts of the Ubuntu file system may be accessed by remote Linux or UNIX systems. These settings can be declared in the */etc/exports* file, which will need to be modified to export the directories for remote access via NFS. The syntax for an export line in this file is as follows:

```
<export> <host1>(<options>) <host2>(<options>)...
```

In the above line, <export> is replaced by the directory to be exported, <host1> is the name or IP address of the system to which access is being granted and <options> represents the restrictions that are to be imposed on that access (read only, read write etc). Multiple host and options entries may be placed on the same line if required. For example, the following line grants read only permission to the */datafiles* directory to a host with the IP address of 192.168.2.38:

```
/datafiles 192.168.2.38(ro, no_subtree_check)
```

The use of wildcards is permitted in order to apply an export to multiple hosts. For example, the following line permits read write access to */home/demo* to all external hosts:

```
/home/demo *(rw)
```

A full list of options supported by the exports file may be found by reading the exports man page:

```
# man exports
```

For the purposes of this chapter, we will configure the */etc/exports* file as follows:

```
/tmp        *(rw,sync, no_subtree_check)
/vol1       192.168.2.21(ro,sync, no_subtree_check)
```

Once configured, the table of exported file systems maintained by the NFS server needs to be updated with the latest */etc/exports* settings using the *exportfs* command as follows:

```
# exportfs -a
```

It is also possible to view the current share settings from the command-line using the *exportfs* tool:

```
# exportfs
```

The above command will generate the following output:

```
/tmp            <world>
/vol1           192.168.2.21
```

21.4 Accessing Shared Ubuntu Folders

The shared folders may be accessed from a client system by mounting them manually from the command-line. Before attempting to mount a remote NFS folder, the *nfs-common* package should first be installed on the client system:

```
# apt install nfs-common
```

To mount a remote folder from the command-line, open a terminal window and create a directory where you would like the remote shared folder to be mounted:

```
# mkdir /home/demo/tmp
```

Next enter the command to mount the remote folder using either the IP address or hostname of the remote NFS server, for example:

```
# mount -t nfs 192.168.1.115:/tmp /home/demo/tmp
```

The remote */tmp* folder will then be mounted on the local system. Once mounted, the */home/demo/tmp* folder will contain the remote folder and all its contents.

Options may also be specified when mounting a remote NFS filesystem. The following command, for example, mounts the same folder, but configures it to be read-only:

```
# mount -t nfs -o ro 192.168.1.115:/tmp /home/demo/tmp
```

21.5 Mounting an NFS Filesystem on System Startup

It is also possible to configure an Ubuntu system to automatically mount a remote file system each time the system starts up by editing the */etc/fstab* file. When loaded into an editor, it will likely resemble the following:

```
UUID=84982a2e-0dc1-4612-9ffa-13baf91ec558 /      ext4    errors=remount-ro 0   1
/swapfile                                 none   swap    sw                0   0
```

To mount, for example, a folder with the path */tmp* which resides on a system with the IP address 192.168.1.115 in the local folder with the path */home/demo/tmp* (note that this folder must already exist) add the following line to the */etc/fstab* file:

```
192.168.1.115:/tmp      /home/demo/tmp          nfs     rw              0 0
```

Next time the system reboots the */tmp* folder located on the remote system will be mounted on the local */home/demo/tmp* mount point. All the files in the remote folder can then be accessed as if they reside on the local hard disk drive.

21.6 Unmounting an NFS Mount Point

Once a remote file system is mounted using NFS it can be unmounted using the *umount* command with the local mount point as the command-line argument. The following command, for example, will unmount our example filesystem mount point:

```
# umount /home/demo/tmp
```

21.7 Accessing NFS Filesystems in Cockpit

In addition to mounting a remote NFS file system on a client using the command-line, it is also possible to perform mount operations from within the Cockpit web interface. Assuming that Cockpit has been installed and configured on the client system, log into the Cockpit interface from within a web browser and select the *Storage* option from the left-hand navigation panel. If the Storage option is not listed, the *cockpit-storaged* package will need to be installed:

```
# apt install cockpit-storaged
```

Once the Cockpit service has restarted, log back into the Cockpit interface at which point the Storage option should now be visible.

Once selected, the main storage page will include a section listing any currently mounted NFS file systems as illustrated in Figure 21-1:

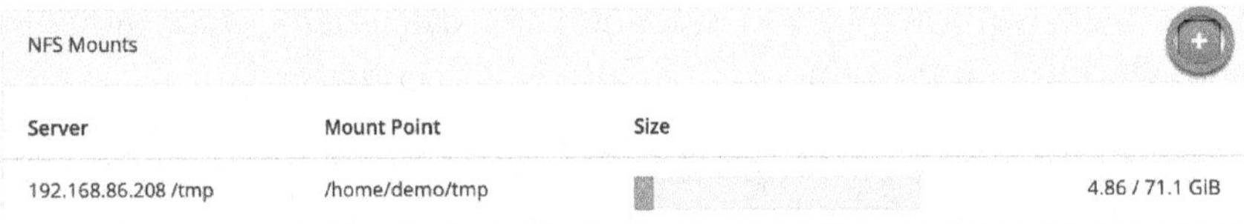

Figure 21-1

To mount a remote filesystem, click on the '+' button highlighted above and enter information about the remote NFS server and file system share together with the local mount point and any necessary options into the resulting dialog before clicking on the *Add* button:

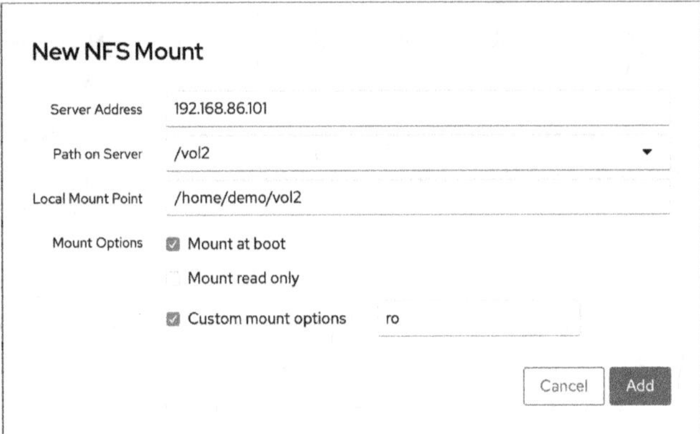

Figure 21-2

To modify, unmount or remove an NFS filesystem share, select the corresponding mount in the NFS Mounts list (Figure 21-1 above) to display the page shown in Figure 21-3 below:

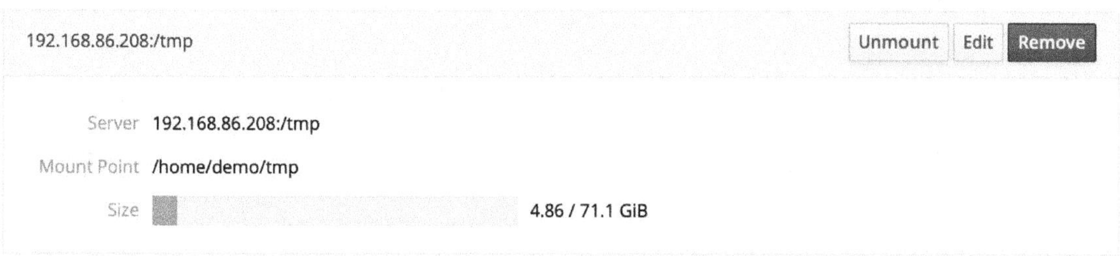

Figure 21-3

Within this screen perform tasks such as changing the server or mount points or unmounting the file system. The Remove option unmounts the file system and deletes the entry from the */etc/fstab* file so that it does not re-mount next time the system reboots.

21.8 Summary

The Network File System (NFS) is a client/server-based system, originally developed by Sun Microsystems, which provides a way for Linux and Unix systems to share filesystems over a network. NFS allows a client system to access and (subject to permissions) modify files located on a remote server as though those files are stored on a local filesystem. This chapter has provided an overview of NFS and outlined the options available for configuring both client and server systems using the command-line or the Cockpit web interface.

Chapter 22

22. Sharing Files between Ubuntu and Windows Systems with Samba

Although Linux has made some inroads into the desktop market, its origins and future are very much server-based. It is not surprising therefore that Ubuntu has the ability to act as a file server. It is also extremely common for Ubuntu and Windows systems to be used side by side in networked environments. It is a common requirement, therefore, that files on an Ubuntu system be accessible to Linux, UNIX and Windows-based systems over network connections. Similarly, shared folders and printers residing on Windows systems may also need to be accessible from Ubuntu based systems.

Windows systems share resources such as file systems and printers using a protocol known as Server Message Block (SMB). In order for an Ubuntu system to serve such resources over a network to a Windows system and vice versa it must, therefore, support SMB. This is achieved using technology called Samba. In addition to providing integration between Linux and Windows systems, Samba may also be used to provide folder sharing between Linux systems (as an alternative to NFS which was covered in the previous chapter).

In this chapter we will look at the steps necessary to share file system resources and printers on an Ubuntu system with remote Windows and Linux systems, and to access Windows resources from Ubuntu.

22.1 Accessing Windows Resources from the GNOME Desktop

Before getting into more details of Samba sharing, it is worth noting that if all you want to do is access Windows shared folders from within the Ubuntu GNOME desktop then support is already provided within the GNOME Files application. The Files application is located in the dash as highlighted in Figure 22-1:

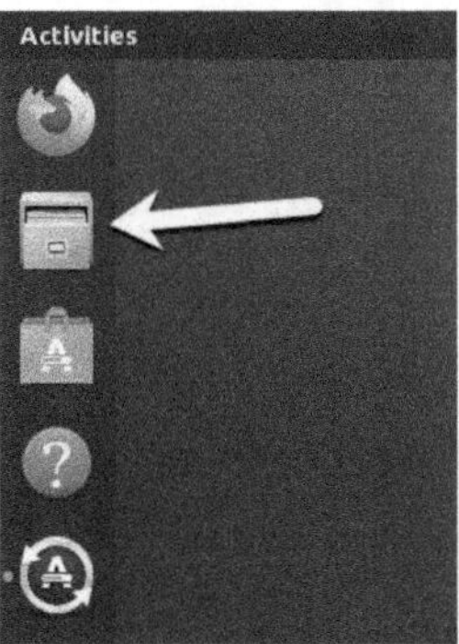

Figure 22-1

Once launched, select the *Other Locations* option in the left-hand navigation panel followed by the Windows Network icon in the main panel to browse available windows resources:

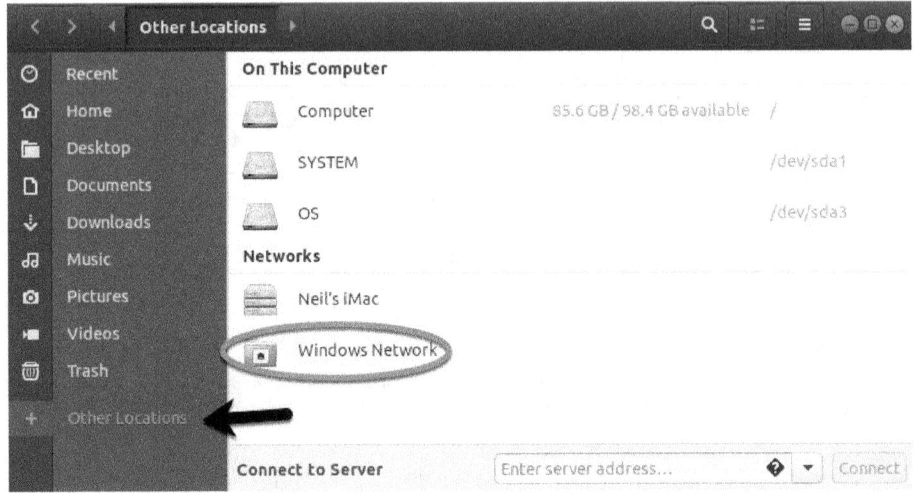

Figure 22-2

22.2 Samba and Samba Client

Samba allows both Ubuntu resources to be shared with Windows systems and Windows resources to be shared with Ubuntu systems. Ubuntu accesses Windows resources using the Samba client. Ubuntu resources, on the other hand, are shared with Windows systems by installing and configuring the Samba service.

22.3 Installing Samba on an Ubuntu System

The default settings used during the Ubuntu installation process do not typically install the necessary Samba packages. Unless you specifically requested that Samba be installed it is unlikely that you have Samba installed on your system. To check whether Samba is installed, open a terminal window and run the following command:

```
# apt -qq list samba-common samba smbclient
```

Any missing packages can be installed using the *apt* command-line tool:

```
# apt install samba-common samba smbclient
```

22.4 Configuring the Ubuntu Firewall to Enable Samba

Next, the firewall currently protecting the Ubuntu system needs to be configured to allow Samba traffic.

If you are using the Uncomplicated Firewall (ufw) run the following command:

```
# ufw allow samba
```

Alternatively, if you are using firewalld, run the *firewall-cmd* command as follows:

```
# firewall-cmd --permanent --add-port={139/tcp,445/tcp}
# firewall-cmd --reload
```

Before starting the Samba service a number of configuration steps are necessary to define how the Ubuntu system will appear to Windows systems, and the resources which are to be shared with remote clients. The majority of these configuration tasks take place within the */etc/samba/smb.conf* file.

22.5 Configuring the *smb.conf* File

Samba is a highly flexible and configurable system that provides many different options for controlling how resources are shared on Windows networks. This flexibility can lead to the sense that Samba is overly complex to work with. In reality, however, many of the configuration options are not needed by the typical installation, and the learning curve to set up a basic configuration is actually quite short.

For the purposes of this chapter we will look at joining an Ubuntu system to a Windows workgroup and setting up a directory as a shared resource that can be accessed by a specific user. This is a configuration known as a *standalone* Samba server. More advanced configurations such as integrating Samba within an Active Directory environment are also available, though these are outside the scope of this book.

The first step in configuring Samba is to edit the */etc/samba/smb.conf* file.

22.5.1 Configuring the [global] Section

The *smb.conf* file is divided into sections. The first section is the [global] section where settings can be specified that apply to the entire Samba configuration. While these settings are global, each option may be overridden within other sections of the configuration file.

The first task is to define the name of the Windows workgroup on which the Ubuntu resources are to be shared. This is controlled via the *workgroup =* directive of the [global] section which by default is configured as follows:

```
workgroup = WORKGROUP
```

Begin by changing this to the actual name of the workgroup if necessary.

In addition to the workgroup setting, the other settings indicate that this is a standalone server on which the shared resources will be protected by user passwords. Before moving on to configuring the resources to be shared, other parameters also need to be added to the [global] section as follows:

```
[global]
.
.
        netbios name = LinuxServer
.
.
```

The “netbios name” property specifies the name by which the server will be visible to other systems on the network.

22.5.2 Configuring a Shared Resource

The next step is to configure the shared resources (in other words the resources that will be accessible from other systems on the Windows network). In order to achieve this, the section is given a name by which it will be referred to when shared. For example, if we plan to share the */sampleshare* directory of our Ubuntu system, we might entitle the section [sampleshare]. In this section a variety of configuration options are possible. For the purposes of this example, however, we will simply define the directory that is to be shared, indicate that the directory is both browsable and writable and declare the resource public so that guest users are able to gain access:

```
[sampleshare]
        comment = Example Samba share
        path = /sampleshare
        browseable = Yes
        public = yes
        writable = yes
```

To restrict access to specific users, the "valid users" property may be used, for example:

```
valid users = demo, bobyoung, marcewing
```

22.5.3 Removing Unnecessary Shares

The *smb.conf* file is pre-configured with sections for sharing printers and the home folders of the users on the system. If these resources do not need to be shared, the corresponding sections can be commented out so that they are ignored by Samba. In the following example, the [homes] section has been commented out:

```
.
.
#[homes]
#       comment = Home Directories
#       valid users = %S, %D%w%S
#       browseable = No
#       read only = No
#       inherit acls = Yes
.
.
```

22.6 Creating a Samba User

Any user that requires access to a Samba shared resource must be configured as a Samba User and assigned a password. This task is achieved using the *smbpasswd* command-line tool. Consider, for example, that a user named *demo* is required to be able to access the */sampleshare* directory of our Ubuntu system from a Windows system. In order to fulfill this requirement we must add *demo* as a Samba user as follows:

```
# smbpasswd -a demo
New SMB password:
Retype new SMB password:
Added user demo.
```

Now that we have completed the configuration of a very basic Samba server, it is time to test our configuration file and then start the Samba services.

22.7 Testing the *smb.conf* File

The settings in the *smb.conf* file may be checked for errors using the *testparm* command-line tool as follows:

```
# testparm
Load smb config files from /etc/samba/smb.conf
rlimit_max: increasing rlimit_max (1024) to minimum Windows limit (16384)
WARNING: The "syslog" option is deprecated
Processing section "[printers]"
Processing section "[print$]"
Processing section "[sampleshare]"
Loaded services file OK.
Server role: ROLE_STANDALONE

Press enter to see a dump of your service definitions

# Global parameters
[global]
        dns proxy = No
        log file = /var/log/samba/log.%m
        map to guest = Bad User
        max log size = 1000
        netbios name = LINUXSERVER
        obey pam restrictions = Yes
        pam password change = Yes
        panic action = /usr/share/samba/panic-action %d
        passwd chat = *Enter\snew\s*\spassword:* %n\n *Retype\snew\s*\spassword:*
%n\n *password\supdated\ssuccessfully* .
        passwd program = /usr/bin/passwd %u
        security = USER
        server role = standalone server
        server string = %h server (Samba, Ubuntu)
        syslog = 0
        unix password sync = Yes
        usershare allow guests = Yes
        wins support = Yes
        idmap config * : backend = tdb

[printers]
        browseable = No
        comment = All Printers
        create mask = 0700
```

```
        path = /var/spool/samba
        printable = Yes

[print$]
        comment = Printer Drivers
        path = /var/lib/samba/printers

[sampleshare]
        comment = Example Samba share
        guest ok = Yes
        path = /sampleshare
        read only = No
```

22.8 Starting the Samba and NetBIOS Name Services

In order for an Ubuntu server to operate within a Windows network both the Samba (SMB) and NetBIOS nameservice (NMB) services must be started. Optionally, also enable the services so that they start each time the system boots:

```
# systemctl enable smbd
# systemctl start smbd
# systemctl enable nmbd
# systemctl start nmbd
```

Before attempting to connect from a Windows system, use the *smbclient* utility to verify that the share is configured:

```
# smbclient -U demo -L localhost
Enter WORKGROUP\demo's password:

        Sharename       Type      Comment
        ---------       ----      -------
        print$          Disk      Printer Drivers
        sampleshare     Disk      Example Samba share
        IPC$            IPC       IPC Service (demo-server2 server (Samba, Ubuntu))
        Officejet_Pro_8600_C7C718_ Printer
        Officejet_6600_971B9B_ Printer
Reconnecting with SMB1 for workgroup listing.

        Server               Comment
        ---------            -------

        Workgroup            Master
        ---------            -------
        WORKGROUP            LINUXSERVER
```

22.9 Accessing Samba Shares

Now that the Samba resources are configured and the services are running, it is time to access the shared resource from a Windows system. On a suitable Windows system on the same workgroup as the Ubuntu system, open Windows Explorer and navigate to the Network panel. At this point, explorer should search the network and list any systems using the SMB protocol that it finds. The following figure illustrates an Ubuntu system named LINUXSERVER located using Windows Explorer on a Windows 10 system:

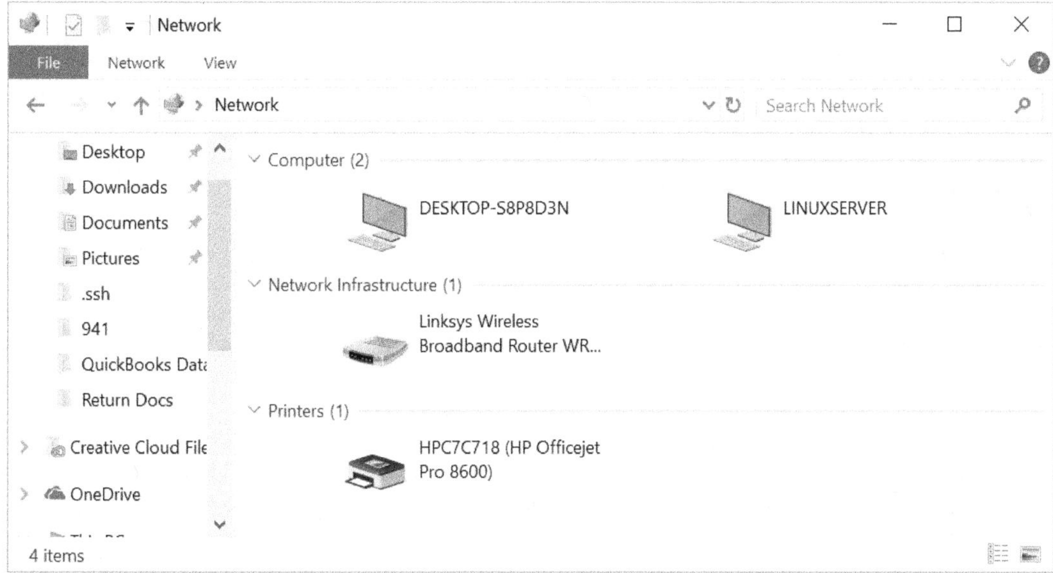

Figure 22-3

Double clicking on the LINUXSERVER host will prompt for the name and password of a user with access privileges. In this case it is the demo account that we configured using the *smbpasswd* tool:

Figure 22-4

Entering the username and password will result in the shared resources configured for that user appearing in the explorer window, including the previously configured */sampleshare* resource:

Figure 22-5

Double clicking on the */sampleshare* shared resource will display a listing of the files and directories contained therein.

If you are unable to see the Linux system or have problems accessing the shared folder, try mapping the Samba share to a local Windows drive as follows:

1. Open Windows File Explorer, right-click on the Network entry in the left-hand panel and select *Map network drive...* from the resulting menu.

2. From the Map Network Drive dialog, select a drive letter before entering the path to the shared folder. For example:

```
\\LinuxServer\sampleshare
```

Enable the checkbox next to *Connect using different credentials.* If you do not want the drive to be mapped each time you log into the Windows system, turn off the corresponding check box:

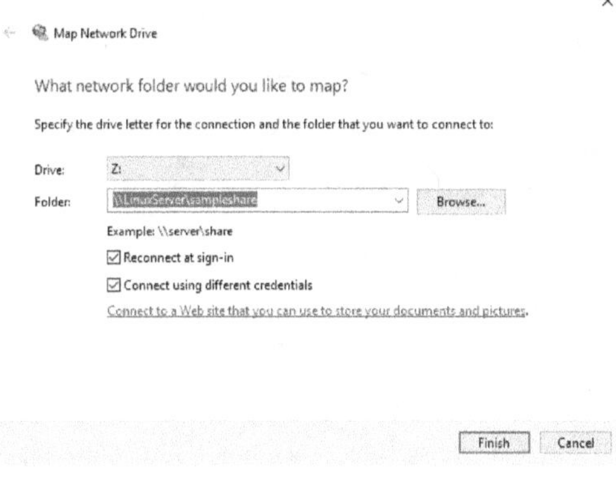

Figure 22-6

With the settings entered, click on the Finish button to map the drive, entering the username and password for the Samba user configured earlier in the chapter when prompted. After a short delay the content of the Samba share will appear in a new File Explorer window.

22.10 Accessing Windows Shares from Ubuntu

As previously mentioned, Samba is a two way street, allowing not only Windows systems to access files and printers hosted on an Ubuntu system, but also allowing the Ubuntu system to access shared resources on Windows systems. This is achieved using the smbclient package which was installed at the start of this chapter. If it is not currently installed, install it from a terminal window as follows:

```
# apt install smbclient
```

Shared resources on a Windows system can be accessed either from the Ubuntu desktop using the Files application, or from the command-line prompt using the *smbclient* and *mount* tools. The steps in this section assume that appropriate network sharing settings have been enabled on the Windows system.

To access any shared resources on a Windows system using the GNOME desktop, begin by launching the Files application and selecting the *Other Locations* option. This will display the screen shown in Figure 22-7 below including an icon for the Windows Network (if one is detected):

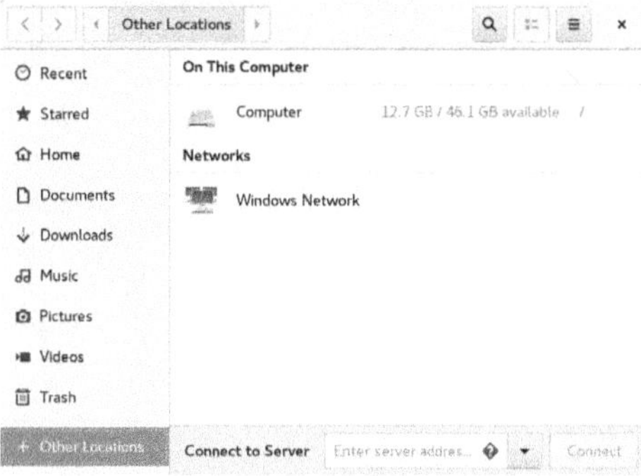

Figure 22-7

Selecting the Windows Network option will display the Windows systems detected on the network and allow access to any shared resources.

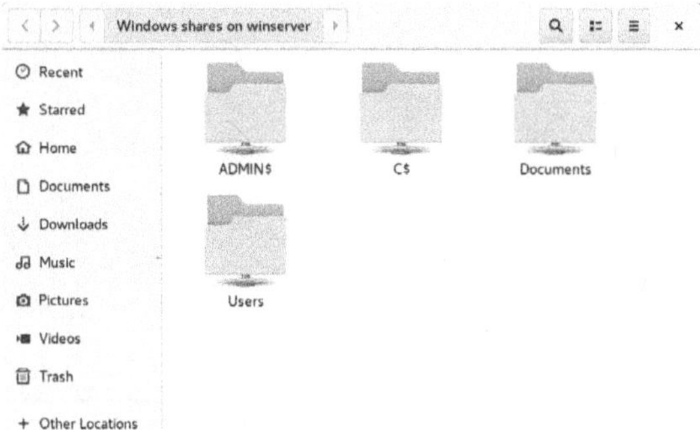

Figure 22-8

Alternatively, the *Connect to Server* option may be used to connect to a specific system. Note that the name or IP address of the remote system must be prefixed by *smb://* and may be followed by the path to a specific shared resource, for example:

```
smb://WinServer10/Documents
```

22.11 Summary

In this chapter we have looked at how to configure an Ubuntu system to act as both a Samba client and server allowing the sharing of resources with Windows based systems. Topics covered included the installation of Samba client and server packages and configuration of Samba as a standalone server.

Chapter 23

23. An Overview of Virtualization Techniques

Virtualization is generically defined as the ability to run multiple operating systems simultaneously on a single computer system. While not necessarily a new concept, Virtualization has come to prominence in recent years because it provides a way to fully utilize the CPU and resource capacity of a server system while providing stability (in that if one virtualized guest system crashes, the host and any other guest systems continue to run).

Virtualization is also useful in terms of trying out different operating systems without having to configure dual boot environments. For example, you can run Windows in a virtual machine without having to re-partition the disk, shut down Ubuntu and then boot from Windows. You simply start up a virtualized version of Windows as a guest operating system. Similarly, virtualization allows you to run other Linux distributions from within an Ubuntu system, providing concurrent access to both operating systems.

When deciding on the best approach to implementing virtualization it is important to have a clear understanding of the different virtualization solutions that are currently available. The purpose of this chapter, therefore, is to describe in general terms the virtualization techniques in common use today.

23.1 Guest Operating System Virtualization

Guest OS virtualization, also referred to as application-based virtualization, is perhaps the easiest concept to understand. In this scenario the physical host computer system runs a standard unmodified operating system such as Windows, Linux, UNIX or macOS. Running on this operating system is a virtualization application which executes in much the same way as any other application such as a word processor or spreadsheet would run on the system. It is within this virtualization application that one or more virtual machines are created to run the guest operating systems on the host computer.

The virtualization application is responsible for starting, stopping and managing each virtual machine and essentially controlling access to physical hardware resources on behalf of the individual virtual machines. The virtualization application also engages in a process known as binary rewriting which involves scanning the instruction stream of the executing guest system and replacing any privileged instructions with safe emulations. This has the effect of making the guest system think it is running directly on the system hardware, rather than in a virtual machine within an application.

The following figure provides an illustration of guest OS based virtualization:

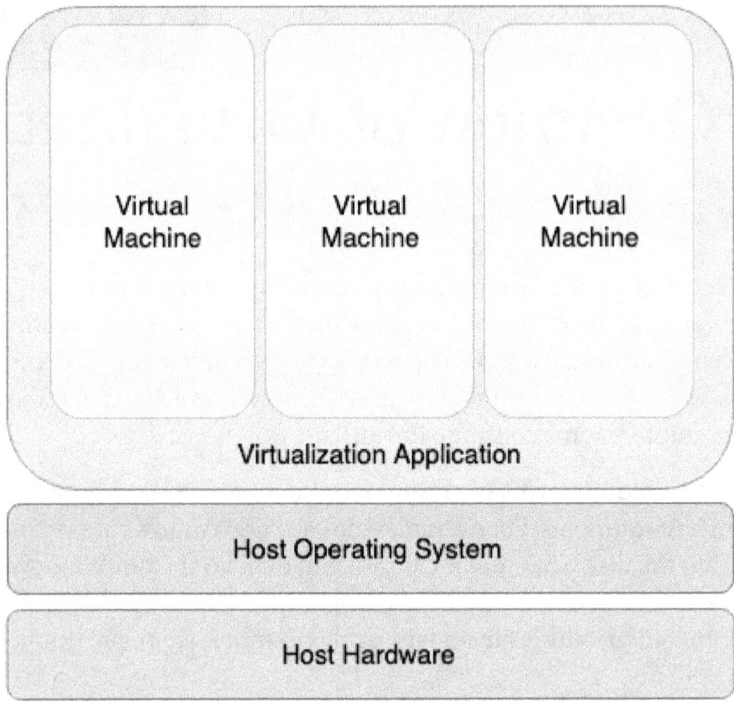

Figure 23-1

As outlined in the above diagram, the guest operating systems operate in virtual machines within the virtualization application which, in turn, runs on top of the host operating system in the same way as any other application. Clearly, the multiple layers of abstraction between the guest operating systems and the underlying host hardware are not conducive to high levels of virtual machine performance. This technique does, however, have the advantage that no changes are necessary to either host or guest operating systems and no special CPU hardware virtualization support is required.

23.2 Hypervisor Virtualization

In hypervisor virtualization, the task of a hypervisor is to handle resource and memory allocation for the virtual machines in addition to providing interfaces for higher level administration and monitoring tools. Hypervisor based solutions are categorized as being either Type-1 or Type-2.

Type-2 hypervisors (sometimes referred to as *hosted hypervisors*) are installed as software applications that run on top of the host operating system, providing virtualization capabilities by coordinating access to resources such as the CPU, memory and network for guest virtual machines. Figure 23-2 illustrates the typical architecture of a system using Type-2 hypervisor virtualization:

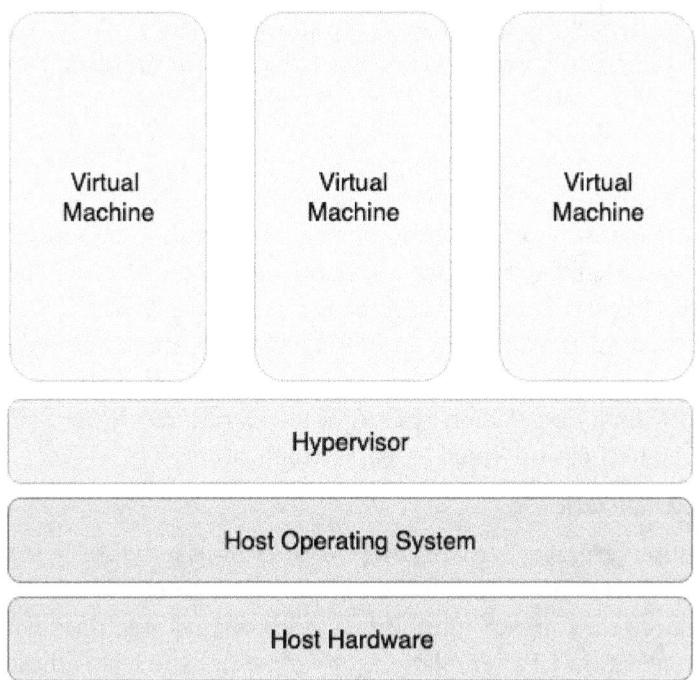

Figure 23-2

To understand how Type-1 hypervisors work, it helps to understand a little about Intel x86 processor architecture. The x86 family of CPUs provides a range of protection levels known as *rings* in which code can execute. Ring 0 has the highest level privilege and it is in this ring that the operating system kernel normally runs. Code executing in ring 0 is said to be running in system space, kernel mode or supervisor mode. All other code such as applications running on the operating system operate in less privileged rings, typically ring 3.

In contrast to Type-2 hypervisors, Type-1 hypervisors (also referred to as *metal* or *native hypervisors*) run directly on the hardware of the host system in ring 0. Clearly, with the hypervisor occupying ring 0 of the CPU, the kernels for any guest operating systems running on the system must run in less privileged CPU rings. Unfortunately, most operating system kernels are written explicitly to run in ring 0 for the simple reason that they need to perform tasks that are only available in that ring, such as the ability to execute privileged CPU instructions and directly manipulate memory. A number of different solutions to this problem have been devised in recent years, each of which is described below:

23.2.1 Paravirtualization

Under paravirtualization, the kernel of the guest operating system is modified specifically to run on the hypervisor. This typically involves replacing any privileged operations that will only run in ring 0 of the CPU with calls to the hypervisor (known as *hypercalls*). The hypervisor, in turn, performs the task on behalf of the guest kernel. This typically limits support to open source operating systems such as Linux which may be freely altered and proprietary operating systems where the owners have agreed to make the necessary code modifications to target a specific hypervisor. These issues notwithstanding, the ability of the guest kernel to communicate directly with the hypervisor results in greater performance levels compared to other virtualization approaches.

23.2.2 Full Virtualization

Full virtualization provides support for unmodified guest operating systems. The term unmodified refers to operating system kernels which have not been altered to run on a hypervisor and therefore still execute privileged operations as though running in ring 0 of the CPU. In this scenario, the hypervisor provides CPU emulation to handle and modify privileged and protected CPU operations made by unmodified guest operating system kernels. Unfortunately this emulation process requires both time and system resources to operate resulting in inferior performance levels when compared to those provided by paravirtualization.

23.2.3 Hardware Virtualization

Hardware virtualization leverages virtualization features built into the latest generations of CPUs from both Intel and AMD. These technologies, known as Intel VT and AMD-V respectively, provide extensions necessary to run unmodified guest virtual machines without the overheads inherent in full virtualization CPU emulation. In very simplistic terms these processors provide an additional privilege mode (referred to as ring -1) above ring 0 in which the hypervisor can operate, thereby leaving ring 0 available for unmodified guest operating systems.

The following figure illustrates the Type-1 hypervisor approach to virtualization:

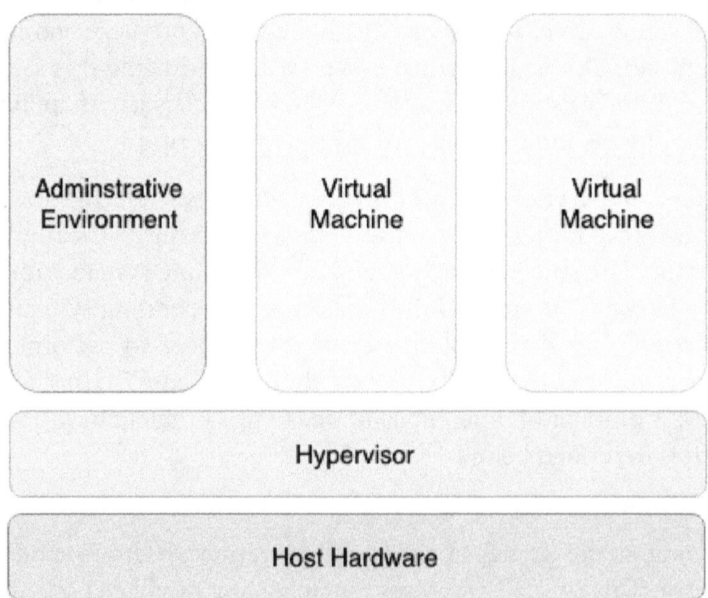

Figure 23-3

As outlined in the above illustration, in addition to the virtual machines, an administrative operating system and/or management console also runs on top of the hypervisor allowing the virtual machines to be managed by a system administrator.

23.3 Virtual Machine Networking

Virtual machines will invariably need to be connected to a network to be of any practical use. One option is for the guest to be connected to a virtual network running within the operating system of the host computer. In this configuration any virtual machines on the virtual network can see each other but access to the external network is provided by Network Address Translation (NAT). When using the virtual network and NAT, each virtual machine is represented on the external network (the network to which the host is connected) using the IP address of the host system. This is the default behavior for KVM virtualization on Ubuntu and generally requires no additional configuration. Typically, a single virtual network is created by default, represented by the name *default* and the device *virbr0*.

In order for guests to appear as individual and independent systems on the external network (i.e. with their own IP addresses), they must be configured to share a physical network interface on the host. The quickest way to achieve this is to configure the virtual machine to use the "direct connection" network configuration option (also referred to a MacVTap) which will provide the guest system with an IP address on the same network as the host. Unfortunately, while this gives the virtual machine access to other systems on the network, it is not possible to establish a connection between the guest and the host when using the MacVTap driver.

A better option is to configure a *network bridge* interface on the host system to which the guests can connect. This provides the guest with an IP address on the external network while also allowing the guest and host to communicate, a topic which is covered in the chapter entitled *"Creating an Ubuntu KVM Networked Bridge Interface"*.

23.4 Summary

Virtualization is defined as the ability to run multiple guest operating systems within a single host operating system. A number of approaches to virtualization have been developed including guest operating system and hypervisor virtualization. Hypervisor virtualization falls into two categories known as Type-1 and Type-2. Type-2 virtualization solutions are categorized as para-virtualization, full virtualization and hardware virtualization, the latter making use of special virtualization features of some Intel and AMD processor models.

Virtual machine guest operating systems have a number of options in terms of networking including NAT, direct connection (MacVTap) and network bridge configurations.

Chapter 24

24. Installing KVM Virtualization on Ubuntu

Earlier versions of Ubuntu provided two virtualization platforms in the form of Kernel-based Virtual Machine (KVM) and Xen. In recent releases, support for Xen has been removed leaving KVM as the only bundled virtualization option supplied with Ubuntu. In addition to KVM, third party solutions are available in the form of products such as VMware and Oracle VirtualBox. Since KVM is supplied with Ubuntu, however, this is the virtualization solution that will be covered in this and subsequent chapters.

Before plunging into installing and running KVM it is worth taking a little time to talk about how it fits into the various types of virtualization outlined in the previous chapter.

24.1 An Overview of KVM

KVM is categorized as a Type-1 hypervisor virtualization solution that implements full virtualization with support for unmodified guest operating systems using Intel VT and AMD-V hardware virtualization support.

KVM differs from many other Type-1 solutions in that it turns the host Linux operating system itself into the hypervisor, allowing bare metal virtualization to be implemented while still running a full, enterprise level host operating system.

24.2 KVM Hardware Requirements

Before proceeding with this chapter we need to take a moment to discuss the hardware requirements for running virtual machines within a KVM environment. First and foremost, KVM virtualization is only available on certain processor types. As previously discussed, these processors must include either Intel VT or AMD-V technology.

To check for virtualization support, run the following command in a terminal window:

```
# lscpu | grep Virtualization:
```

If the system contains a CPU with Intel VT support, the above command will provide the following output:

```
Virtualization:       VT-x
```

Alternatively, the following output will be displayed when a CPU with AMD-V support is detected:

```
Virtualization:       AMD-V
```

If the CPU does not support virtualization, no output will be displayed by the above *lscpu* command.

Note that while the above commands only report whether the processor supports the respective feature, it does not indicate whether the feature is currently enabled in the BIOS. In practice virtualization support is typically disabled by default in the BIOS of most systems. It is recommended, therefore, that you check your BIOS settings to ensure the appropriate virtualization technology is enabled before proceeding with this tutorial.

Unlike a dual booting environment, a virtualized environment involves the running of two or more complete operating systems concurrently on a single computer system. This means that the system must have enough physical memory, disk space and CPU processing power to comfortably accommodate all these systems in parallel. Before beginning the configuration and installation process check on the minimum system requirements for both Ubuntu and your chosen guest operating systems and verify that your host system has sufficient resources to handle the requirements of both systems.

24.3 Preparing Ubuntu for KVM Virtualization

Unlike Xen, it is not necessary to run a special version of the kernel in order to support KVM. As a result KVM support is already available for use with the standard kernel via the installation of a KVM kernel module, thereby negating the need to install and boot from a special kernel.

To avoid conflicts, however, if a Xen enabled kernel is currently running on the system, reboot the system and select a non-Xen kernel from the boot menu before proceeding with the remainder of this chapter.

The tools required to setup and maintain a KVM-based virtualized system are not installed by default unless specifically selected during the Ubuntu operating system installation process. To install the KVM tools from the command prompt, execute the following command in a terminal window:

```
# apt install qemu-kvm libvirt-clients libvirt-daemon-system bridge-utils
```

If you have access to a graphical desktop environment the *virt-manager* package is also recommended:

```
# apt install virt-manager
```

24.4 Verifying the KVM Installation

It is worthwhile checking that the KVM installation worked correctly before moving forward. When KVM is installed and running, two modules will have been loaded into the kernel. The presence or otherwise of these modules can be verified in a terminal window by running the following command:

```
# lsmod | grep kvm
```

Assuming that the installation was successful the above command should generate output similar to the following:

```
# lsmod | grep kvm
kvm_intel              237568  0
kvm                    737280  1 kvm_intel
```

```
irqbypass              16384  1 kvm
```

Note that if the system contains an AMD processor the kvm module will likely read *kvm_amd* rather than *kvm_intel.*

The installation process should also have configured the libvirtd daemon to run in the background. Once again using a terminal window, run the following command to ensure libvirtd is running:

```
# systemctl status libvirtd
 libvirtd.service - Virtualization daemon
   Loaded: loaded (/usr/lib/systemd/system/libvirtd.service; enabled; vendor
preset: enabled)
   Active: active (running) since Wed 2019-03-06 14:41:22 EST; 3min 54s ago
```

If the process is not running, it may be started as follows:

```
# systemctl enable --now libvirtd
# systemctl start libvirtd
```

If the desktop environment is available, run the *virt-manager* tool by selecting Activities and entering "virt" into the search box. When the Virtual Machine Manager icon appears, click on it to launch it. When loaded, the manager should appear as illustrated in the following figure:

Figure 24-1

If the QEMU/KVM entry is not listed, select the *File -> Add Connection* menu option and, in the resulting dialog, select the QEMU/KVM Hypervisor before clicking on the Connect button:

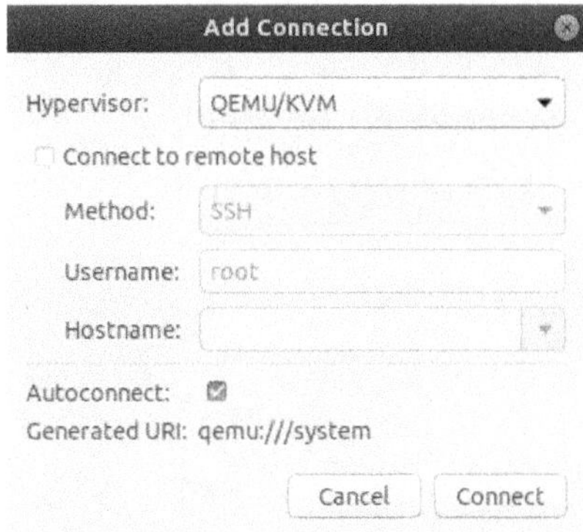

Figure 24-2

If the manager is not currently connected to the virtualization processes, right-click on the entry listed and select Connect from the popup menu.

24.5 Summary

KVM is a Type-1 hypervisor virtualization solution that implements full virtualization with support for unmodified guest operating systems using Intel VT and AMD-V hardware virtualization support. It is the default virtualization solution bundled with Ubuntu and can be installed quickly and easily on any Ubuntu system with appropriate processor support. With KVM support installed and enabled, the next few chapters will outline some of the options for installing and managing virtual machines on an Ubuntu host.

Chapter 25

25. Creating KVM Virtual Machines using Cockpit and virt-manager

KVM-based virtual machines can easily be configured on Ubuntu using either the *virt-install* command-line tool, the *virt-manager* GUI tool or the Virtual Machines module of the Cockpit web console. For the purposes of this chapter we will use Cockpit and the *virt-manager* tool to install a Fedora distribution as a KVM guest on an Ubuntu host.

The command-line approach to virtual machine creation will be covered in the next chapter entitled *"Creating KVM Virtual Machines with virt-install and virsh"*.

25.1 Installing the Cockpit Virtual Machines Module

By default, the virtual machines module may not be included in a standard Cockpit installation. Assuming that Cockpit is installed and configured, the virtual machines module may be installed as follows:

```
# apt install cockpit-machines
```

Once installed, the Virtual Machines option (marked A in Figure 25-1) will appear in the navigation panel next time you log into the Cockpit interface:

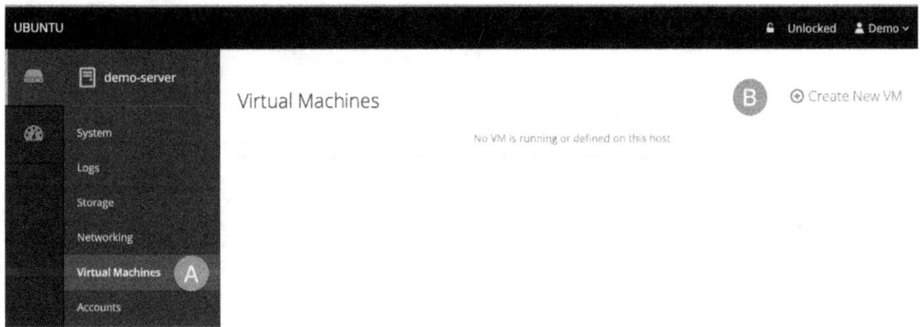

Figure 25-1

25.2 Creating a Virtual Machine in Cockpit

To create a virtual machine in Cockpit, simply click on the *Create VM* button marked B in Figure 25-1 to display the creation dialog.

Within the dialog, enter a name for the machine and choose whether the installation media is in the form of an ISO accessible via a URL or a local filesystem path. Ideally, also select the vendor and operating system type information for the guest. While not essential, this will aid the system in optimizing the virtual machine for the guest.

Also specify the size of the virtual disk drive to be used for the operating system installation and the amount of memory to be allocated to the virtual machine:

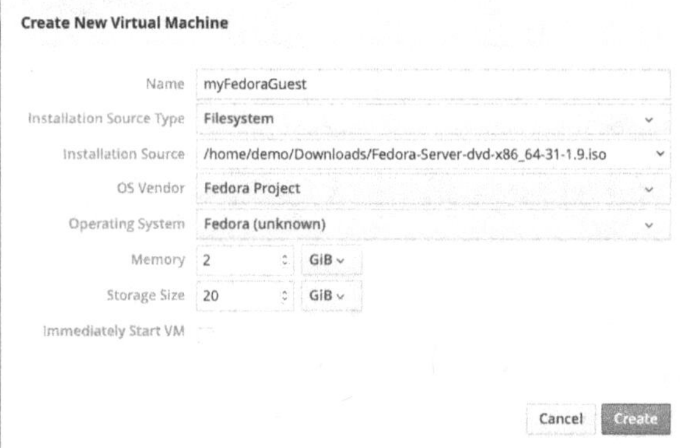

Figure 25-2

For this example, leave the *Immediately Start VM* option unselected and, once the new virtual machine has been configured, click on the *Create* button to build the virtual machine. After the creation process is complete, the new VM will appear in Cockpit as shown in Figure 25-3:

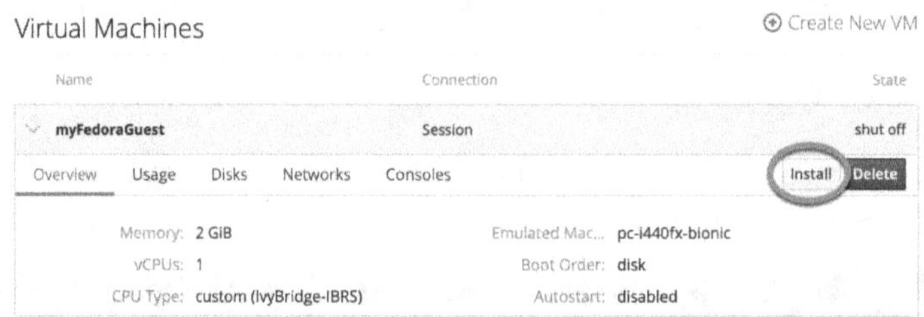

Figure 25-3

As described in *"An Overview of Virtualization Techniques"*, KVM provides virtual machines with a number of options in terms of network configuration. To view the network settings of a virtual machine, click on the Networks tab as shown in Figure 25-4:

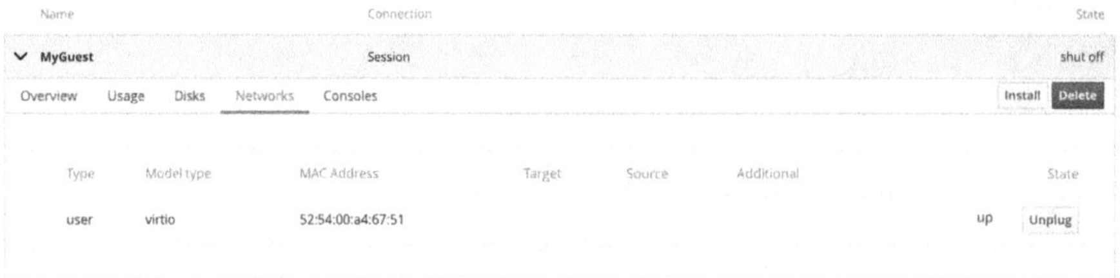

Figure 25-4

In the resulting dialog, the Network Type menu may be used to change the type of network connection, for example from virtual network (NAT) to direct (MacVTap).

25.3 Starting the Installation

To start the new virtual machine and begin installing the guest operating system from the designated installation media, click on the *Install* button highlighted in Figure 25-3 above. Cockpit will start the virtual machine and switch to the Consoles view where the guest OS screen will appear:

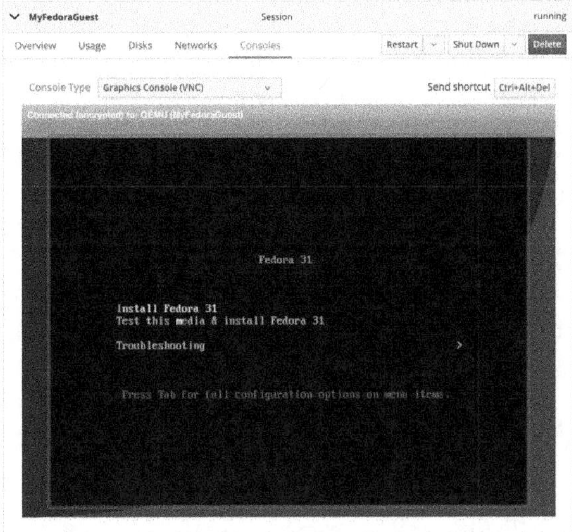

Figure 25-5

If the installation fails, check the message to see if it reads as follows:

```
unsupported configuration: CPU mode 'custom' for x86_64 kvm domain on x86_64 host
is not supported by hypervisor
```

To resolve this issue, delete the newly created virtual machine, reboot the system and then recreate the machine.

Alternatively, check whether the message reads as follows:

```
Could not open '<path to iso image>': Permission denied
Domain installation does not appear to have been successful.
```

This usually occurs because the QEMU emulator runs as a user named qemu which does not have access to the directory in which the ISO installation image is located. To resolve this issue, open a terminal window (or connect with SSH if the system is remote), change directory to the location of the ISO image file and add the qemu user to the access control list (ACL) of the parent directory as follows:

```
# cd /path/to/iso/directory
# setfacl --modify u:qemu:x ..
```

After making this change, check the setting as follows:

```
# getfacl ..
# file: ..
```

```
# owner: demo
# group: demo
user::rwx
user:qemu:--x
group::---
mask::--x
other::---
```

Once these changes have been made, click on the Install button once again to complete the installation.

To complete the installation, interact with the screen in the Consoles view just as you would if you were installing the operating system on physical hardware.

It is also possible to connect with and display the graphical console for the VM from outside the Cockpit browser session using the *virt-viewer* tool. To install *virt-viewer* on an Ubuntu system, run the following command:

```
# apt install virt-viewer
```

The *virt-viewer* tool is also available for Windows systems and can be downloaded from the following URL:

https://virt-manager.org/download/

To connect with a virtual machine running on the local host, simply run *virt-viewer* and select the virtual machine to which you wish to connect from the resulting dialog:

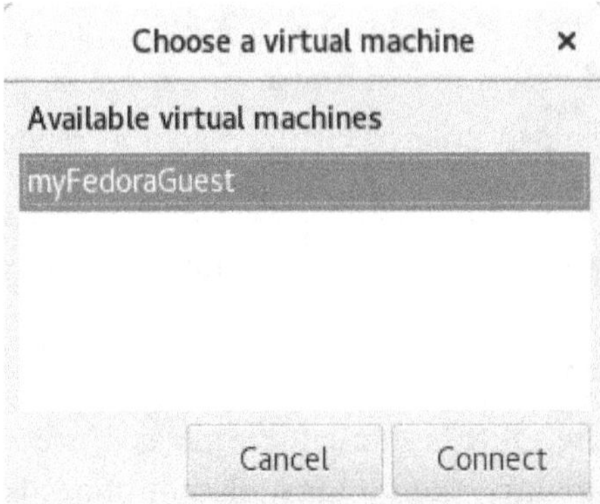

Figure 25-6

Alternatively, it is also possible to specify the virtual machine name and bypass the selection dialog entirely, for example:

```
# virt-viewer myFedoraGuest
```

To connect a *virt-viewer* instance to a virtual machine running on a remote host using SSH, the following command can be used:

```
$ virt-viewer --connect qemu+ssh://<user>@<host>/system <guest name>
```

For example:

```
$ virt-viewer --connect qemu+ssh://root@192.168.1.122/system MyFedoraGuest
```

When using this technique it is important to note that you will be prompted twice for the user password before the connection will be fully established.

Once the virtual machine has been created, the Cockpit interface can be used to monitor the machine and perform tasks such as rebooting, shutting down or deleting the guest system. An option is also included on the *Disks* panel to add additional disks to the virtual machine configuration.

25.4 Creating a Virtual Machine using virt-manager

With the caveat that *virt-manager* is now deprecated and will be removed once the Virtual Machines Cockpit extension is fully implemented, the remainder of this chapter will explore the use of this tool to create new virtual machines.

25.5 Starting the Virtual Machine Manager

Begin by launching Virtual Machine Manager from the command-line in a terminal window by running *virt-manager*. Once loaded, the virtual machine manager will prompt for the password of the currently active user prior to displaying the following screen:

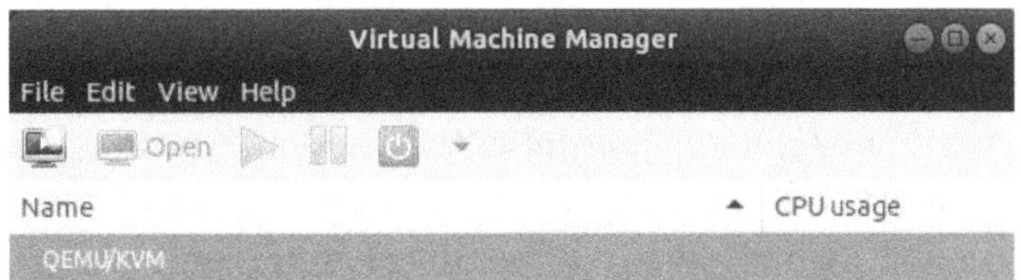

Figure 25-7

The main screen lists the current virtual machines running on the system. At this point there should only be one, the hypervisor running on the host system. By default the manager should be connected to the host. If it is not, connect to the host system by right-clicking on the entry in the list and selecting *Connect* from the popup menu.

To create a new virtual system, click on the new virtual machine button (the far left button on the toolbar) or right-click on the hypervisor entry and select *New* from the resulting menu to display the first screen of the New VM wizard. In the Name field enter a suitably descriptive name for the virtual system. On this screen, also select the location of the media from which the guest operating system will be installed. This can either be a CD or DVD drive, an ISO image file accessible to the local host, a network install using HTTP, FTP, NFS or PXE or the disk image from an existing virtual machine:

Figure 25-8

25.6 Configuring the KVM Virtual System

Clicking *Forward* will display a screen seeking additional information about the installation process. The screen displayed and information required will depend on selections made in the preceding screen. For example, if a CD, DVD or ISO was selected, this screen will ask for the specific location of the ISO file or physical media device. This screen also attempts to identify the type and version of the guest operating system to be installed (for example the Windows version or Linux distribution) based on the installation media specified. If it is unable to do so, uncheck the *Automatically detect from installation media / source* option, type in the first few characters of the operating system name and select an option from the list of possible matches:

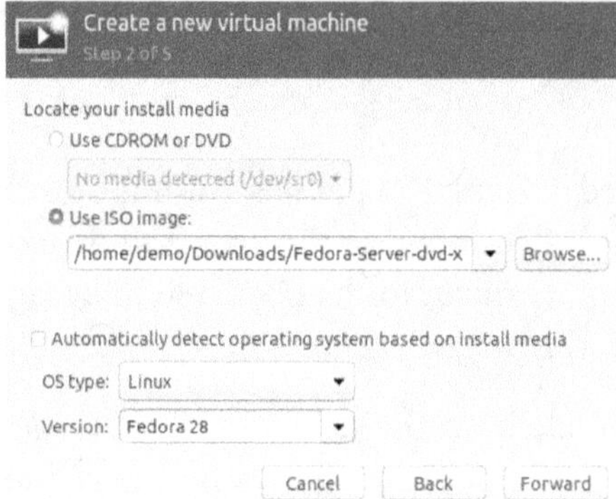

Figure 25-9

Once these settings are complete, click the *Forward* button to configure CPU and memory settings. The optimal settings will depend on the number of CPUs and amount of physical memory present in the host together with the requirements of other applications and virtual machines that will run in parallel with the new virtual machine:

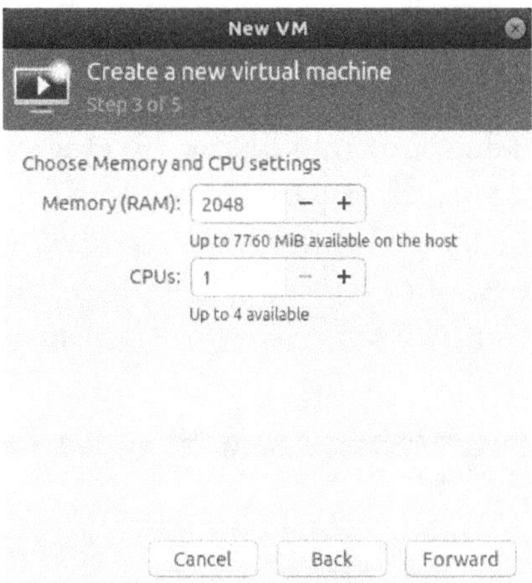

Figure 25-10

25.7 Working with Storage Volumes and Storage Pools

The last item to configure before creating the virtual machine is the storage space for the guest operating system and corresponding user data. This takes the form of a virtual disk image or pre-existing storage. A virtual disk drive is essentially an image file located on the file system of the host computer which is seen by the virtual machine as a physical disk drive. After clicking the Forward button within virt-manager, the following screen will appear:

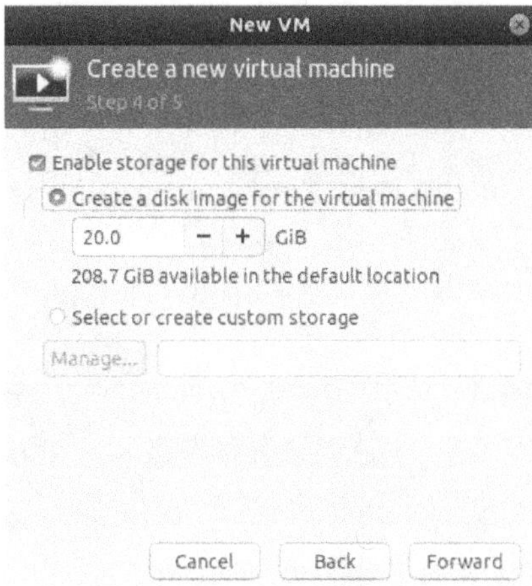

Figure 25-11

When a virtual machine is created it will usually have associated with it at least one virtual disk drive. The images that represent these virtual disk drives are stored in *storage pools*. A storage pool can take the form of an existing directory on a local filesystem, a filesystem partition, physical disk device, Logical Volume Management (LVM) volume group or even a remote network file system (NFS).

Each storage pool is divided into one or more *storage volumes*. Storage volumes are typically individual image files, each representing a single virtual disk drive, but can also take the form of physical disk partitions, entire disk drives or LVM volume groups.

If no changes are made in the dialog shown in Figure 25-11 above, a default storage pool will be used into which virtual machine images may be stored. This default storage pool occupies space on the root filesystem and will be located within the */var/lib/libvirt/images* directory of the local system. To create a new storage pool or use an existing one, enable the *Select or create custom storage* option before clicking on the Manage... button to display the screen shown in Figure 25-12:

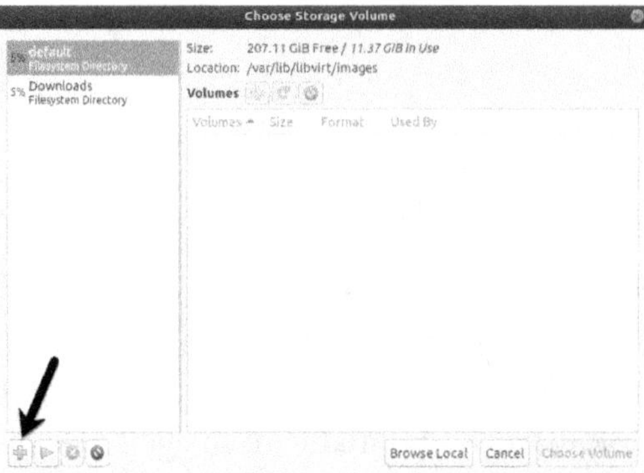

Figure 25-12

As we can see, the above configuration has two storage pools, one representing the installation media (which, in this case, is an ISO image located in the user's Downloads directory) and the default storage pool located in */var/lib/libvirt/images.*

To create a custom pool, click on the Add Pool button highlighted in Figure 25-12 above. In the resulting dialog (Figure 25-13) select the type of pool from the list (for the purposes of this example, a filesystem directory will be used) and give the pool a name before clicking on the Forward button:

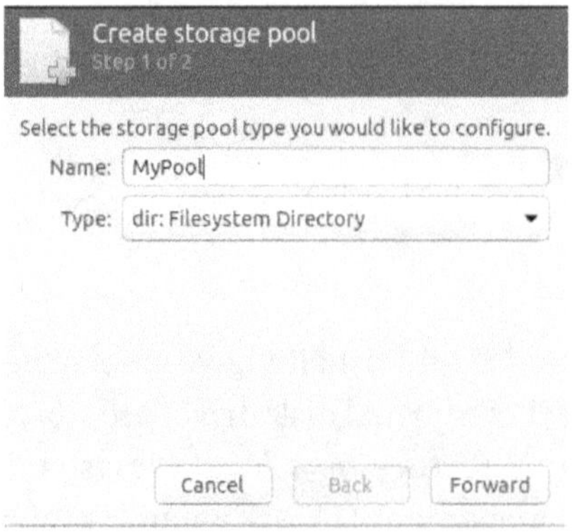

Figure 25-13

On the subsequent screen, navigate to a directory in which to store the new pool (opening a terminal window and creating the directory if it does not already exist). Once the location has been selected, open it to close the browse dialog, then click on Finish to create the storage. The new pool should now be listed in the storage selection dialog:

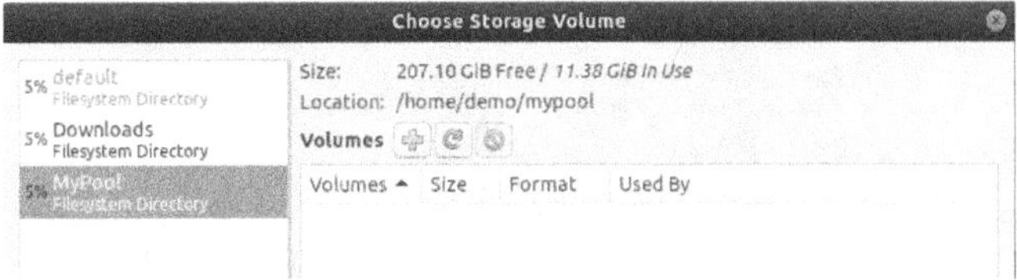

Figure 25-14

In the storage volume dialog, select the MyPool entry in the left hand panel, followed by the + button in the main panel to create a new storage volume:

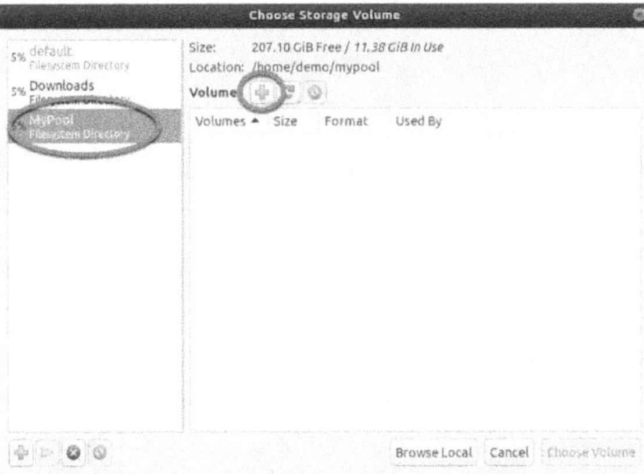

Figure 25-15

In the configuration screen (Figure 25-16), name the storage volume, select the volume size and click on the Finish button to create the volume and assign it to the virtual machine:

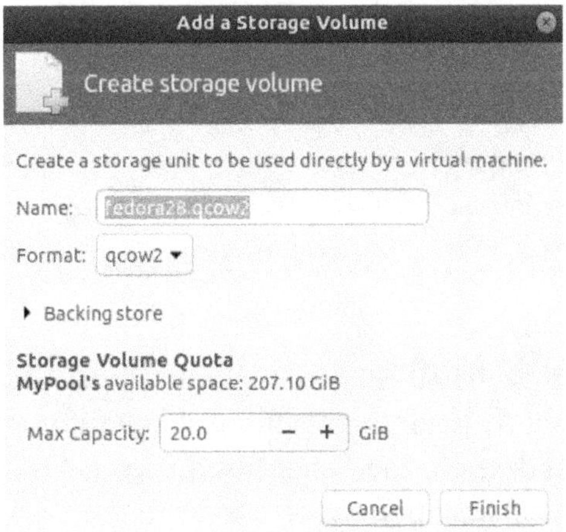

Figure 25-16

Once these settings are configured, select the new volume and click on the Choose Volume button. Click the *Forward* button once more. The final screen displays a summary of the configuration. Review the information displayed. Advanced options are also available to change the virtual network configuration for the guest as shown in Figure 25-17:

Figure 25-17

25.8 Starting the KVM Virtual Machine

Click on the *Finish* button to begin the creation process. The virtualization manager will create the disk and configure the virtual machine before starting the guest system. The new virtual machine will appear in the main *virt-manager* window with the status set to *Running* as illustrated in Figure 25-18:

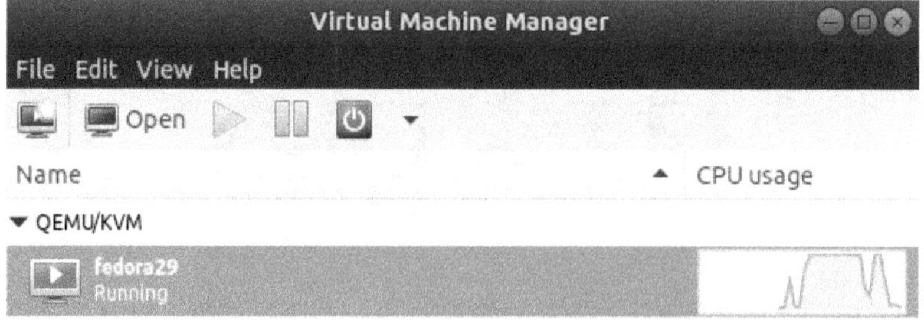

Figure 25-18

By default, the console for the virtual machine should appear in the virtual machine viewer window. To view the console of the running machine at any future time, ensure that it is selected in the virtual machine list and select the *Open* button from the toolbar. The virtual machine viewer should be ready for the installation process to begin:

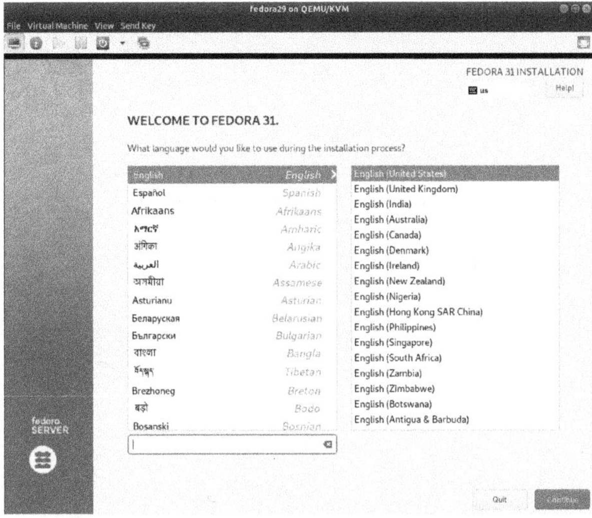

Figure 25-19

From this point on, simply follow the operating system installation instructions to install the guest OS in the KVM virtual machine.

25.9 Summary

This chapter has outlined two different ways to create new KVM-based virtual machines on an Ubuntu host system. The first option covered involves the use of the Cockpit web-based interface to create and manage virtual machines. This has the advantage of not requiring access to a desktop environment running on the host system. An alternative option is to use the *virt-manager* graphical tool. With these basics covered, the next chapter will cover the creation of virtual machines from the command-line.

Chapter 26

26. Creating KVM Virtual Machines with virt-install and virsh

In the previous chapter we explored the creation of KVM guest operating systems on an Ubuntu host using Cockpit and the *virt-manager* graphical tool. In this chapter we will turn our attention to the creation of KVM-based virtual machines using the *virt-install* and *virsh* command-line tools. These tools provide all the capabilities of the *virt-manager* and Cockpit options with the added advantage that they can be used within scripts to automate virtual machine creation. In addition, the *virsh* command allows virtual machines to be created based on a specification contained within a configuration file.

The *virt-install* tool is supplied to allow new virtual machines to be created by providing a list of command-line options. This chapter assumes that the necessary KVM tools are installed. For details on these requirements read the chapter entitled *"Installing KVM Virtualization on Ubuntu"*.

26.1 Running virt-install to build a KVM Guest System

The *virt-install* utility accepts a wide range of command-line arguments that are used to provide configuration information related to the virtual machine being created. Some of these command-line options are mandatory (specifically name, memory and disk storage must be provided) while others are optional.

At a minimum, a *virt-install* command will typically need the following arguments:

- **--name** - The name to be assigned to the virtual machine.
- **--memory** - The amount of memory to be allocated to the virtual machine.
- **--disk** - The name and location of an image file to be used as storage for the virtual machine. This file will be created by *virt-install* during the virtual machine creation unless the **--import** option is specified to indicate an existing image file is to be used.
- **--cdrom** or **--location** - Specifies the local path or the URL of a remote ISO image containing the installation media for the guest operating system.

A summary of all the arguments available for use when using *virt-install* can be found in the man page:

```
$ man virt-install
```

26.2 An Example Ubuntu virt-install Command

With reference to the above command-line argument list, we can now look at an example command-line construct using the *virt-install* tool.

Note that in order to be able to display the virtual machine and complete the installation, a *virt-viewer* instance will need to be connected to the virtual machine after it is started by the *virt-install* utility. By default, *virt-install* will attempt to launch *virt-viewer* automatically once the virtual machine starts running. If *virt-viewer* is not available, *virt-install* will wait until a *virt-viewer* connection is established. The *virt-viewer* session may be running locally on the host system if it has a graphical desktop, or a connection may be established from a remote client as outlined in the chapter entitled *"Creating KVM Virtual Machines using Cockpit and virt-manager"*.

The following command creates a new KVM virtual machine configured to run Fedora using KVM para-virtualization. It creates a new 10GB disk image, assigns 1024MB of RAM to the virtual machine and configures a virtual CD device for the installation media ISO image:

```
# virt-install --name MyFedora --memory 1024 --disk path=/tmp/myFedora.
img,size=10 --network network=default --os-variant fedora28 --cdrom /tmp/Fedora-
Server-dvd-x86_64-29-1.2.iso
```

As the creation process runs, the *virt-install* command will display status updates of the creation progress:

```
Starting install...
Allocating 'MyFedora.img'                                 |  10 GB  00:00:01
Domain installation still in progress. Waiting for installation to complete.
```

Once the guest system has been created, the *virt-viewer* screen will appear containing the operating system installer loaded from the specified installation media:

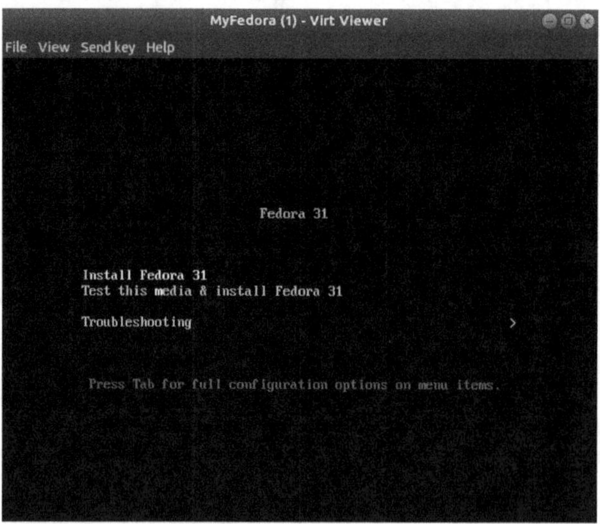

Figure 26-1

From this point, follow the standard installation procedure for the guest operating system.

26.3 Starting and Stopping a Virtual Machine from the Command-Line

Having created the virtual machine from the command-line it stands to reason that you may also need to start it from the command-line in the future. This can be achieved using the virsh command-line utility, referencing the name assigned to the virtual machine during the creation process. For example:

```
# virsh start MyFedora
```

Similarly, the virtual machine may be sent a shutdown signal as follows:

```
# virsh shutdown MyFedora
```

If the virtual machine fails to respond to the shutdown signal and does not begin a graceful shutdown the virtual machine may be destroyed (with the attendant risks of data loss) using the destroy directive:

```
# virsh destroy MyFedora
```

26.4 Creating a Virtual Machine from a Configuration File

The *virsh create* command can take as an argument the name of a configuration file on which to base the creation of a new virtual machine. The configuration file uses XML format. Arguably the easiest way to create a configuration file is to dump out the configuration of an existing virtual machine and modify it for the new one. This can be achieved using the *virsh dumpxml* command. The following command outputs the configuration data for a virtual machine domain named MyFedora to a file named *MyFedora.xml*:

```
# virsh dumpxml MyFedora > MyFedora.xml
```

Once the file has been generated, load it into an editor to review and change the settings for the new virtual machine.

At the very least, the <name>, <uuid> and image file path <source file> must be changed in order to avoid conflict with the virtual machine from which the configuration was taken. In the case of the UUID, this line can simply be deleted from the file.

The virtualization type, memory allocation and number of CPUs to name but a few options may also be changed if required. Once the file has been modified, the new virtual machine may be created as follows:

```
# virsh create MyFedora.xml
```

26.5 Summary

KVM provides the *virt-install* and *virsh* command-line tools as a quick and efficient alternative to using the Cockpit and *virt-manager* tools to create and manage virtual machine instances. These tools have the advantage that they can be used from within scripts to automate the creation and management of virtual machines. The *virsh* command also includes the option to create VM instances from XML-based configuration files.

Chapter 27

27. Creating an Ubuntu KVM Networked Bridge Interface

By default, the KVM virtualization environment on Ubuntu creates a virtual network to which virtual machines may connect. It is also possible to configure a direct connection using a MacVTap driver, though as outlined in the chapter entitled *"An Overview of Virtualization Techniques"*, this approach does not allow the host and guest systems to communicate.

The goal of this chapter is to cover the steps involved in creating a network bridge on Ubuntu enabling guest systems to share one or more of the host system's physical network connections while still allowing the guest and host systems to communicate.

In the remainder of this chapter we will cover the steps necessary to configure an Ubuntu network bridge for use by KVM-based guest operating systems.

27.1 Identifying the Network Management System

The steps to create a network bridge will differ depending on whether the host system is using Network Manager or Netplan for network management. If you installed Ubuntu using the desktop installation media then you most likely have a system running Network Manager. If, on the other hand, you installed from the server or Network installer image, then your system is most likely using Netplan.

To identify which networking system is being used, open a Terminal window and change directory to */etc/netplan*. If you are using Network Manager this directory will contain a file named *01-network-manager-all.yaml* with the following content:

```
# Let NetworkManager manage all devices on this system
network:
  version: 2
  renderer: NetworkManager
```

Alternatively, if the directory contains a file named either *01-netcfg.yaml* or *50-cloud-init.yaml* with content similar to the following, then your system is using Netplan:

```
network:
  version: 2
  renderer: networkd
  ethernets:
    eno1:
      dhcp4: yes
```

Having identified your network management system, follow the corresponding steps in the remainder of this chapter.

27.2 Getting the Netplan Network Settings

Before creating the network bridge on a Netplan based system, begin by obtaining information about the current network configuration using the *networkctl* command as follows:

```
# networkctl status -a
● 1: lo
       Link File: /lib/systemd/network/99-default.link
    Network File: n/a
            Type: loopback
           State: carrier (unmanaged)
         Address: 127.0.0.1
                  ::1

● 2: eno1
       Link File: /lib/systemd/network/99-default.link
    Network File: /run/systemd/network/10-netplan-eno1.network
            Type: ether
           State: routable (configured)
            Path: pci-0000:00:19.0
          Driver: e1000e
          Vendor: Intel Corporation
           Model: 82579LM Gigabit Network Connection (Lewisville)
      HW Address: fc:4d:d4:3b:e4:0f (Universal Global Scientific Industrial Co., 
Ltd.)
         Address: 192.168.86.214
                  fe80::fe4d:d4ff:fe3b:e40f
         Gateway: 192.168.86.1
             DNS: 192.168.86.1
  Search Domains: lan

● 3: virbr0
       Link File: /lib/systemd/network/99-default.link
    Network File: n/a
            Type: ether
           State: no-carrier (unmanaged)
          Driver: bridge
      HW Address: 52:54:00:2d:f4:2a
         Address: 192.168.122.1

● 4: virbr0-nic
       Link File: /lib/systemd/network/99-default.link
    Network File: n/a
            Type: ether
           State: off (unmanaged)
          Driver: tun
```

```
    HW Address: 52:54:00:2d:f4:2a
```

In the above output we can see that the host has an Ethernet network connection established via a device named *eno1* and the default bridge interface named *virbr0* which provides access to the NAT-based virtual network to which KVM guest systems are connected by default. The output also lists the loopback interface (lo).

27.3 Creating a Netplan Network Bridge

The creation of a network bridge on an Ubuntu system using Netplan involves the addition of an entry to the */etc/netplan/01-netcfg.yaml* file. Using your preferred editor, open the file and add a *bridges* entry beneath the current content as follows (substituting *eno1* for the connection name on your system):

```
network:
  version: 2
  renderer: networkd
  ethernets:
    eno1:
      dhcp4: yes

  bridges:
    br0:
      interfaces: [eno1]
      dhcp4: yes
```

Note that the *bridges:* line must be indented by two spaces. Without this indentation, the netplan tool will fail with the following error when run:

```
Error in network definition: unknown key 'bridges'
```

Once the changes have been made, apply them using the following command:

```
# netplan apply
```

Note that this command will switch the network from the current connection to the bridge resulting in the system being assigned a different IP address by the DHCP server. If you are connected via a remote SSH session this will cause you to lose contact with the server. If you would prefer to assign a static IP address to the bridge connection, modify the bridge declaration as follows (making sure to turn off DHCP for both IPv4 and IPv6):

```
network:
  version: 2
  renderer: networkd
  ethernets:
    eno1:
      dhcp4: no
      dhcp6: no

  bridges:
```

```
    br0:
      interfaces: [eno1]
      dhcp4: no
      addresses: [192.168.86.230/24]
      gateway4: 192.168.86.1
      nameservers:
        addresses: [192.168.86.1]
```

After running the netplan apply command, check that the bridge is now configured and ready for use within KVM virtual machines:

```
# networkctl status -a
● 1: lo
       Link File: /lib/systemd/network/99-default.link
    Network File: n/a
            Type: loopback
           State: carrier (unmanaged)
         Address: 127.0.0.1
                  ::1

● 2: eno1
       Link File: /lib/systemd/network/99-default.link
    Network File: /run/systemd/network/10-netplan-eno1.network
            Type: ether
           State: carrier (configured)
            Path: pci-0000:00:19.0
          Driver: e1000e
          Vendor: Intel Corporation
           Model: 82579LM Gigabit Network Connection (Lewisville)
      HW Address: fc:4d:d4:3b:e4:0f (Universal Global Scientific Industrial Co.,
.
.
● 5: br0
       Link File: /lib/systemd/network/99-default.link
    Network File: /run/systemd/network/10-netplan-br0.network
            Type: ether
           State: routable (configured)
          Driver: bridge
      HW Address: b6:56:ed:e9:d5:75
         Address: 192.168.86.230
                  fe80::b456:edff:fee9:d575
         Gateway: 192.168.86.1
             DNS: 192.168.86.1
```

27.4 Getting the Current Network Manager Settings

A network bridge can be created using the NetworkManager command-line interface tool (*nmcli*). The NetworkManager is installed and enabled by default on Ubuntu desktop systems and is responsible for detecting and connecting to network devices in addition to providing an interface for managing networking configurations.

A list of current network connections on the host system can be displayed as follows:

```
# nmcli con show
NAME                UUID                                  TYPE      DEVICE
Wired connection 1  56f32c14-a4d2-32c8-9391-f51967efa173  ethernet  eno1
virbr0              59bf4111-e0d2-4e6c-b8d4-cb70fa6d695e  bridge    virbr0
```

In the above output we can see that the host has an Ethernet network connection established via a device named *eno1* and the default bridge interface named *virbr0* which provides access to the NAT-based virtual network to which KVM guest systems are connected by default.

Similarly, the following command can be used to identify the devices (both virtual and physical) that are currently configured on the system:

```
# nmcli device show
GENERAL.DEVICE:                         eno1
GENERAL.TYPE:                           ethernet
GENERAL.HWADDR:                         FC:4D:D4:3B:E4:0F
GENERAL.MTU:                            1500
GENERAL.STATE:                          100 (connected)
GENERAL.CONNECTION:                     Wired connection 1
GENERAL.CON-PATH:                       /org/freedesktop/NetworkManager/
ActiveConnection/1
WIRED-PROPERTIES.CARRIER:               on
IP4.ADDRESS[1]:                         192.168.86.207/24
IP4.GATEWAY:                            192.168.86.1
IP4.ROUTE[1]:                           dst = 0.0.0.0/0, nh = 192.168.86.1, mt =
100
IP4.ROUTE[2]:                           dst = 192.168.86.0/24, nh = 0.0.0.0, mt =
100
IP4.ROUTE[3]:                           dst = 169.254.0.0/16, nh = 0.0.0.0, mt =
1000
IP4.DNS[1]:                             192.168.86.1
IP4.DOMAIN[1]:                          lan
IP6.ADDRESS[1]:                         fe80::d3e2:c3dc:b69b:cd30/64
IP6.GATEWAY:                            --
IP6.ROUTE[1]:                           dst = ff00::/8, nh = ::, mt = 256,
table=255
IP6.ROUTE[2]:                           dst = fe80::/64, nh = ::, mt = 256
IP6.ROUTE[3]:                           dst = fe80::/64, nh = ::, mt = 100
```

```
GENERAL.DEVICE:                         virbr0
GENERAL.TYPE:                           bridge
GENERAL.HWADDR:                         52:54:00:9D:19:E5
GENERAL.MTU:                            1500
GENERAL.STATE:                          100 (connected)
GENERAL.CONNECTION:                     virbr0
GENERAL.CON-PATH:                       /org/freedesktop/NetworkManager/
ActiveConnection/2
IP4.ADDRESS[1]:                         192.168.122.1/24
IP4.GATEWAY:                            --
IP4.ROUTE[1]:                           dst = 192.168.122.0/24, nh = 0.0.0.0, mt
= 0
IP6.GATEWAY:                            --
.
.
```

The above partial output indicates that the host system on which the command was executed contains a physical Ethernet device (eno1) and the virtual bridge (virbr0).

The *virsh* command may also be used to list the virtual networks currently configured on the system:

```
# virsh net-list --all
 Name                 State      Autostart     Persistent
----------------------------------------------------------
 default              active     yes           yes
```

At this point, the only virtual network present is the default network provided by virbr0. Now that some basic information about the current network configuration has been obtained, the next step is to create a network bridge connected to the physical network device (in this case the device named eno1).

27.5 Creating a Network Manager Bridge from the Command-Line

The first step in creating the network bridge is to add a new connection to the network configuration. This can be achieved using the *nmcli* tool, specifying that the connection is to be a bridge and providing names for both the connection and the interface:

```
# nmcli con add ifname br0 type bridge con-name br0
```

Once the connection has been added, a bridge slave interface needs to be established between physical device eno1 (the slave) and the bridge connection br0 (the master) as follows:

```
# nmcli con add type bridge-slave ifname eno1 master br0
```

At this point, the NetworkManager connection list should read as follows:

```
# nmcli con show
NAME                UUID                                  TYPE      DEVICE
Wired connection 1  56f32c14-a4d2-32c8-9391-f51967efa173  ethernet  eno1
br0                 8416607e-c6c1-4abb-8583-1661689b95a9  bridge    br0
```

```
virbr0              dffab88d-1588-4e69-8d1c-2148090aa5ee  bridge    virbr0
bridge-slave-eno1   43383092-6434-448f-b735-0cbea39eb38f  ethernet  --
```

The next step is to start up the bridge interface. If the steps to configure the bridge are being performed over a network connection (i.e. via SSH) this step can be problematic because the current eno1 connection must be closed down before the bridge connection can be brought up. This means that the current connection will be lost before the bridge connection can be enabled to replace it, potentially leaving the remote host unreachable.

If you are accessing the host system remotely this problem can be avoided by creating a shell script to perform the network changes. This will ensure that the bridge interface is enabled after the eno1 interface is brought down, allowing you to reconnect to the host after the changes are complete. Begin by creating a shell script file named *bridge.sh* containing the following commands:

```
#!/bin/bash
nmcli con down "Wired connection 1"
nmcli con up br0
```

Once the script has been created, execute it as follows:

```
# sh ./bridge.sh
```

When the script executes, the connection will be lost when the eno1 connection is brought down. After waiting a few seconds, however, it should be possible to reconnect to the host once the br0 connection has been activated.

If you are working locally on the host, the two *nmcli* commands can be run within a terminal window without any risk of losing connectivity:

```
# nmcli con down "Wired connection 1"
# nmcli con up br0
```

Once the bridge is up and running, the connection list should now include both the bridge and the bridge-slave connections:

```
# nmcli con show
NAME                UUID                                  TYPE      DEVICE
br0                 8416607e-c6c1-4abb-8583-1661689b95a9  bridge    br0
bridge-slave-eno1   43383092-6434-448f-b735-0cbea39eb38f  ethernet  eno1
virbr0              dffab88d-1588-4e69-8d1c-2148090aa5ee  bridge    virbr0
Wired connection 1  56f32c14-a4d2-32c8-9391-f51967efa173  ethernet  --
```

Note that the Wired Connection 1 connection is still listed but is actually no longer active. To exclude inactive connections from the list, simply use the --active flag when requesting the list:

```
# nmcli con show --active
NAME               UUID                                  TYPE      DEVICE
br0                8416607e-c6c1-4abb-8583-1661689b95a9  bridge    br0
bridge-slave-eno1  43383092-6434-448f-b735-0cbea39eb38f  ethernet  eno1
virbr0             dffab88d-1588-4e69-8d1c-2148090aa5ee  bridge    virbr0
```

27.6 Declaring the KVM Bridged Network

At this point, the bridge connection is present on the system but is not visible to the KVM environment. Running the *virsh* command should still list the default network as being the only available network option:

```
# virsh net-list --all
 Name                 State      Autostart     Persistent
----------------------------------------------------------
 default              active     yes           yes
```

Before the bridge can be used by a virtual machine it must be declared and added to the KVM network configuration. This involves the creation of a definition file and, once again, the use of the *virsh* command-line tool.

Begin by creating a definition file for the bridge network named *bridge.xml* that reads as follows:

```
<network>
  <name>br0</name>
  <forward mode="bridge"/>
  <bridge name="br0" />
</network>
```

Next, use the file to define the new network:

```
# virsh net-define ./bridge.xml
```

Once the network has been defined, start it and, if required, configure it to autostart each time the system reboots:

```
# virsh net-start br0
# virsh net-autostart br0
```

Once again list the networks to verify that the bridge network is now accessible within the KVM environment:

```
# virsh net-list --all
 Name                 State      Autostart     Persistent
----------------------------------------------------------
 br0                  active     yes           yes
 default              active     yes           yes
```

27.7 Using a Bridge Network in a Virtual Machine

To create a virtual machine that makes use of the bridge network, use the *virt-install* --network option and specify the br0 bridge name. For example:

```
# virt-install --name MyFedora --memory 1024 --disk path=/tmp/myFedora.
img,size=10 --network network=br0 --os-variant fedora28 --cdrom /home/demo/
Downloads/Fedora-Server-dvd-x86_64-29-1.2.iso
```

When the guest operating system is running it will appear on the same physical network as the host system and will no longer be on the NAT-based virtual network.

To modify an existing virtual machine so that it uses the bridge, use the *virsh edit* command. This command loads the XML definition file into an editor where changes can be made and saved:

```
# virsh edit GuestName
```

By default, the file will be loaded into the vi editor. To use a different editor, simply change the $EDITOR environment variable, for example:

```
# export EDITOR=gedit
```

To change from the default virtual network, locate the <interface> section of the file which will read as follows for a NAT based configuration:

```
<interface type='network'>
      <mac address='<your mac address here>'/>
      <source network='default'/>
      <model type='virtio'/>
      <address type='pci' domain='0x0000' bus='0x01' slot='0x00' function='0x0'/>
</interface>
```

Alternatively, if the virtual machine was using a direct connection, the entry may read as follows:

```
<interface type='direct'>
      <mac address='<your mac address here>'/>
      <source dev='eno1' mode='vepa'/>
      <model type='virtio'/>
      <address type='pci' domain='0x0000' bus='0x01' slot='0x00' function='0x0'/>
```

To use the bridge, change the source network property to read as follows before saving the file:

```
<interface type='network'>
      <mac address='<your mac address here>'/>
      <source network='br0'/>
      <model type='virtio'/>
      <address type='pci' domain='0x0000' bus='0x01' slot='0x00' function='0x0'/>
</interface>
```

If the virtual machine is already running, the change will not take effect until it is restarted.

27.8 Creating a Bridge Network using nm-connection-editor

If either local or remote desktop access is available on the host system, much of the bridge configuration process can be performed using the *nm-connection-editor* graphical tool. To use this tool, open a Terminal window within the desktop and enter the following command:

```
# nm-connection-editor
```

When the tool has loaded, the window shown in Figure 27-1 will appear listing the currently configured network connections (essentially the same output as that generated by the *nmcli con show* command):

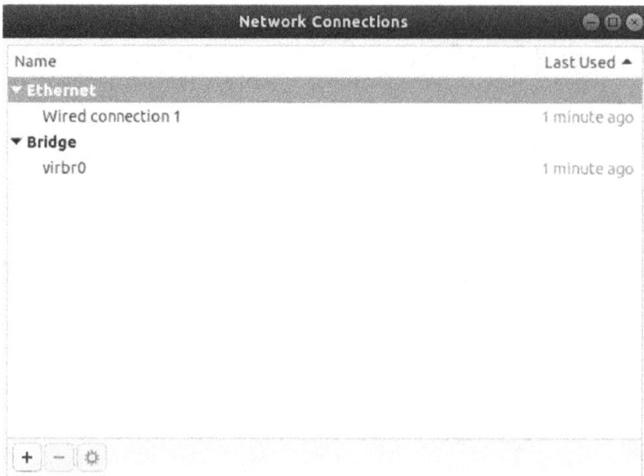

Figure 27-1

To create a new connection, click on the '+' button located in the bottom left-hand corner of the window. From the resulting dialog (Figure 27-2) select the Bridge option from the menu:

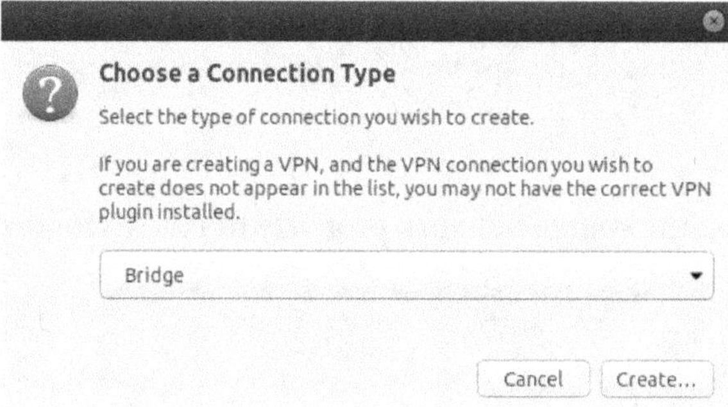

Figure 27-2

With the bridge option selected, click on the *Create...* button to proceed to the bridge configuration screen. Begin by changing both the connection and interface name fields to br0 before clicking on the *Add* button located to the right of the Bridge connections list as highlighted in Figure 27-3:

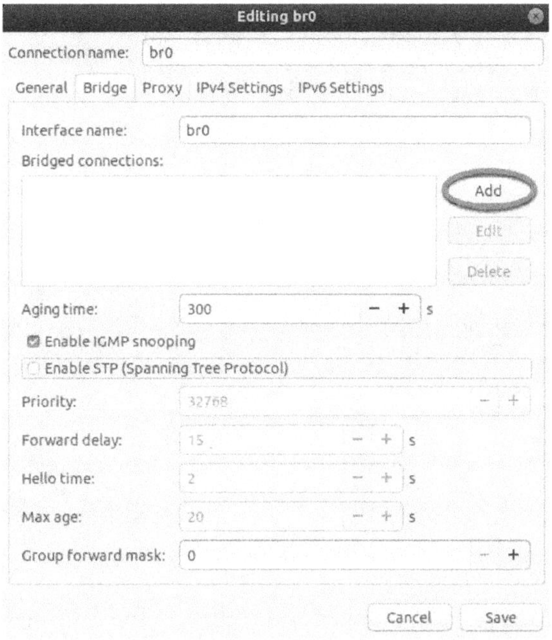

Figure 27-3

From the connection type dialog (Figure 27-4) change the menu setting to *Ethernet* before clicking on the *Create...* button:

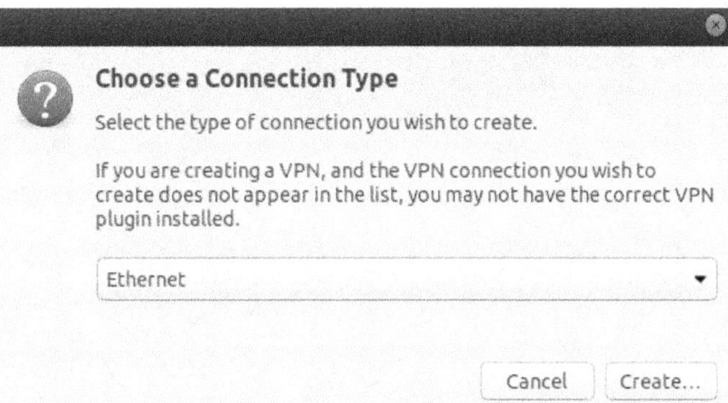

Figure 27-4

Another dialog will now appear in which the bridge slave connection needs to be configured. Within this dialog, select the physical network to which the bridge is to connect (for example *eno1*) from the Device menu:

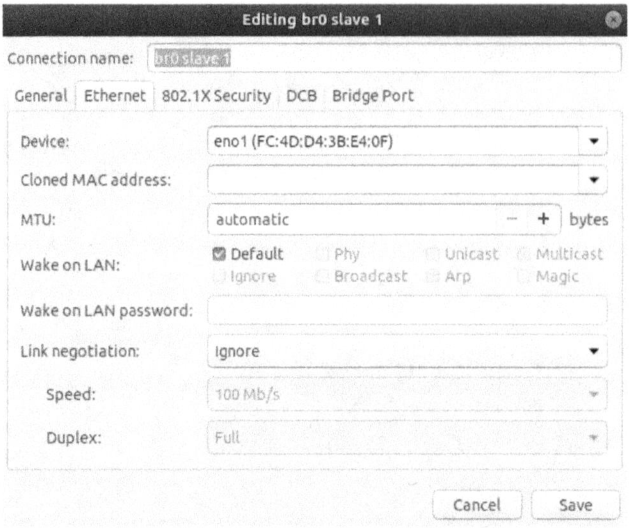

Figure 27-5

Click on the *Save* button to apply the changes and return to the *Editing br0* dialog (as illustrated in Figure 27-3 above). Within this dialog, click on the *Save* button to create the bridge. On returning to the main window, the new bridge and slave connections should now be listed:

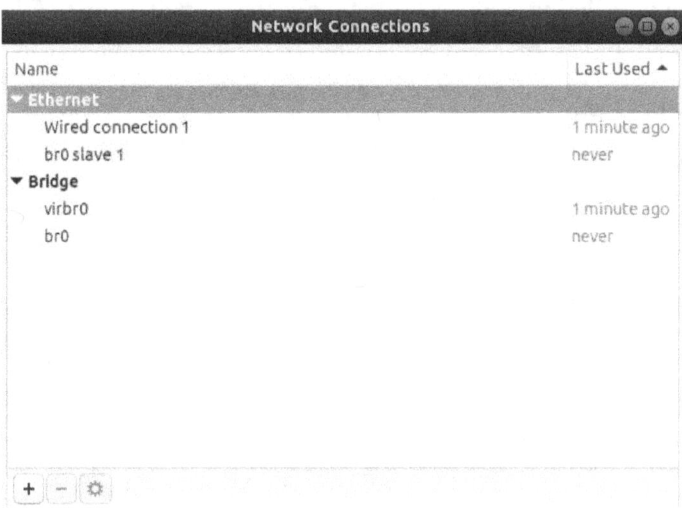

Figure 27-6

All that remains is to bring down the original eno1 connection and bring up the br0 connection using the steps outlined in the previous chapter (remembering to perform these steps in a shell script if the host is being accessed remotely):

```
# nmcli con down "Wired connection 1"
# nmcli con up br0
```

It will also be necessary, as it was when creating the bridge using the command-line tool, to add this bridge to the KVM network configuration. To do so, simply repeat the steps outlined in the section above entitled *"Declaring the KVM Bridged Network"*. Once this step has been taken, the bridge is ready to be used by guest virtual machines.

27.9 Summary

By default, KVM virtual machines are connected to a virtual network that uses NAT to provide access to the network to which the host system is connected. If the guests are required to appear on the network with their own IP addresses, the guests need to be configured to share the physical network interface of the host system. As outlined in this chapter, this can be achieved using either the *nmcli* or *nm-connection-editor* tools to create a networked bridge interface.

Chapter 28

28. Managing KVM using the virsh Command-Line Tool

In previous chapters we have covered the installation and configuration of KVM-based guest operating systems on Ubuntu. This chapter is dedicated to exploring some additional areas of the *virsh* tool that have not been covered in previous chapters, and how it may be used to manage KVM-based guest operating systems from the command-line.

28.1 The virsh Shell and Command-Line

The *virsh* tool is both a command-line tool and an interactive shell environment. When used in the command-line mode, the command is simply issued at the command prompt with sets of arguments appropriate to the task to be performed.

To use the options as command-line arguments, use them at a terminal command prompt as shown in the following example:

```
# virsh <option>
```

The *virsh* tool, when used in shell mode, provides an interactive environment from which to issue sequences of commands.

To run commands in the *virsh* shell, run the following command:

```
# virsh
Welcome to virsh, the virtualization interactive terminal.

Type:  'help' for help with commands
       'quit' to quit

virsh #
```

At the *virsh #* prompt enter the options you wish to run. The following *virsh* session, for example, lists the current virtual machines, starts a virtual machine named FedoraVM and then obtains another listing to verify the VM is running:

```
# virsh
Welcome to virsh, the virtualization interactive terminal.

Type:  'help' for help with commands
       'quit' to quit

virsh # list
 Id    Name                           State
```

```
-----------------------------------------------------
 8      RHEL8VM                        running
 9      CentOS7VM                      running

virsh # start FedoraVM
Domain FedoraVM started

virsh # list
 Id     Name                            State
-----------------------------------------------------
 8      RHEL8VM                        running
 9      CentOS7VM                      running
10      FedoraVM                       running

virsh#
```

The *virsh* tool supports a wide range of commands, a full listing of which may be obtained using the help option:

```
# virsh help
```

Additional details on the syntax for each command may be obtained by specifying the command after the help directive:

```
# virsh help restore
  NAME
    restore - restore a domain from a saved state in a file

  SYNOPSIS
    restore <file> [--bypass-cache] [--xml <string>] [--running] [--paused]

  DESCRIPTION
    Restore a domain.

  OPTIONS
    [--file] <string>  the state to restore
    --bypass-cache     avoid file system cache when restoring
    --xml <string>     filename containing updated XML for the target
    --running          restore domain into running state
    --paused           restore domain into paused state
```

In the remainder of this chapter we will look at some of these commands in more detail.

28.2 Listing Guest System Status

The status of the guest systems on an Ubuntu virtualization host may be viewed at any time using the *list* option of the *virsh* tool. For example:

```
# virsh list
```

The above command will display output containing a line for each guest similar to the following:

```
virsh # list
 Id     Name                          State
----------------------------------------------------
 8      RHEL8VM                      running
 9      CentOS7VM                    running
10      FedoraVM                     running
```

28.3 Starting a Guest System

A guest operating system can be started using the *virsh* tool combined with the start option followed by the name of the guest operating system to be launched. For example:

```
# virsh start myGuestOS
```

28.4 Shutting Down a Guest System

The *shutdown* option of the *virsh* tool, as the name suggests, is used to shutdown a guest operating system:

```
# virsh shutdown guestName
```

Note that the shutdown option allows the guest operating system to perform an orderly shutdown when it receives the shutdown instruction. To instantly stop a guest operating system the *destroy* option may be used (with the risk of file system damage and data loss):

```
# virsh destroy guestName
```

28.5 Suspending and Resuming a Guest System

A guest system can be suspended and resumed using the *virsh* tool's suspend and resume options. For example, to suspend a specific system:

```
# virsh suspend guestName
```

Similarly, to resume the paused system:

```
# virsh resume guestName
```

Note that a suspended session will be lost if the host system is rebooted. Also, be aware that a suspended system continues to reside in memory. To save a session such that it no longer takes up memory and can be restored to its exact state (even after a reboot), it is necessary to save and restore the guest.

28.6 Saving and Restoring Guest Systems

A running guest operating system can be saved and restored using the *virsh* utility. When saved, the current status of the guest operating system is written to disk and removed from system memory. A saved system may subsequently be restored at any time (including after a host system reboot).

To save a guest:

```
# virsh save guestName path_to_save_file
```

To restore a saved guest operating system session:

```
# virsh restore path_to_save_file
```

28.7 Rebooting a Guest System

To reboot a guest operating system:

```
# virsh reboot guestName
```

28.8 Configuring the Memory Assigned to a Guest OS

To configure the memory assigned to a guest OS, use the *setmem* option of the *virsh* command. For example, the following command reduces the memory allocated to a guest system to 256MB:

```
# virsh setmem guestName 256
```

Note that acceptable memory settings must fall within the memory available to the current Domain. This may be increased using the *setmaxmem* option.

28.9 Summary

The *virsh* tool provides a wide range of options for creating, monitoring and managing guest virtual machines. As outlined in this chapter, the tool can be used in either command-line or interactive modes.

Chapter 29

29. An Introduction to Linux Containers

The preceding chapters covered the concept of virtualization with a particular emphasis on creating and managing virtual machines using KVM. This chapter will introduce a related technology in the form of Linux Containers. While there are some similarities between virtual machines and containers, there are also some key differences that will be outlined in this chapter along with an introduction to the concepts and advantages of Linux Containers. The chapter will also provide an overview of some of the Ubuntu container management tools. Once the basics of containers have been covered in this chapter, the next chapter will work through some practical examples of creating and running containers on Ubuntu.

29.1 Linux Containers and Kernel Sharing

In simple terms, Linux containers can be thought of as a lightweight alternative to virtualization. In a virtualized environment, a virtual machine is created that contains and runs the entire guest operating system. The virtual machine, in turn, runs on top of an environment such as a hypervisor that manages access to the physical resources of the host system.

Containers work by using a concept referred to as *kernel sharing* which takes advantage of the architectural design of Linux and UNIX-based operating systems.

In order to understand how kernel sharing and containers work it helps to first understand the two main components of Linux or UNIX operating systems. At the core of the operating system is the kernel. The kernel, in simple terms, handles all the interactions between the operating system and the physical hardware. The second key component is the root file system which contains all the libraries, files and utilities necessary for the operating system to function. Taking advantage of this structure, containers each have their own root file system but share the kernel of the host operating system. This structure is illustrated in the architectural diagram in Figure 29-1 below.

This type of resource sharing is made possible by the ability of the kernel to dynamically change the current root file system (a concept known as *change root* or *chroot*) to a different root file system without having to reboot the entire system. Linux containers are essentially an extension of this capability combined with a *container runtime*, the responsibility of which is to provide an interface for executing and managing the containers on the host system. A number of container runtimes are available including Docker, lxd, containerd and CRI-O.

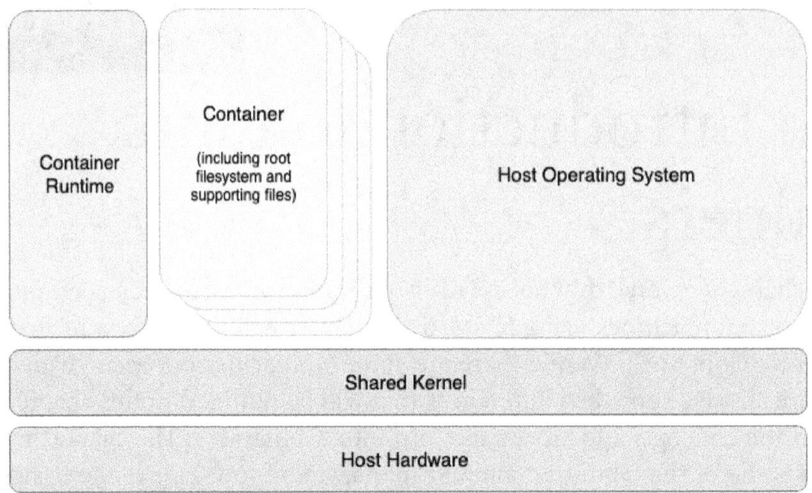

Figure 29-1

29.2 Container Uses and Advantages

The main advantage of containers is that they require considerably less resource overhead than virtualization allowing many container instances to be run simultaneously on a single server, and can be started and stopped rapidly and efficiently in response to demand levels. Containers run natively on the host system providing a level of performance that cannot be matched by a virtual machine.

Containers are also extremely portable and can be migrated between systems quickly and easily. When combined with a container management system such as Docker, OpenShift and Kubernetes, it is possible to deploy and manage containers on a vast scale spanning multiple servers and cloud platforms, potentially running thousands of containers.

Containers are frequently used to create lightweight execution environments for applications. In this scenario, each container provides an isolated environment containing the application together with all of the runtime and supporting files required by that application to run. The container can then be deployed to any other compatible host system that supports container execution and run without any concerns that the target system may not have the necessary runtime configuration for the application - all of the application's dependencies are already in the container.

Containers are also useful when bridging the gap between development and production environments. By performing development and QA work in containers, those containers can then be passed to production and launched safe in the knowledge that the applications are running in the same container environments in which they were developed and tested.

Containers also promote a modular approach to deploying large and complex solutions. Instead of developing applications as single monolithic entities, containers can be used to design applications as groups of interacting modules, each running in a separate container.

One possible drawback of containers is the fact that the guest operating systems must be compatible with the version of the kernel which is being shared. It is not, for example, possible to run Microsoft Windows in a container on a Linux system. Nor is it possible for a Linux guest system designed for the 2.6 version of the kernel to share a 2.4 version kernel. These requirements are not, however, what containers were designed for. Rather than being seen as limitations, therefore, these restrictions should be viewed as some of the key advantages of containers in terms of providing a simple, scalable and reliable deployment platform.

29.3 Ubuntu Container Tools

There a number of options available for creating and managing containers on Ubuntu. One option is to download and install the standard tools provided by Docker. In this book, however, we are going to focus on a new set of tools that have been developed by Red Hat, Inc. and are widely used on other Linux distributions such as CentOS, Fedora and Red Hat Enterprise Linux. There are a number of reasons for this choice. First, these tools are fully compatible with the tools supplied by Docker (including using the same command-line options). More importantly, these tools have the advantage that they can be used without the need to have the Docker daemon running in the background. This container tool set consists of the following utilities:

- **buildah** – A command-line tool for building container images.
- **podman** – A command-line based container runtime and management tool. Performs tasks such as downloading container images from remote registries and inspecting, starting and stopping images.
- **skopeo** – A command-line utility used to convert container images, copy images between registries and inspect images stored in registries without the need to download them.
- **runc** – A lightweight container runtime for launching and running containers from the command-line.

All of the above tools are compliant with the Open Container Initiative (OCI), a set of specifications designed to ensure that containers conform to the same standards between competing tools and platforms.

29.4 The Docker Registry

Although Ubuntu is provided with a set of tools designed to be used in place of those provided by Docker, those tools still need access to Ubuntu images for use when building containers. For this purpose, the Ubuntu team maintains a set of Ubuntu container images within the Docker Hub. The Docker Hub is an online container *registry* made of multiple *repositories*, each containing a wide range of container images available for download when building containers. The images within a repository are each assigned a *repository tag* (for example, 18.04, latest etc) which can be referenced when performing an image download. The following, for example, is the URL of the Ubuntu 18.04 image contained within the Docker Hub:

```
docker://docker.io/library/ubuntu:18.04
```

In addition to downloading (referred to as "pulling" in container terminology) container images from Docker and other third party hosts registries, you can also use registries to store your own images. This can be achieved either by hosting your own registry, or by making use of existing services such as those provided by Docker, Amazon AWS, Google Cloud, Microsoft Azure and IBM Cloud to name a few of the many options.

29.5 Container Networking

By default, containers are connected to a network using a Container Networking Interface (CNI) bridged network stack. In the bridged configuration, all the containers running on a server belong to the same subnet and, as such, are able to communicate with each other. The containers are also connected to the external network by bridging the host system's network connection. Similarly, the host is able to access the containers via a virtual network interface (usually named cni0) which will have been created as part of the container tool installation.

29.6 Summary

Linux Containers offer a lightweight alternative to virtualization and take advantage of the structure of the Linux and Unix operating systems. Linux Containers essentially share the kernel of the host operating system, with each container having its own root file system containing the files, libraries and applications. Containers are highly efficient and scalable and provide an ideal platform for building and deploying modular enterprise level solutions. A number of tools and platforms are available for building, deploying and managing containers including third-party solutions and those provided with Ubuntu.

Chapter 30

30. Working with Containers on Ubuntu

Now that the basics of Linux Containers have been covered in the previous chapter, this chapter will demonstrate how to create and manage containers using the Podman, Skopeo and Buildah tools on Ubuntu. It is intended that by the end of this chapter you will have a clearer understanding of how to create and manage containers on Ubuntu and will have gained a knowledge foundation on which to continue exploring the power of Linux Containers.

30.1 Installing the Container Tools

Before starting with containers, the first step is to install all of the container tools outlined in the previous chapter using the following commands:

```
# apt install curl
# . /etc/os-release
# sh -c "echo 'deb https://download.opensuse.org/repositories/devel:/kubic:/
libcontainers:/stable/xUbuntu_${VERSION_ID}/ /' > /etc/apt/sources.list.d/devel:k
ubic:libcontainers:stable.list"
# curl -L https://download.opensuse.org/repositories/devel:/kubic:/
libcontainers:/stable/xUbuntu_${VERSION_ID}/Release.key | sudo apt-key add -
# apt update
# apt install podman skopeo buildah
```

30.2 Pulling a Container Image

For this example, the most recent Ubuntu release will be pulled from the registry. Before pulling an image, however, information about the image repository can be obtained using the *skopeo* tool, for example:

```
# skopeo inspect docker://docker.io/ubuntu
{
    "Name": "docker.io/library/ubuntu",
    "Digest": "sha256:bec5a2727be7fff3d308193cfde3491f8fba1a2ba392b7546b43a051853
a341d",
    "RepoTags": [
        "10.04",
        "12.04.5",
        "12.04",
        "12.10",
        "13.04",
        "13.10",
        "14.04.1",
        "14.04.2",
```

```
        "14.04.3",
        "14.04.4",
        "14.04.5",
        "14.04",
        "14.10",
        "15.04",
.
.
    ],
    "Created": "2020-03-20T19:20:22.835345724Z",
    "DockerVersion": "18.09.7",
    "Labels": null,
    "Architecture": "amd64",
    "Os": "linux",
    "Layers": [
        "sha256:5bed26d33875e6da1d9ff9a1054c5fef3bbeb22ee979e2acf72528de007b",
        "sha256:f11b29a9c7306674a9479158c1b4259938af11b979ac02030cc1095e9ed1",
        "sha256:930bda195c84cf132344bf38edcad255317380503fef234a9ce3bff0f4dd",
        "sha256:78bf9a5ad49e4ae42a83f4995ade4efc08fd38299cf05bc041e8cdda2a36"
    ],
    "Env": [
        "PATH=/usr/local/sbin:/usr/local/bin:/usr/sbin:/usr/bin:/sbin:/bin"
    ]
}
```


For example, to pull the latest Ubuntu image:

```
$ podman pull docker://docker.io/ubuntu:latest
Trying to pull docker://docker.io/ubuntu:latest...
Getting image source signatures
Copying blob 5bed26d33875 done
Copying blob f11b29a9c730 done
Copying blob 78bf9a5ad49e done
Copying blob 930bda195c84 done
Copying config 4e5021d210 done
Writing manifest to image destination
Storing signatures
4e5021d210f65ebe915670c7089120120bc0a303b90208592851708c1b8c04bd
```

Verify that the image has been stored by asking *podman* to list all local images:

```
$ podman images
REPOSITORY                  TAG      IMAGE ID       CREATED       SIZE
docker.io/library/ubuntu    latest   4e5021d210f6   3 weeks ago   66.6 MB
```

Details about a local image may be obtained by running the *podman inspect* command:

```
$ podman inspect ubuntu:latest
```

This command should output the same information as the *skopeo* command performed on the remote image earlier in this chapter.

30.3 Running the Image in a Container

The image pulled from the registry is a fully operational image that is ready to run in a container without modification. To run the image, use the *podman run* command. In this case the *–rm* option will be specified to indicate that we want to run the image in a container, execute one command and then have the container exit. In this case, the *cat* tool will be used to output the content of the */etc/passwd* file located on the container root filesystem:

```
$ podman run --rm ubuntu:latest cat /etc/passwd
root:x:0:0:root:/root:/bin/bash
daemon:x:1:1:daemon:/usr/sbin:/usr/sbin/nologin
bin:x:2:2:bin:/bin:/usr/sbin/nologin
sys:x:3:3:sys:/dev:/usr/sbin/nologin
sync:x:4:65534:sync:/bin:/bin/sync
games:x:5:60:games:/usr/games:/usr/sbin/nologin
man:x:6:12:man:/var/cache/man:/usr/sbin/nologin
lp:x:7:7:lp:/var/spool/lpd:/usr/sbin/nologin
mail:x:8:8:mail:/var/mail:/usr/sbin/nologin
news:x:9:9:news:/var/spool/news:/usr/sbin/nologin
uucp:x:10:10:uucp:/var/spool/uucp:/usr/sbin/nologin
proxy:x:13:13:proxy:/bin:/usr/sbin/nologin
www-data:x:33:33:www-data:/var/www:/usr/sbin/nologin
backup:x:34:34:backup:/var/backups:/usr/sbin/nologin
list:x:38:38:Mailing List Manager:/var/list:/usr/sbin/nologin
irc:x:39:39:ircd:/var/run/ircd:/usr/sbin/nologin
gnats:x:41:41:Gnats Bug-Reporting System (admin):/var/lib/gnats:/usr/sbin/nologin
nobody:x:65534:65534:nobody:/nonexistent:/usr/sbin/nologin
_apt:x:100:65534::/nonexistent:/usr/sbin/nologin
```

Compare the content of the */etc/passwd* file within the container with the */etc/passwd* file on the host system and note that it lacks all of the additional users that are present on the host confirming that the *cat* command was executed within the container environment. Also note that the container started, ran the command and exited all within a matter of seconds. Compare this to the amount of time it takes to start a full operating system, perform a task and shutdown a virtual machine and you begin to appreciate the speed and efficiency of containers.

To launch a container, keep it running and access the shell, the following command can be used:

```
$ podman run --name=mycontainer -it ubuntu:latest /bin/bash
root@4b49ddeb2987:/#
```

In this case, an additional command-line option has been used to assign the name "mycontainer" to the container. Though optional, this makes the container easier to recognize and reference as an alternative to using the automatically generated container ID.

While the container is running, run *podman* in a different terminal window to see the status of all containers on the system

```
$ podman ps -a
CONTAINER ID  IMAGE                           COMMAND    CREATED
STATUS                PORTS  NAMES
4b49ddeb2987  docker.io/library/ubuntu:latest  /bin/bash  About a minute ago  Up
About a minute ago         mycontainer
```

To execute a command in a running container from the host, simply use the *podman exec* command, referencing the name of the running container and the command to be executed. The following command, for example, starts up a second bash session in the container named *mycontainer*:

```
$ podman exec -it mycontainer /bin/bash
root@4b49ddeb2987:/#
```

Note that though the above example referenced the container name the same result can be achieved using the container ID as listed by the *podman ps -a* command:

```
$ podman exec -it 4b49ddeb2987 /bin/bash
root@4b49ddeb2987:/#
```

Alternatively, the *podman attach* command will also attach to a running container and access the shell prompt:

```
$ podman attach mycontainer
root@4b49ddeb2987:/#
```

Once the container is up and running, any additional configuration changes can be made and packages installed just like any other Ubuntu system.

30.4 Managing a Container

Once launched, a container will continue to run until it is stopped via *podman*, or the command that was launched when the container was run exits. Running the following command on the host, for example, will cause the container to exit:

```
$ podman stop mycontainer
```

Alternatively, pressing the Ctrl-D keyboard sequence within the last remaining bash shell of the container would cause both the shell and container to exit. Once it has exited, the status of the container will change accordingly:

```
$ podman ps -a
CONTAINER ID  IMAGE                           COMMAND    CREATED         STATUS
PORTS  NAMES
4b49ddeb2987  docker.io/library/ubuntu:latest  /bin/bash  6 minutes ago  Exited
(127) About a minute ago          mycontainer
```

Although the container is no longer running, it still exists and contains all of the changes that were made to the configuration and file system. If you installed packages, made configuration changes or added files, these changes will persist within "mycontainer". To verify this, simply restart the container as follows:

```
$ podman start mycontainer
```

After starting the container, use the *podman exec* command once again to execute commands within the container as outlined previously. For example, to once again gain access to a shell prompt:

```
$ podman exec -it mycontainer /bin/bash
```

A running container may also be paused and resumed using the *podman pause* and *unpause* commands as follows:

```
$ podman pause mycontainer
$ podman unpause mycontainer
```

30.5 Saving a Container to an Image

Once the container guest system is configured to your requirements there is a good chance that you will want to create and run more than one container of this particular type. To do this, the container needs to be saved as an image to local storage so that it can be used as the basis for additional container instances. This is achieved using the *podman commit* command combined with the name or ID of the container and the name by which the image will be stored, for example:

```
$ podman commit mycontainer  myubuntu_image
```

Once the image has been saved, check that it now appears in the list of images in the local repository:

```
$ podman images
REPOSITORY                  TAG      IMAGE ID       CREATED          SIZE
localhost/myubuntu_image    latest   8ad685d49482   47 seconds ago   66.6 MB
docker.io/library/ubuntu    latest   4e5021d210f6   3 weeks ago      66.6 MB
```

The saved image can now be used to create additional containers identical to the original:

```
$ podman run --name=mycontainer2 -it localhost/myubuntu_image /bin/bash
```

30.6 Removing an Image from Local Storage

To remove an image from local storage once it is no longer needed, simply run the *podman rmi* command, referencing either the image name or ID as output by the *podman images* command. For example, to remove the image named *myubuntu_image* created in the previous section, run *podman* as follows:

```
$ podman rmi localhost/myubuntu_image
```

Note before an image can be removed, any containers based on that image must first be removed.

30.7 Removing Containers

Even when a container has exited or been stopped, it still exists and can be restarted at any time. If a container is no longer needed, it can be deleted using the *podman rm* command as follows after the container has been stopped:

```
# podman rm mycontainer2
```

30.8 Building a Container with Buildah

Buildah allows new containers to be built either from existing containers, an image or entirely from scratch. Buildah also includes the ability to mount the file system of a container so that it can be accessed and modified from the host.

The following *buildah* command, for example, will build a container from the Ubuntu Base image (if the image has not already been pulled from the registry, *buildah* will download it before creating the container):

```
$ buildah from docker://docker.io/library/ubuntu:latest
```

The result of running this command will be a container named *ubuntu-working-container* that is ready to run:

```
$ buildah run ubuntu-working-container cat /etc/passwd
```

30.9 Summary

This chapter has worked through the creation and management of Linux Containers on Ubuntu using the *podman*, *skopeo* and *buildah* tools.

Chapter 31

31. Setting Up an Ubuntu Web Server

Among the many packages that make up the Ubuntu operating system is the Apache web server. In fact the scalability and resilience of Ubuntu makes it an ideal platform for hosting even the most heavily trafficked web sites.

In this chapter we will explain how to configure an Ubuntu system using Apache to act as a web server, including both secure (HTTPS) and insecure (HTTP) configurations.

31.1 Requirements for Configuring an Ubuntu Web Server

To set up your own web site you need a computer (or cloud server instance), an operating system, a web server, a domain name, a name server and an IP address.

In terms of an operating system, we will, of course, assume you are using Ubuntu. As previously mentioned, Ubuntu supports the Apache web server which can easily be installed once the operating system is up and running. A domain name can be registered with any domain name registration service.

If you are running Ubuntu on a cloud instance, the IP address assigned by the provider will be listed in the server overview information. If you are hosting your own server and your internet service provider (ISP) has assigned a static IP address then you will need to associate your domain with that address. This is achieved using a name server and all domain registration services will provide this service for you.

If you do not have a static IP address (i.e. your ISP provides you with a dynamic address which changes frequently) then you can use one of a number of free Dynamic DNS (DDNS or DynDNS for short) services which map your dynamic IP address to your domain name.

Once you have your domain name and your name server configured the next step is to install and configure your web server.

31.2 Installing the Apache Web Server Packages

The current release of Ubuntu typically does not install the Apache web server by default. To check whether the server is already installed, run the following command:

```
# apt -qq list apache
```

If *apt* generates output similar to the following, the apache server is already installed:

```
apache2/bionic-updates,bionic-security,now 2.4.29-1ubuntu4.13 amd64 [installed]
```

If the apt output does not list the package or include the [installed] status, run the following command at the command prompt to perform the Apache installation:

```
# apt install apache2
```

31.3 Configuring the Firewall

Before starting and testing the Apache web server, the firewall will need to be modified to allow the web server to communicate with the outside world. By default, the HTTP and HTTPS protocols use ports 80 and 443 respectively so, depending on which protocols are being used, either one or both of these ports will need to be opened. If your Ubuntu system is being protected by the Uncomplicated Firewall, the following command can be used to enable only insecure web traffic (HTTP):

```
# ufw allow Apache
```

To enable only secure (HTTPS) traffic:

```
# ufw allow 'Apache Secure'
```

Alternatively, enable both secure and insecure web traffic as follows:

```
# ufw allow 'Apache Full'
```

If you are using firewalld, the following commands can be used to open the HTTP and HTTPS ports. When opening the ports, be sure to specify the firewall zone that applies to the internet facing network connection:

```
# firewall-cmd --permanent --zone=<zone> --add-port=80/tcp
# firewall-cmd --permanent --zone=<zone> --add-port=443/tcp
```

After opening the necessary ports, be sure to reload the firewall settings:

```
# firewall-cmd --reload
```

On cloud hosted servers, it may also be necessary to enable the appropriate port for the server instance within the cloud console. Check the documentation for the cloud provider for steps on how to do this.

31.4 Port Forwarding

If the Ubuntu system hosting the web server sits on a network protected by a firewall (either another computer running a firewall, or a router or wireless base station containing built-in firewall protection) you will need to configure the firewall to forward port 80 and/or port 443 to your web server system. The mechanism for performing this differs between firewalls and devices so check your documentation to find out how to configure port forwarding.

31.5 Starting the Apache Web Server

Once the Apache server is installed and the firewall configured, the next step is to verify that the server is running and start it if necessary.

To check the status of the Apache service from the command-line, enter the following at the command-prompt:

```
# systemctl status apache2
```

If the above command indicates that the httpd service is not running, it can be launched from the command-line as follows:

```
# systemctl start apache2
```

If you would like the Apache httpd service to start automatically when the system boots, run the following command:

```
# systemctl enable apache2
```

31.6 Testing the Web Server

Once the installation is complete the next step is to verify the web server is up and running.

If you have access (either locally or remotely) to the desktop environment of the server, simply start up a web browser and enter *http://127.0.0.1* in the address bar (127.0.0.1 is the loop-back network address which tells the system to connect to the local machine). If everything is set up correctly, the browser should load the page shown in Figure 31-1:

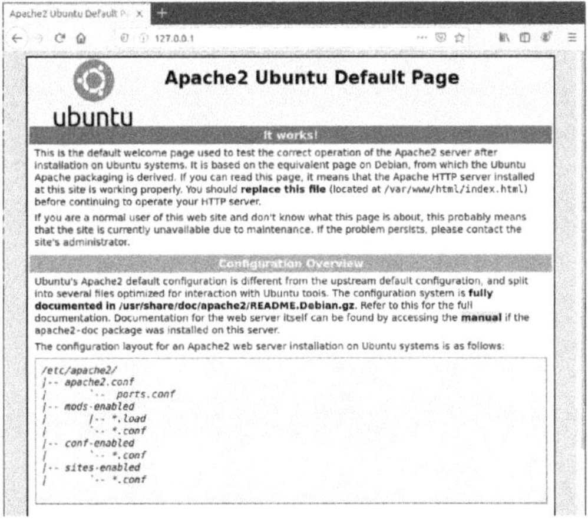

Figure 31-1

If the desktop environment is not available, connect either from another system on the same local network as the server, or using the external IP address assigned to the system if it is hosted remotely.

31.7 Configuring the Apache Web Server for Your Domain

The next step in setting up your web server is to configure it for your domain name. To configure the web server, begin by changing directory to */etc/apache2* which, in turn, contains a number of files and sub-directories. The main configuration file is named *apache2.conf* and serves as the central point for organizing the modular configuration files located in the sub-directories. For example, the *apache2.conf* file includes a line to import the configuration settings declared in the files located in the *sites-enabled* folder:

```
# Include the virtual host configurations:
IncludeOptional sites-enabled/*.conf
```

Similarly, the *apache2.conf* file imports the *ports.conf* file, which defines the ports on which the Apache server listens for network traffic.

Setting Up an Ubuntu Web Server

To configure a web site domain on Ubuntu, begin by changing directory to */etc/apache2*. In this directory you will find two sub-directories, *sites-available* and *sites-enabled*. Change directory into sites-available. In this directory you will find a default file which may be used as a template for your own site.

Copy the default file to a new file with a name which matches your domain name. For example:

```
# cp 000-default.conf myexample.conf
```

Edit your myexample.com file using your favorite editor where it will appear as follows:

```
<VirtualHost *:80>
        # The ServerName directive sets the request scheme, hostname and port
that
        # the server uses to identify itself. This is used when creating
        # redirection URLs. In the context of virtual hosts, the ServerName
        # specifies what hostname must appear in the request's Host: header to
        # match this virtual host. For the default virtual host (this file) this
        # value is not decisive as it is used as a last resort host regardless.
        # However, you must set it for any further virtual host explicitly.
        #ServerName www.example.com

        ServerAdmin webmaster@localhost
        DocumentRoot /var/www/html

        # Available loglevels: trace8, ..., trace1, debug, info, notice, warn,
        # error, crit, alert, emerg.
        # It is also possible to configure the loglevel for particular
        # modules, e.g.
        #LogLevel info ssl:warn

        ErrorLog ${APACHE_LOG_DIR}/error.log
        CustomLog ${APACHE_LOG_DIR}/access.log combined

        # For most configuration files from conf-available/, which are
        # enabled or disabled at a global level, it is possible to
        # include a line for only one particular virtual host. For example the
        # following line enables the CGI configuration for this host only
        # after it has been globally disabled with "a2disconf".
        #Include conf-available/serve-cgi-bin.conf
</VirtualHost>
```

The ServerAdmin directive defines an administrative email address for people wishing to contact the web master for your site. Change this to an appropriate email address where you can be contacted:

```
ServerAdmin webmaster@myexample.com
```

Next the ServerName directive needs to be uncommented (in other words remove the '#' character prefix) and defined so that the web server knows which virtual host this configuration file refers to:

```
ServerName myexample.com
```

In the next stage we need to define where the web site files are going to be located using the DocumentRoot directive. The tradition is to use */var/www/domain-name*:

```
DocumentRoot /var/www/myexample.com
```

Having completed the changes we now need to enable the site as follows:

```
# a2ensite myexample.conf
```

This command creates a symbolic link from the *myexample.conf* file in the *sites-available* directory to the sites-enabled folder.

With the site enabled, run the following command to disable the default test site:

```
# a2dissite 000-default.conf
```

Next, create the */var/www/myexample.com* directory and place an *index.html* file in it. For example:

```
<html>
<title>Sample Web Page</title>
<body>
Welcome to MyExample.com
</body>
</html>
```

With these changes made, run the apache2ctl command to check the configuration files for errors:

```
# apache2ctl configtest
Syntax OK
```

If no errors are reported, reload the Apache web server to make sure it picks up our new settings:

```
# systemctl reload apache2
```

Finally, check that the server configuration is working by opening a browser window and navigating to the site using the domain name instead of the IP address. The web page that loads should be the one defined in the *index.html* file created above.

31.8 The Basics of a Secure Web Site

The web server and web site created so far in this chapter use the HTTP protocol on port 80 and, as such, is considered to be insecure. The problem is that the traffic between the web server and the client (typically a user's web browser) is transmitted in *clear text*. In other words the data is unencrypted and susceptible to interception. While not a problem for general web browsing, this is a serious weakness when performing tasks such as logging into web sites or transferring sensitive information such as identity or credit card details.

These days, web sites are expected to use HTTPS which uses either Secure Socket Layer (SSL) or

Transport Layer Security (TLS) to establish secure, encrypted communication between web server and client. This security is established through the use of public, private and session encryption together with certificates.

To support HTTPS, a web site must have a certificate issued by a trusted authority known as a Certificate Authority (CA). When a browser connects to a secure web site, the web server sends back a copy of the web site's SSL certificate which also contains a copy of the site's public key. The browser then validates the authenticity of the certificate with trusted certificate authorities.

If the certificate is found to be valid, the browser uses the public key sent by the server to encrypt a session key and passes it to the server. The server decrypts the session key using the private key and uses it to send an encrypted acknowledgment to the browser. Once this process is complete, the browser and server use the session key to encrypt all subsequent data transmissions until the session ends.

31.9 Configuring Apache for HTTPS

By default, the Apache server does not include the necessary module to implement a secure HTTPS web site. The first step, therefore, is to enable the Apache *mod_ssl* module on the server system as follows:

```
# a2enmod ssl
```

Restart httpd after the installation completes to load the new module into the Apache server:

```
# systemctl restart apache2
```

Check that the module has loaded into the server using the following command:

```
# apache2ctl -M | grep ssl_module
 ssl_module (shared)
```

Once the ssl module is installed, repeat the steps from the previous section of this chapter to create a configuration file for the website, this time using the *sites-available/default-ssl.conf* file as the template for the site configuration file.

Assuming that the module is installed, the next step is to generate an SSL certificate for the web site.

31.10 Obtaining an SSL Certificate

The certificate for a web site must be obtained from a Certificate Authority. A number of options are available at a range of prices. By far the best option, however, is to obtain a free certificate from Let's Encrypt at the following URL:

https://letsencrypt.org/

The process of obtaining a certificate from Let's Encrypt simply involves installing and running the *Certbot* tool. This tool will scan the Apache configuration files on the server and provides the option to generate certificates for any virtual hosts configured on the system. It will then generate the certificate and add virtual host entries to the Apache configuration specifically for the corresponding web sites.

Use the following steps to install the certbot tool on your Ubuntu system:

```
# apt update
# apt install software-properties-common
# add-apt-repository universe
# add-apt-repository ppa:certbot/certbot
# apt install certbot python-certbot-apache
```

Once certbot is installed, run it as follows:

```
# certbot --apache
```

After requesting an email address and seeking terms of service acceptance, Certbot will list the domains found in the *sites-available* folder and provide the option to select one or more of those sites for which a certificate is to be installed. Certbot will then perform some checks before obtaining and installing the certificate on the system:

```
Which names would you like to activate HTTPS for?
- - - - - - - - - - - - - - - - - - - - - - - - - - - - - - - - - - - - - - - -
1: myexample.com
- - - - - - - - - - - - - - - - - - - - - - - - - - - - - - - - - - - - - - - -
Select the appropriate numbers separated by commas and/or spaces, or leave input
blank to select all options shown (Enter 'c' to cancel): 1
Obtaining a new certificate
Performing the following challenges:
http-01 challenge for ebooktricity.com
Enabled Apache rewrite module
Waiting for verification...
Cleaning up challenges
Created an SSL vhost at /etc/apache2/sites-available/myexample-le-ssl.conf
Deploying Certificate to VirtualHost /etc/apache2/sites-available/myexample-le-
ssl.conf
Enabling available site: /etc/apache2/sites-available/myexample-le-ssl.conf
```

Certbot will also have created a new file named *myexample-le-ssl.conf* in the */etc/apache2/sites-available* directory containing a secure virtual host entry for each domain name for which a certificate has been generated and enabled the site so that a link to the file is made in the */etc/apache2/sites-enabled* directory. These entries will be similar to the following:

```
<IfModule mod_ssl.c>
<VirtualHost *:443>
.
.
        ServerName ebooktricity.com
        ServerAdmin webmaster@ebooktricity.com
        DocumentRoot /var/www/ebooktricity.com
.
```

```
.
        ErrorLog ${APACHE_LOG_DIR}/error.log
        CustomLog ${APACHE_LOG_DIR}/access.log combined
.
.
SSLCertificateFile /etc/letsencrypt/live/ebooktricity.com/fullchain.pem
SSLCertificateKeyFile /etc/letsencrypt/live/ebooktricity.com/privkey.pem
Include /etc/letsencrypt/options-ssl-apache.conf
</VirtualHost>
</IfModule>
```

Finally, Certbot will ask whether future HTTP web requests should be redirected by the server to HTTPS. In other words, if a user attempts to access *http://www.myexample.com* the web server will redirect the user to *https://www.myexample.com*:

```
Please choose whether or not to redirect HTTP traffic to HTTPS, removing HTTP
access.
- - - - - - - - - - - - - - - - - - - - - - - - - - - - - - - - - - - - - - - -
1: No redirect - Make no further changes to the webserver configuration.
2: Redirect - Make all requests redirect to secure HTTPS access. Choose this for
new sites, or if you're confident your site works on HTTPS. You can undo this
change by editing your web server's configuration.
- - - - - - - - - - - - - - - - - - - - - - - - - - - - - - - - - - - - - - - -
Select the appropriate number [1-2] then [enter] (press 'c' to cancel): 2
```

If you are currently testing the HTTPS configuration and would like to keep the HTTP version live until later, select the *No redirect* option. Otherwise, redirecting to HTTPS is generally recommended.

Once the certificate has been installed, test it in a browser at the following URL (replacing myexample.com with your own domain name):

```
https://www.ssllabs.com/ssltest/analyze.html?d=www.myexample.com
```

If the certificate configuration was successful, the SSL Labs report will provide a high rating as shown in Figure 31-2:

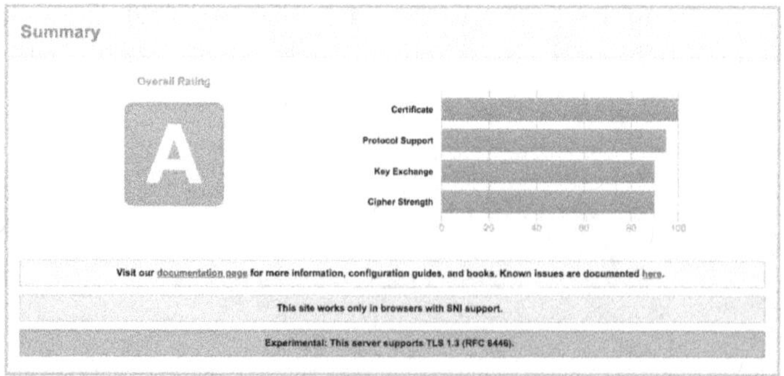

Figure 31-2

As a final test, open a browser window and navigate to your domain using the https:// prefix. The page should load as before and the browser should indicate that the connection between the browser and server is secure (usually indicated by a padlock icon in the address bar which can be clicked for additional information):

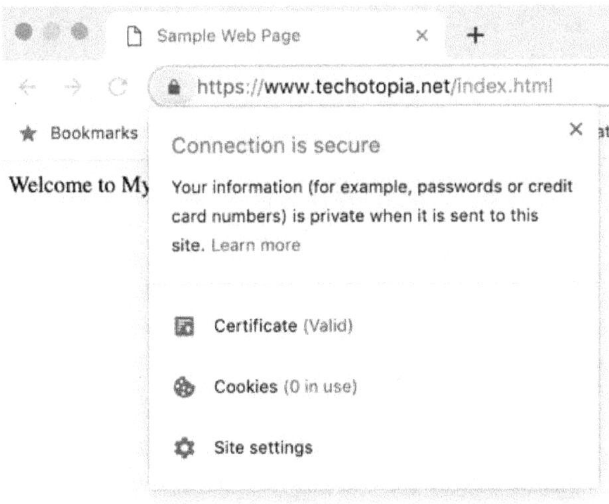

Figure 31-3

31.11 Summary

An Ubuntu system can be used to host web sites by installing the Apache web server. Both insecure (HTTP) and secure (HTTPS) web sites can be deployed on Ubuntu. Secure web sites use either Secure Socket Layer (SSL) or Transport Layer Security (TLS) to establish encrypted communication between the web server and client through the use of public, private and session encryption together with a certificate issued by a trusted Certificate Authority.

Chapter 32

32. Configuring an Ubuntu Postfix Email Server

Along with acting as a web server, email is one of the primary uses of an Ubuntu system, particularly in business environments. Given both the importance and popularity of email it is surprising to some people to find out how complex the email structure is on a Linux system and this complexity can often be a little overwhelming to the Ubuntu newcomer.

The good news is that much of the complexity is there to allow experienced email administrators to implement complicated configurations for large scale enterprise installations. The fact is, for most Linux administrators it is relatively straight forward to set up a basic email system so that users can send and receive electronic mail.

In this chapter of Ubuntu Essentials, we will explain the basics of Linux-based email configuration and step through configuring a basic email environment. In the interests of providing the essentials, we will leave the complexities of the email system for more advanced books on the subject.

32.1 The structure of the Email System

There are a number of components that make up a complete email system. Below is a brief description of each one:

32.1.1 Mail User Agent

This is the part of the system that the typical user is likely to be most familiar with. The Mail User Agent (MUA), or mail client, is the application that is used to write, send and read email messages. Anyone who has written and sent a message on any computer has used a Mail User Agent of one type or another.

Typical Graphical MUA's on Linux are Evolution, Thunderbird and KMail. For those who prefer a text based mail client, there are also the more traditional *pine* and *mail* tools.

32.1.2 Mail Transfer Agent

The Mail Transfer Agent (MTA) is the part of the email system that does much of the work of transferring the email messages from one computer to another (either on the same local network or over the internet to a remote system). Once configured correctly, most users will not have any direct interaction with their chosen MTA unless they wish to re-configure it for any reason. There are many choices of MTA available for Linux including sendmail, Postfix, Fetchmail, Qmail and Exim.

32.1.3 Mail Delivery Agent

Another part of the infrastructure that is typically hidden from the user, the Mail Delivery Agent (MDA) sits in the background and performs filtering of the email messages between the Mail Transfer Agent and the mail client (MUA). The most popular form of MDA is a spam filter to remove all the unwanted email messages from the system before they reach the inbox of the user's mail client (MUA). Popular MDAs are Spamassassin and Procmail. It is important to note that some Mail User Agent applications (such as Evolution, Thunderbird and KMail) include their own MDA filtering. Others, such as Pine and Basla, do not. This can be a source of confusion to the Linux beginner.

32.1.4 SMTP

SMTP is an acronym for Simple Mail Transport Protocol. This is the protocol used by the email systems to transfer mail messages from one server to another. This protocol is essentially the communications language that the MTAs use to talk to each other and transfer messages back and forth.

32.1.5 SMTP Relay

SMTP Relay is a protocol that allows an external SMTP server to be used to send emails instead of hosting a local SMTP server. This will typically involve using a service such as MailJet, SendGrid or MailGun. These services avoid the necessity to configure and maintain your own SMTP server and often provide additional benefits such as analytics.

32.2 Configuring an Ubuntu Email Server

Many systems use the Sendmail MTA to transfer email messages and on many Linux distributions this is the default Mail Transfer Agent. Sendmail is, however, a complex system that can be difficult for beginner and experienced user alike to understand and configure. It is also falling from favor because it is considered to be slower at processing email messages than many of the more recent MTAs available.

Many system administrators are now using Postfix or Qmail to handle email. Both are faster and easier to configure than Sendmail.

For the purposes of this chapter, therefore, we will look at Postfix as an MTA because of its simplicity and popularity. If you would prefer to use Sendmail there are many books that specialize in the subject and that will do the subject much more justice than we can in this chapter.

As a first step, this chapter will cover the configuration of an Ubuntu system to act as a full email server. Later in the chapter, the steps to make use of an SMTP Relay service will also be covered.

32.3 Postfix Pre-Installation Steps

The first step before installing Postfix is to make sure that Sendmail is not already running on your system. You can check for this using the following command:

```
# systemctl status sendmail
```

If sendmail is not installed, the tool will display a message similar to the following:

```
Unit sendmail.service could not be found.
```

If sendmail is running on your system it is necessary to stop it before installing and configuring Postfix. To stop sendmail, run the following command:

```
# systemctl stop sendmail
```

The next step is to ensure that sendmail does not get restarted automatically when the system is rebooted:

```
# systemctl disable  sendmail
```

Sendmail is now switched off and configured so that it does not auto start when the system is booted. Optionally, to completely remove sendmail from the system, run the following command:

```
# apt remove sendmail
```

32.4 Firewall/Router Configuration

Since the sending and receiving of email messages involves network connections, the firewall will need to be configured to allow SMTP traffic. If firewalld is active, use the *firewall-cmd* tool will as follows:

```
# firewall-cmd --permanent --add-service=smtp
```

Alternatively, if ufw is enabled, configure it to allow SMTP traffic using the following command:

```
# ufw allow Postfix
```

It will also be important to configure any other firewall or router between the server and the internet to allow connections on port 25, 143 and 587 and, if necessary, to configure port forwarding for those ports to the corresponding ports on the email server.

With these initial steps completed, we can now move on to installing Postfix.

32.5 Installing Postfix on Ubuntu

By default, the Ubuntu installation process installs postfix for most configurations. To verify if postfix is already installed, use the following *apt* command:

```
# apt -qq list postfix
```

If *apt* reports that postfix is not installed, it may be installed as follows:

```
# apt install postfix
```

In most cases the Internet Site option will be the most useful option. This will configure some basic settings designed to send and receive messages associated with your web site domain name. With this option selection, tap the Enter key to proceed to the next screen:

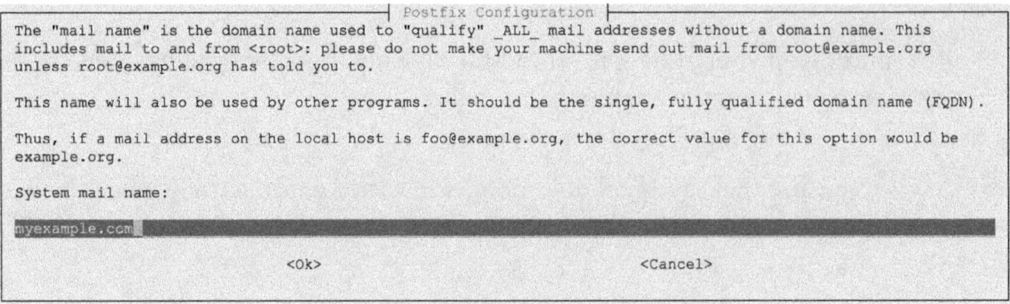

Postfix Configuration
The "mail name" is the domain name used to "qualify" _ALL_ mail addresses without a domain name. This includes mail to and from <root>: please do not make your machine send out mail from root@example.org unless root@example.org has told you to.
This name will also be used by other programs. It should be the single, fully qualified domain name (FQDN).
Thus, if a mail address on the local host is foo@example.org, the correct value for this option would be example.org.
System mail name:
myexample.com
<Ok>
<Cancel>

Figure 32-1

On the above screen, enter your domain name before pressing the Enter key once again.

32.6 Configuring Postfix

The main configuration settings for postfix are located in the */etc/postfix/main.cf* file. There are many resources on the internet that provide detailed information on postfix so this section will focus on the basic options required to get email up and running. Even though the apt installation set up some basic configuration options, it tends to miss some settings and guess incorrectly for others so be sure to carefully review the *main.cf* file.

The key options in the *main.cf* file are:

```
myhostname = mta1.domain.com
mydomain = domain.com
myorigin = $mydomain
mydestination = $myhostname, localhost.$mydomain, localhost, $mydomain
inet_interfaces = $myhostname
mynetworks = subnet
```

Other settings will have either been set up for you by the installation process or are not needed unless you are feeling adventurous and want to configure a more sophisticated email system.

The format of *myhostname* is *host.domain.extension.* If, for example, your Linux system is named MyLinuxHost and your internet domain is MyDomain.com you would set the myhostname option as follows:

```
myhostname = mylinuxhost.mydomain.com
```

The *mydomain* setting is just the domain part of the above setting. For example:

```
mydomain = mydomain.com
```

The *myorigin* setting defines the name of the domain from which output email appears to come from when it arrives in the recipient's inbox and should be set to your domain name:

```
myorigin = $mydomain
```

Perhaps one of the most crucial parameters, *mydestination* relates to incoming messages and declares the domains for which this server is the final delivery destination. Any incoming email messages addressed to a domain name not on this list will be considered a relay request which, subject to the *mynetworks* setting (outlined below), will typically result in a delivery failure.

The *inet_interfaces* setting defines the network interfaces on the system via which postfix is permitted to receive email and is generally set to *all:*

```
inet_interfaces = all
```

The *mynetworks* setting defines which external systems are trusted to use the server as an SMTP relay. Possible values for this setting are as follows:

- **host** - Only the local system is trusted. Attempts by all external clients to use the server as a relay will be rejected.
- **subnet** - Only systems on the same network subnet are permitted to use the server as a relay. If, for example, the server has an IP address of 192.168.1.29, a client system with an IP address of 192.168.1.30 would be able to use the server as a relay.
- **class** - Any systems within the same IP address class (A, B and C) may use the server as a relay.

Trusted IP addresses may also be defined manually by specifying subnets, address ranges or referencing pattern files. The following example declares the local host and the subnet 192.168.0.0 as trusted IP addresses.

```
mynetworks = 192.168.0.0/24, 127.0.0.0/8
```

For this example, set the property to *subnet* so that any other systems on the same local network as the server are able to send email via SMTP relay while external systems are prevented from doing so.

```
mynetworks = subnet
```

The key settings within a *main.cf* file might, therefore, read as follows:

```
smtpd_banner = $myhostname ESMTP $mail_name (Ubuntu)
biff = no

# appending .domain is the MUA's job.
append_dot_mydomain = no
readme_directory = no

compatibility_level = 2

smtpd_tls_cert_file=/etc/ssl/certs/ssl-cert-snakeoil.pem
smtpd_tls_key_file=/etc/ssl/private/ssl-cert-snakeoil.key
smtpd_use_tls=yes
smtpd_tls_session_cache_database = btree:${data_directory}/smtpd_scache
smtp_tls_session_cache_database = btree:${data_directory}/smtp_scache

smtpd_relay_restrictions = permit_mynetworks permit_sasl_authenticated defer_
unauth_destination
```

```
myhostname = hostname.myexample.com
alias_maps = hash:/etc/aliases
alias_database = hash:/etc/aliases
mydomain = myexample.com
myorigin = $mydomain
mydestination = $myhostname, myexample.com, localhost.localdomain, localhost
relayhost =
mynetworks = 127.0.0.0/8 [::ffff:127.0.0.0]/104 [::1]/128
mailbox_size_limit = 0
recipient_delimiter = +
inet_interfaces = all
inet_protocols = all
```

32.7 Configuring DNS MX Records

When you registered and configured your domain name with a registrar, a number of default values will have been configured in the DNS settings. One of these is the so-called *Mail Exchanger (MX)* record. This record essentially defines where email addressed to your domain should be sent and is usually set by default to a mail server provided by your registrar. If you are hosting your own mail server, the MX record should be set to your domain or the IP address of your mail server. The steps on how to make this change will depend on your domain registrar but generally involves editing the DNS information for the domain and either adding or editing an existing MX record so that it points to your email server.

32.8 Starting Postfix on an Ubuntu System

Once the */etc/postfix/main.cf* file is configured with the correct settings it is now time to start up postfix. This can be achieved from the command-line as follows:

```
# systemctl start postfix
```

If postfix was already running, make sure the configuration changes are loaded using the following command:

```
# systemctl reload postfix
```

To configure postfix to start automatically at system startup, run the following command:

```
# systemctl enable postfix
```

The postfix process should now start up. The best way to verify that everything is working is to check your mail log. This is typically in the */var/log/mail.log* file and should now contain an entry resembling the following output:

```
Mar 25 11:21:48 demo-server postfix/postfix-script[5377]: starting the Postfix mail system
Mar 25 11:21:48 demo-server postfix/master[5379]: daemon started -- version 3.3.1, configuration /etc/postfix
```

As long as no error messages have been logged, you have successfully installed and started postfix and are ready to test the postfix configuration.

32.9 Testing Postfix

An easy way to test the postfix configuration is to send an email message between local users on the system. To perform a quick test, use the *mail* tool as follows (where *name* and *mydomain* are replaced by the name of a user on the system and your domain name respectively):

```
# mail name@mydomain.com
```

If the mail tool is not available, it can be installed as follows:

```
# apt install mailutils
```

When prompted, enter a subject for the email message and then enter message body text. To send the email message, simply press Ctrl-D. For example:

```
# mail demo@mydomain.com
Subject: Test email message
This is a test message.
EOT
```

Run the *mail* command again, this time as the other user and verify that the message was sent and received:

```
$ mail
"/var/mail/demo": 1 message 1 new
>N   1 demo              Wed Apr 15 15:30  13/475   Test email message
?
```

If the message does not appear, check the log file (*/var/log/mail.log*) for errors. A successful mail delivery will appear in the log file as follows:

```
Mar 25 13:41:37 demo-server postfix/pickup[7153]: 94FAF61E8F4A: uid=0 from=<root>
Mar 25 13:41:37 demo-server postfix/cleanup[7498]: 94FAF61E8F4A: message-id=<20190325174137.94FAF61E8F4A@demo-server.mydomain.com>
Mar 25 13:41:37 demo-server postfix/qmgr[7154]: 94FAF61E8F4A: from=<root@mydomain.com>, size=450, nrcpt=1 (queue active)
Mar 25 13:41:37 demo-server postfix/local[7500]: 94FAF61E8F4A: to=<neil@mydomain.com>, relay=local, delay=0.12, delays=0.09/0.01/0/0.02, dsn=2.0.0, status=sent (delivered to mailbox)
Mar 25 13:41:37 demo-server postfix/qmgr[7154]: 94FAF61E8F4A: removed
```

Once local email is working, try sending an email to an external address (such as a GMail account), Also, test that incoming mail works by sending an email from an external account to a user on your domain. In each case, check the */var/log/mail.log* file for explanations of any errors.

32.10 Sending Mail via an SMTP Relay Server

An alternative to configuring a mail server to handle outgoing email messages is to use an SMTP Relay service. As previously discussed, a number of services are available, most of which can be found by performing a web search for "SMTP Relay Service". Most of these services will require you to verify your domain in some way and will provide MX records with which to update your DNS settings. You will also be provided with a username and password which need to be added to the postfix configuration. The remainder of this section makes the assumption that postfix is already installed on your system and that all of the initial steps required by your chosen SMTP Relay provider have been completed.

Begin by editing the */etc/postfix/main.cf* file and configuring the *myhostname* parameter with your domain name:

```
myhostname = mydomain.com
```

Next, create a new file in */etc/postfix* named *sasl_passwd* and add a line containing the mail server host provided by the relay service and the user name and password. For example:

```
[smtp.myprovider.com]:587 neil@mydomain.com:mypassword
```

Note that port 587 has also been specified in the above entry. Without this setting, postfix will default to using port 25 which is blocked by default by most SMTP relay service providers.

With the password file created, use the *postmap* utility to generate the hash database containing the mail credentials:

```
# postmap /etc/postfix/sasl_passwd
```

Before proceeding, take some additional steps to secure your postfix credentials:

```
# chown root:root /etc/postfix/sasl_passwd /etc/postfix/sasl_passwd.db
# chmod 0600 /etc/postfix/sasl_passwd /etc/postfix/sasl_passwd.db
```

Edit the *main.cf* file once again and add an entry to specify the relay server:

```
relayhost = [smtp.myprovider.com]:587
```

Remaining within the *main.cf* file, add the following lines to configure the authentication settings for the SMTP server:

```
smtp_use_tls = yes
smtp_sasl_auth_enable = yes
smtp_sasl_password_maps = hash:/etc/postfix/sasl_passwd
smtp_tls_CAfile = /etc/ssl/certs/ca-bundle.crt
smtp_sasl_security_options = noanonymous
smtp_sasl_tls_security_options = noanonymous
```

Finally, restart the postfix service:

```
# systemctl restart postfix
```

Once the service has restarted, try sending and receiving mail using either the *mail* tool or your preferred mail client.

32.11 Summary

A complete, end-to-end email system consists of a Mail User Agent (MUA), Mail Transfer Agent (MTA), Mail Delivery Agent (MDA) and the SMTP protocol. Ubuntu provides a number of options in terms of MTA solutions, one of the more popular being Postfix. This chapter has outlined how to install, configure and test postfix on an Ubuntu system both to act as a mail server and to send and receive email using a third party SMTP relay server.

Chapter 33

33. Adding a New Disk Drive to an Ubuntu System

One of the first problems encountered by users and system administrators these days is that systems tend to run out of disk space to store data. Fortunately disk space is now one of the cheapest IT commodities. In the next two chapters we will look at the steps necessary to configure Ubuntu to use the space provided via the installation of a new physical or virtual disk drive.

33.1 Mounted File Systems or Logical Volumes

There are two ways to configure a new disk drive on an Ubuntu system. One very simple method is to create one or more Linux partitions on the new drive, create Linux file systems on those partitions and then mount them at specific mount points so that they can be accessed. This approach will be covered in this chapter.

Another approach is to add the new space to an existing volume group or create a new volume group. When Ubuntu is installed with the logical volume management option selected a volume group is created and named *ubuntu-vg*. Within this volume group are three logical volumes named *root*, *home* and *swap* that are used to store the / and /home file systems and swap partition respectively. By configuring the new disk as part of a volume group we are able to increase the disk space available to the existing logical volumes. Using this approach we are able, therefore, to increase the size of the /home file system by allocating some or all of the space on the new disk to the *home* volume. This topic will be discussed in detail in *"Adding a New Disk to an Ubuntu Volume Group and Logical Volume"*.

33.2 Finding the New Hard Drive

This tutorial assumes that a new physical or virtual hard drive has been installed on the system and is visible to the operating system. Once added, the new drive should automatically be detected by the operating system. Typically, the disk drives in a system are assigned device names beginning hd or sd followed by a letter to indicate the device number. For example, the first device might be */dev/sda*, the second */dev/sdb* and so on.

The following is output from a typical system with only one disk drive connected to a SATA controller:

```
# ls /dev/sd*
/dev/sda  /dev/sda1  /dev/sda2
```

This shows that the disk drive represented by */dev/sda* is itself divided into 2 partitions, represented by */dev/sda1* and */dev/sda2*.

The following output is from the same system after a second hard disk drive has been installed:

```
# ls /dev/sd*
/dev/sda /dev/sda1 /dev/sda2 /dev/sdb
```

As shown above, the new hard drive has been assigned to the device file */dev/sdb*. Currently the drive has no partitions shown (because we have yet to create any).

At this point we have a choice of creating partitions and file systems on the new drive and mounting them for access or adding the disk as a physical volume as part of a volume group. To perform the former continue with this chapter, otherwise read *"Adding a New Disk to an Ubuntu Volume Group and Logical Volume"* for details on configuring Logical Volumes.

33.3 Creating Linux Partitions

The next step is to create one or more Linux partitions on the new disk drive. This is achieved using the *fdisk* utility which takes as a command-line argument the device to be partitioned:

```
# fdisk /dev/sdb
Welcome to fdisk (util-linux 2.32.1).
Changes will remain in memory only, until you decide to write them.
Be careful before using the write command.

Device does not contain a recognized partition table.
Created a new DOS disklabel with disk identifier 0xbd09c991.

Command (m for help):
```

In order to view the current partitions on the disk enter the p command:

```
Command (m for help): p
Disk /dev/sdb: 8 GiB, 8589934592 bytes, 16777216 sectors
Units: sectors of 1 * 512 = 512 bytes
Sector size (logical/physical): 512 bytes / 512 bytes
I/O size (minimum/optimal): 512 bytes / 512 bytes
Disklabel type: dos
Disk identifier: 0xbd09c991
```

As we can see from the above *fdisk* output, the disk currently has no partitions because it is a previously unused disk. The next step is to create a new partition on the disk, a task which is performed by entering n (for new partition) and p (for primary partition):

```
Command (m for help): n
Partition type
   p   primary (0 primary, 0 extended, 4 free)
   e   extended (container for logical partitions)
Select (default p): p
Partition number (1-4, default 1):
```

In this example we only plan to create one partition which will be partition 1. Next we need to specify where the partition will begin and end. Since this is the first partition we need it to start at the first available sector and since we want to use the entire disk we specify the last sector as the end. Note that if you wish to create multiple partitions you can specify the size of each partition by sectors, bytes, kilobytes or megabytes.

```
Partition number (1-4, default 1): 1
First sector (2048-16777215, default 2048):
Last sector, +sectors or +size{K,M,G,T,P} (2048-16777215, default 16777215):

Created a new partition 1 of type 'Linux' and of size 8 GiB.

Command (m for help):
```

Now that we have specified the partition, we need to write it to the disk using the w command:

```
Command (m for help): w
The partition table has been altered.
Calling ioctl() to re-read partition table.
Syncing disks.
```

If we now look at the devices again we will see that the new partition is visible as */dev/sdb1*:

```
# ls /dev/sd*
/dev/sda /dev/sda1 /dev/sda2 /dev/sdb /dev/sdb1
```

The next step is to create a file system on our new partition.

33.4 Creating a File System on a Disk Partition

We now have a new disk installed, it is visible to Ubuntu and we have configured a Linux partition on the disk. The next step is to create a Linux file system on the partition so that the operating system can use it to store files and data. The easiest way to create a file system on a partition is to use the *mkfs.xfs* utility:

```
# apt install xfsprogs
# mkfs.xfs /dev/sdb1
meta-data=/dev/sdb1          isize=512    agcount=4, agsize=524224 blks
         =                   sectsz=512   attr=2, projid32bit=1
         =                   crc=1        finobt=1, sparse=1, rmapbt=0
         =                   reflink=1
data     =                   bsize=4096   blocks=2096896, imaxpct=25
         =                   sunit=0      swidth=0 blks
naming   =version 2          bsize=4096   ascii-ci=0, ftype=1
log      =internal log       bsize=4096   blocks=2560, version=2
         =                   sectsz=512   sunit=0 blks, lazy-count=1
realtime =none               extsz=4096   blocks=0, rtextents=0
```

In this case we have created an XFS file system. XFS is a high performance file system and includes a number of advantages in terms of parallel I/O performance and the use of journaling.

33.5 An Overview of Journaled File Systems

A journaling filesystem keeps a journal or log of the changes that are being made to the filesystem during disk writing that can be used to rapidly reconstruct corruptions that may occur due to events such as a system crash or power outage.

There are a number of advantages to using a journaling file system. Both the size and volume of data stored on disk drives has grown exponentially over the years. The problem with a non-journaled file system is that following a crash the *fsck* (filesystem consistency check) utility has to be run. The *fsck* utility will scan the entire filesystem validating all entries and making sure that blocks are allocated and referenced correctly. If it finds a corrupt entry it will attempt to fix the problem. The issues here are two-fold. First, the *fsck* utility will not always be able to repair damage and you will end up with data in the *lost+found* directory. This is data that was being used by an application but the system no longer knows where it was referenced from. The other problem is the issue of time. It can take a very long time to complete the *fsck* process on a large file system, potentially leading to unacceptable down time.

A journaled file system, on the other hand, records information in a log area on a disk (the journal and log do not need to be on the same device) during each write. This is a essentially an "intent to commit" data to the filesystem. The amount of information logged is configurable and ranges from not logging anything, to logging what is known as the "metadata" (i.e. ownership, date stamp information etc), to logging the "metadata" and the data blocks that are to be written to the file. Once the log is updated the system then writes the actual data to the appropriate areas of the filesystem and marks an entry in the log to say the data is committed.

After a crash the filesystem can very quickly be brought back on-line using the journal log, thereby reducing what could take minutes using *fsck* to seconds with the added advantage that there is considerably less chance of data loss or corruption.

33.6 Mounting a File System

Now that we have created a new file system on the Linux partition of our new disk drive we need to mount it so that it is accessible and usable. In order to do this we need to create a mount point. A mount point is simply a directory or folder into which the file system will be mounted. For the purposes of this example we will create a */backup* directory to match our file system label (although it is not necessary that these values match):

```
# mkdir /backup
```

The file system may then be manually mounted using the *mount* command:

```
# mount /dev/sdb1 /backup
```

Running the *mount* command with no arguments shows us all currently mounted file systems (including our new file system):

```
# mount
sysfs on /sys type sysfs (rw,nosuid,nodev,noexec,relatime,seclabel)
proc on /proc type proc (rw,nosuid,nodev,noexec,relatime)
```

```
.
.
/dev/sdb1 on /backup type xfs (rw,relatime,attr2,inode64,logbufs=8,logbsize=32k,n
oquota)
```

33.7 Configuring Ubuntu to Automatically Mount a File System

In order to set up the system so that the new file system is automatically mounted at boot time an entry needs to be added to the */etc/fstab* file. The format for an fstab entry is as follows:

```
<device>      <dir>  <type> <options>     <dump> <fsck>
```

These entries can be summarized as follows:

- **<device>** - The device on which the filesystem is to be mounted.
- **<dir>** - The directory that is to act as the mount point for the filesystem.
- **<type>** - The filesystem type (xfs, ext4 etc.)
- **<options>** - Additional filesystem mount options, for example making the filesystem read-only or controlling whether the filesystem can be mounted by any user. Run *man mount* to review a full list of options. Setting this value to *defaults* will use the default settings for the filesystem (rw, suid, dev, exec, auto, nouser, async).
- **<dump>** - Dictates whether the content of the filesystem is to be included in any backups performed by the dump utility. This setting is rarely used and can be disabled with a 0 value.
- **<fsck>** - Whether the filesystem is checked by fsck after a system crash and the order in which filesystems are to be checked. For journaled filesystems such as XFS this should be set to 0 to indicate that the check is not required.

The following example shows an *fstab* file configured to automount our */backup* partition on the /dev/sdb1 partition:

```
/dev/mapper/ubuntu--vg-root /                ext4    errors=remount-ro 0       1
/dev/mapper/ubuntu--vg-swap_1 none             swap    sw                0       0
/dev/sdb1             /backup                xfs     defaults          0       0
```

The */backup* filesystem will now automount each time the system restarts.

33.8 Adding a Disk Using Cockpit

In addition to working with storage using the command-line utilities outlined in this chapter, it is also possible to configure a new storage device using the Cockpit web console. To view the current storage configuration, log into the Cockpit console and select the Storage option as shown in Figure 33-1:

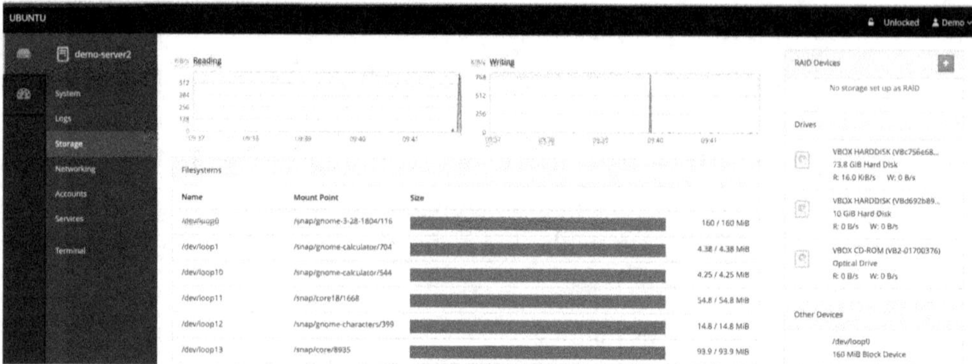

Figure 33-1

To locate the newly added storage, scroll to the bottom of the Storage page until the Drives section comes into view (note that the Drives section may also be located in the top right-hand corner of the screen):

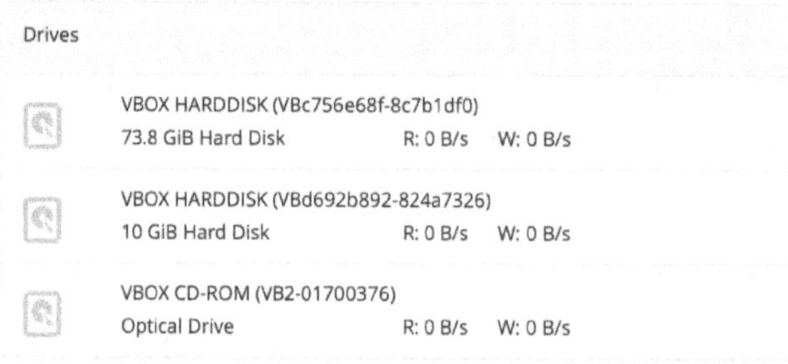

Figure 33-2

In the case of the above figure, the new drive is the 10 GiB drive. Select the new drive to display the Drive screen as shown in Figure 33-3:

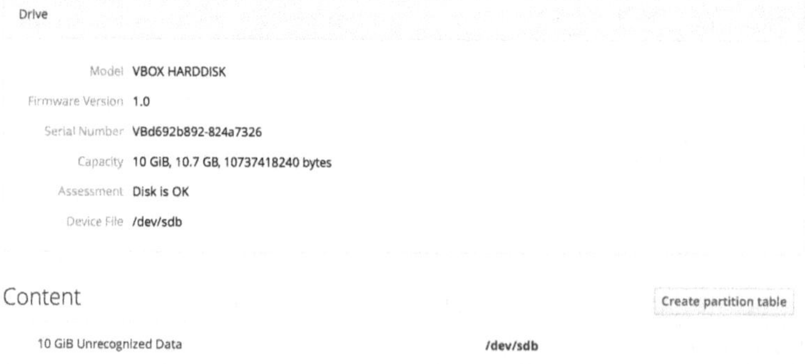

Figure 33-3

Click on the *Create Partition Table* button and, in the resulting dialog, accept the default settings before clicking on the *Format* button:

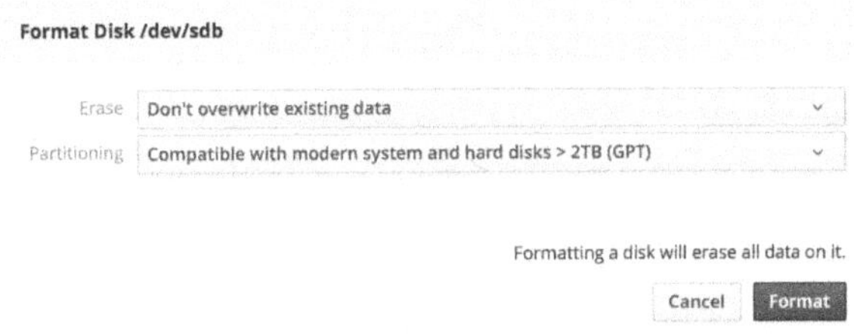

Figure 33-4

On returning to the main Storage screen, click on the *Create Partition* button and use the dialog to specify how much space is to be allocated to this partition, the filesystem type (XFS is recommended) and an optional label, filesystem mount point and mount options. Note that if this new partition does not use all of the available space, additional partitions may subsequently be added to the drive. To change settings such as whether the filesystem is read-only or mounted at boot time, change the Mounting menu option to *Custom* and adjust the toggle button settings:

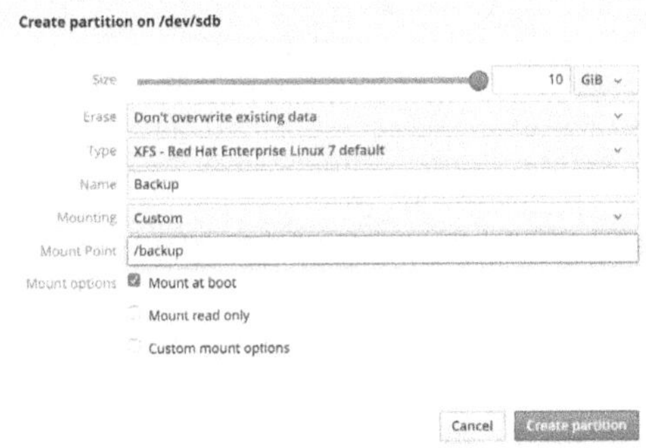

Figure 33-5

Once the settings have been selected, click on the *Create partition* button to commit the change. On completion of the creation process the new partition will be added to the disk, the corresponding filesystem created and mounted at the designated mount point and appropriate changes made to the */etc/fstab* file.

33.9 Summary

This chapter has covered the topic of adding an additional physical or virtual disk drive to an existing Ubuntu system. This is a relatively simple process of making sure the new drive has been detected by the operating system, creating one or more partitions on the drive and then making filesystems on those partitions. Although a number of different filesystem types are available on Ubuntu, XFS is generally the recommended option. Once the filesystems are ready, they can be mounted using the *mount* command. So that the newly created filesystems mount automatically on system startup, additions can be made to the */etc/fstab* configuration file.

Chapter 34

34. Adding a New Disk to an Ubuntu Volume Group and Logical Volume

In the previous chapter we looked at adding a new disk drive to an Ubuntu system, creating a partition and file system and then mounting that file system so that the disk can be accessed. An alternative to creating fixed partitions and file systems is to use Logical Volume Management (LVM) to create logical disks made up of space from one or more physical or virtual disks or partitions. The advantage of using LVM is that space can be added to or removed from logical volumes as needed without the need to spread data over multiple file systems.

Let us take, for example, the root (/) file system of an Ubuntu-based server. Without LVM this file system would be created with a certain size when the operating system is installed. If a new disk drive is installed there is no way to allocate any of that space to the / file system. The only option would be to create new file systems on the new disk and mount them at particular mount points. In this scenario you would have plenty of space on the new file system but the / file system would still be nearly full. The only option would be to move files onto the new file system. With LVM, the new disk (or part thereof) can be assigned to the logical volume containing the root file system thereby dynamically extending the space available.

In this chapter we will look at the steps necessary to add new disk space to both a volume group and a logical volume for the purpose of adding additional space to the root file system of an Ubuntu system.

34.1 An Overview of Logical Volume Management (LVM)

LVM provides a flexible and high level approach to managing disk space. Instead of each disk drive being split into partitions of fixed sizes onto which fixed size file systems are created, LVM provides a way to group together disk space into logical volumes which can be easily resized and moved. In addition, LVM allows administrators to carefully control disk space assigned to different groups of users by allocating distinct volume groups or logical volumes to those users. When the space initially allocated to the volume is exhausted the administrator can simply add more space without having to move the user files to a different file system.

LVM consists of the following components:

34.1.1 Volume Group (VG)

The Volume Group is the high level container which holds one or more logical volumes and physical volumes.

34.1.2 Physical Volume (PV)

A physical volume represents a storage device such as a disk drive or other storage media.

34.1.3 Logical Volume (LV)

A logical volume is the equivalent to a disk partition and, as with a disk partition, can contain a file system.

34.1.4 Physical Extent (PE)

Each physical volume (PV) is divided into equal size blocks known as physical extents.

34.1.5 Logical Extent (LE)

Each logical volume (LV) is divided into equal size blocks called logical extents.

Suppose we are creating a new volume group called VolGroup001. This volume group needs physical disk space in order to function so we allocate three disk partitions */dev/sda1*, */dev/sdb1* and */dev/sdb2*. These become physical volumes in VolGroup001. We would then create a logical volume called LogVol001 within the volume group made up of the three physical volumes.

If we run out of space in LogVol001 we simply add more disk partitions as physical volumes and assign them to the volume group and logical volume.

34.2 Getting Information about Logical Volumes

As an example of using LVM with Ubuntu we will work through an example of adding space to the / file system of a standard Ubuntu installation. Anticipating the need for flexibility in the sizing of the root partition (assuming, of course, that LVM partitioning option was selected during the Ubuntu installation process), Ubuntu sets up the / file system as a logical volume (called *root*) within a volume group called *ubuntu-vg*. Before making any changes to the LVM setup, however, it is important to first gather information.

Running the *mount* command will output information about a range of mount points, including the following entry for the root filesystem:

```
/dev/mapper/ubuntu--vg-root on / type ext4 (rw,relatime,errors=remount-ro)
```

Information about the volume group can be obtained using the *vgdisplay* command:

```
# vgdisplay
  --- Volume group ---
  VG Name               ubuntu-vg
  System ID
  Format                lvm2
  Metadata Areas        1
  Metadata Sequence No  3
  VG Access             read/write
  VG Status             resizable
  MAX LV                0
  Cur LV                2
  Open LV               2
  Max PV                0
  Cur PV                1
```

```
  Act PV                1
  VG Size               <73.75 GiB
  PE Size               4.00 MiB
  Total PE              18879
  Alloc PE / Size       18879 / <73.75 GiB
  Free  PE / Size       0 / 0
  VG UUID               hqaagb-OgB5-3DhK-qLoN-bRHU-jsFm-LrdXtT
```

As we can see in the above example, the *ubuntu-vg* volume group has a physical extent size of 4.00MiB and has a total of approximately 73GB available for allocation to logical volumes. Currently 18879 physical extents are allocated equaling the total capacity. If we want to increase the space allocated to any logical volumes in the *ubuntu-vg* volume group, therefore, we will need to add one or more physical volumes. The *vgs* tool is also useful for displaying a quick overview of the space available in the volume groups on a system:

```
# vgs
  VG        #PV #LV #SN Attr   VSize   VFree
  ubuntu-vg   1   2   0 wz--n- <73.75g    0
```

Information about logical volumes in a volume group may similarly be obtained using the *lvdisplay* command:

```
## lvdisplay
  --- Logical volume ---
  LV Path                /dev/ubuntu-vg/root
  LV Name                root
  VG Name                ubuntu-vg
  LV UUID                iLfsLf-pVzy-yCfd-wKim-EdbW-efvm-J6p1f4
  LV Write Access        read/write
  LV Creation host, time ubuntu, 2020-04-06 11:17:53 -0400
  LV Status              available
  # open                 1
  LV Size                <72.79 GiB
  Current LE             18634
  Segments               1
  Allocation             inherit
  Read ahead sectors     auto
  - currently set to     256
  Block device           253:0

  --- Logical volume ---
  LV Path                /dev/ubuntu-vg/swap_1
  LV Name                swap_1
  VG Name                ubuntu-vg
  LV UUID                14Cr74-x5EW-V1k1-c5z8-8NUn-DTqC-PLEg7F
  LV Write Access        read/write
  LV Creation host, time ubuntu, 2020-04-06 11:17:54 -0400
```

```
  LV Status              available
  # open                 2
  LV Size                980.00 MiB
  Current LE             245
  Segments               1
  Allocation             inherit
  Read ahead sectors     auto
  - currently set to     256
  Block device           253:1
```

As shown in the above example approximately 72 GiB of the space in volume group *ubuntu-vg* is allocated to logical volume *root* (for the / file system) and 980 MiB to *swap_1* (for swap space).

Now that we know what space is being used it is often helpful to understand which devices are providing the space (in other words which devices are being used as physical volumes). To obtain this information we need to run the *pvdisplay* command:

```
# pvdisplay
  --- Physical volume ---
  PV Name               /dev/sda1
  VG Name               ubuntu-vg
  PV Size               <73.75 GiB / not usable 2.00 MiB
  Allocatable           yes (but full)
  PE Size               4.00 MiB
  Total PE              18879
  Free PE               0
  Allocated PE          18879
  PV UUID               nwp55K-Chay-x5eB-kZcc-sonL-cm3E-3SWnKG
```

Clearly the space controlled by logical volume *ubuntu-vg* is provided via a physical volume located on */dev/sda1*.

Now that we know a little more about our LVM configuration we can embark on the process of adding space to the volume group and the logical volume contained within.

34.3 Adding Additional Space to a Volume Group from the Command-Line

Just as with the previous steps to gather information about the current Logical Volume Management configuration of an Ubuntu system, changes to this configuration can be made from the command-line.

In the remainder of this chapter we will assume that a new disk has been added to the system and that it is being seen by the operating system as */dev/sdb*. We shall also assume that this is a new disk that does not contain any existing partitions. If existing partitions are present they should be backed up and then the partitions deleted from the disk using the *fdisk* utility. For example, assuming a device represented by */dev/sdb* containing one partition as follows:

```
# fdisk -l /dev/sdb
Disk /dev/sdb: 10 GiB, 10737418240 bytes, 20971520 sectors
```

```
Units: sectors of 1 * 512 = 512 bytes
Sector size (logical/physical): 512 bytes / 512 bytes
I/O size (minimum/optimal): 512 bytes / 512 bytes
Disklabel type: gpt
Disk identifier: 6C7E15CA-C9B1-4FEB-B10A-BE75F8B6D483

Device     Start      End  Sectors Size Type
/dev/sdb1   2048 20971486 20969439  10G Linux filesystem
```

Once any filesystems on this partition have been unmounted, they can be deleted as follows:

```
# fdisk  /dev/sdb

Welcome to fdisk (util-linux 2.31.1).
Changes will remain in memory only, until you decide to write them.
Be careful before using the write command.

Command (m for help): d
Selected partition 1
Partition 1 has been deleted.

Command (m for help): w
The partition table has been altered.
Calling ioctl() to re-read partition table.
Syncing disks.
```

Before moving to the next step, be sure to remove any entries in the */etc/fstab* file for these filesystems so that the system does not attempt to mount them on the next reboot.

Once the disk is ready, the next step is to convert this disk into a physical volume using the *pvcreate* command (also wiping the dos signature if one exists):

```
# pvcreate /dev/sdb
  Physical volume "/dev/sdb" successfully created.
```

If the creation fails with a message that reads "Device /dev/<device> excluded by a filter", it may be necessary to wipe the disk using the *wipefs* command before creating the physical volume:

```
# wipefs -a /dev/sdb
/dev/sdb: 8 bytes were erased at offset 0x00000200 (gpt): 45 46 49 20 50 41 52 54
/dev/sdb: 8 bytes were erased at offset 0x1fffffe00 (gpt): 45 46 49 20 50 41 52
54
/dev/sdb: 2 bytes were erased at offset 0x000001fe (PMBR): 55 aa
/dev/sdb: calling ioctl to re-read partition table: Success
```

With the physical volume created we now need to add it to the volume group (in this case *ubuntu-vg*)using the *vgextend* command:

```
# vgextend ubuntu-vg /dev/sdb
  Volume group "ubuntu-vg" successfully extended
```

The new physical volume has now been added to the volume group and is ready to be allocated to a logical volume. To do this we run the *lvextend* tool providing the size by which we wish to extend the volume. In this case we want to extend the size of logical volume by 9 GB. Note that we need to provide the path to the logical volume which can be obtained from the *lvdisplay* command (in this case */dev/ubuntu-vg/root*):

```
# lvextend -L+9G /dev/ubuntu-vg/root
  Size of logical volume ubuntu-vg/root changed from <72.79 GiB (18634 extents) to <81.79 GiB (20938 extents).
  Logical volume ubuntu-vg/root successfully resized.
```

The last step in the process is to resize the file system residing on the logical volume so that it uses the additional space. The way this is performed will depend on the filesystem type which can be identified using the following command and checking the Type column:

```
# df -T /
Filesystem                    Type 1K-blocks    Used Available Use% Mounted on
/dev/mapper/ubuntu--vg-root ext4  83890408 5186940  74496972   7% /
```

If root is formatted using the XFS filesystem, this can be achieved using the *xfs_growfs* utility:

```
# xfs_growfs /
```

If, on the other hand, the filesystem is of type ext2, ext3, or ext4, the *resize2fs* utility should be used instead when performing the filesystem resize:

```
# resize2fs /dev/ubuntu-vg/root
```

Once the resize completes, the file system will have been extended to use the additional space provided by the new disk drive. All this has been achieved without moving a single file or even having to restart the server. As far as any users on the system are concerned nothing has changed (except, of course, that there is now more disk space).

34.4 Summary

Volume groups and logical volumes provide an abstract layer on top of the physical storage devices on an Ubuntu system to provide a flexible way to allocate the space provided by multiple disk drives. This allows disk space allocations to be made and changed dynamically without the need to repartition disk drives and move data between filesystems. This chapter has outlined the basic concepts of volume groups, logical volumes and physical volumes while demonstrating how to manage these using command-line tools.

Chapter 35

35. Adding and Managing Ubuntu Swap Space

An important part of maintaining the performance of an Ubuntu system involves ensuring that adequate swap space is available comparable to the memory demands placed on the system. The goal of this chapter, therefore, is to provide an overview of swap management on Ubuntu.

35.1 What is Swap Space?

Computer systems have a finite amount of physical memory that is made available to the operating system. When the operating system begins to approach the limit of the available memory it frees up space by writing memory pages to disk. When any of those pages are required by the operating system they are subsequently read back into memory. The area of the disk allocated for this task is referred to as *swap space*.

35.2 Recommended Swap Space for Ubuntu

The amount of swap recommended for Ubuntu depends on a number of factors including the amount of memory in the system, the workload imposed on that memory and whether the system is required to support hibernation. The current guidelines for Ubuntu swap space are as follows:

Amount of installed RAM	**Recommended swap space**	**Recommended swap space if hibernation enabled**
1GB	1GB	2GB
2GB	1GB	3GB
3GB	2GB	5GB
4GB	2GB	6GB
5GB	2GB	7GB
6GB	2GB	8GB
8GB	3GB	11GB
12GB	3GB	15GB
16GB	4GB	32GB
24GB	5GB	48GB

Table 35-1

For systems with memory configurations exceeding 24GB refer to the following web page for swap space guidelines:

https://help.ubuntu.com/community/SwapFaq

When a system enters hibernation, the current system state is written to the hard disk and the host machine is powered off. When the machine is subsequently powered on, the state of the system is restored from the hard disk drive. This differs from suspension where the system state is stored in RAM. The machine then enters a sleep state whereby power is maintained to the system RAM while other devices are shut down.

35.3 Identifying Current Swap Space Usage

The current amount of swap used by an Ubuntu system may be identified in a number of ways. One option is to output the */proc/swaps* file:

```
# cat /proc/swaps
Filename                Type        Size        Used        Priority
/dev/dm-1               partition   4169724     41484       -2
```

Alternatively, the *swapon* command may be used:

```
# swapon
NAME      TYPE       SIZE  USED PRIO
/dev/dm-1 partition    4G 40.5M   -2
```

To view the amount of swap space relative to the overall available RAM, the *free* command may be used:

```
# free
        total        used        free      shared  buff/cache   available
Mem:  4035436     1428276     2224596       21968      382564     2360172
Swap: 4169724       41484     4128240
```

35.4 Adding a Swap File to an Ubuntu System

Additional swap may be added to the system by creating a file and assigning it as swap. Begin by creating the swap file using the *dd* command. The size of the file can be changed by adjusting the *count=* variable. The following command-line, for example, creates a 2.0 GB file:

```
# dd if=/dev/zero of=/newswap bs=1024 count=2000000
2000000+0 records in
2000000+0 records out
2048000000 bytes (2.0 GB, 1.9 GiB) copied, 3.62697 s, 565 MB/s
```

Before converting the file to a swap file, it is important to make sure the file has secure permissions set:

```
# chmod 0600 /newswap
```

Once a suitable file has been created, it needs to be converted into a swap file using the *mkswap* command:

```
# mkswap /newswap
Setting up swapspace version 1, size = 1.9 GiB (2047995904 bytes)
no label, UUID=4ffc238d-7fde-4367-bd98-c5c46407e535
```

With the swap file created and configured it can be added to the system in real-time using the *swapon* utility:

```
# swapon /newswap
```

Re-running swapon should now report that the new file is now being used as swap:

```
# swapon
NAME       TYPE       SIZE USED PRIO
/dev/dm-1 partition    4G   0B   -2
/newswap  file       1.9G   0B   -3
```

The swap space may be removed dynamically by using the *swapoff* utility as follows:

```
# swapoff /newswap
```

Finally, modify the */etc/fstab* file to automatically add the new swap at system boot time by adding the following line:

```
/newswap    swap    swap   defaults 0 0
```

35.5 Adding Swap as a Partition

As an alternative to designating a file as swap space, entire disk partitions may also be designated as swap. The steps to achieve this are largely the same as those for adding a swap file. Before allocating a partition to swap, however, make sure that any existing data on the corresponding filesystem is either backed up or no longer needed and that the filesystem has been unmounted.

Assuming that a partition exists on a disk drive represented by */dev/sdb1*, for example, the first step would be to convert this into a swap partition, once again using the *mkswap* utility:

```
# mkswap /dev/sdb1
mkswap: /dev/sdb1: warning: wiping old xfs signature.
Setting up swapspace version 1, size = 8 GiB (8587833344 bytes)
no label, UUID=a899c8ec-c410-4569-ba18-ddea03370c7f
```

Next, add the new partition to the system swap and verify that it has indeed been added:

```
# swapon /dev/sdb1
# swapon
NAME       TYPE       SIZE USED PRIO
/dev/dm-1 partition    4G   0B   -2
/dev/sdb1 partition    8G   0B   -3
```

Once again, the */etc/fstab* file may be modified to automatically add the swap partition at boot time as follows:

```
/dev/sdb1    swap    swap   defaults 0 0
```

35.6 Adding Space to an Ubuntu LVM Swap Volume

On systems using Logical Volume Management, an alternative to adding swap via file or disk partition is to extend the logical volume used for the swap space.

The first step is to identify the current amount of swap available and the volume group and logical volume used for the swap space using the *lvdisplay* utility (for more information on LVM, refer to the chapter entitled *"Adding a New Disk to an Ubuntu Volume Group and Logical Volume"*):

```
# lvdisplay
.
.
  --- Logical volume ---
  LV Path                /dev/ubuntu-vg/swap_1
  LV Name                swap_1
  VG Name                ubuntu-vg
  LV UUID                nJPip0-Q6dx-Mfe3-4Aao-gWAa-swDk-7ZiPdP
  LV Write Access        read/write
  LV Creation host, time ubuntu, 2020-01-13 13:16:18 -0500
  LV Status              available
  # open                 2
  LV Size                5.00 GiB
  Current LE             1280
  Segments               1
  Allocation             inherit
  Read ahead sectors     auto
  - currently set to     256
  Block device           253:1
```

Clearly the swap resides on a logical volume named *swap_1* which is part of the volume group named ubuntu-vg. The next step is to verify if there is any space available on the volume group that can be allocated to the swap volume:

```
# vgs
  VG         #PV #LV #SN Attr   VSize   VFree
  ubuntu-vg    2   3   0 wz--n- 197.66g <22.00g
```

If the amount of space available is sufficient to meet additional swap requirements, turn off the swap and extend the swap logical volume to use as much of the available space as needed to meet the system's swap requirements:

```
# lvextend -L+8GB /dev/ubuntu-vg/swap_1
    Logical volume ubuntu_vg/swap_1 successfully resized.
```

Next, reformat the swap volume and turn the swap back on:

```
# mkswap /dev/ubuntu-vg/swap_1
mkswap: /dev/ubuntu-vg/swap_1: warning: wiping old swap signature.
Setting up swapspace version 1, size = 12 GiB (12754874368 bytes)
no label, UUID=241a4818-e51c-4b8c-9bc9-1697fc2ce26e

# swapon /dev/ubuntu-vg/swap_1
```

Having made the changes, check that the swap space has increased:

```
# swapon
NAME      TYPE       SIZE USED PRIO
```

```
/dev/dm-1 partition  12G   0B   -2
```

35.7 Adding Swap Space to the Volume Group

In the above section we extended the swap logical volume to use space that was already available in the volume group. If no space is available in the volume group then it will need to be added before the swap can be extended.

Begin by checking the status of the volume group:

```
# vgs
  VG         #PV #LV #SN Attr   VSize   VFree
  ubuntu-vg   1   2   0 wz--n- <73.75g    0
```

The above output indicates that no space is available within the volume group. Suppose, however, that we have a requirement to add 8 GB to the swap on the system. Clearly, this will require the addition of more space to the volume group. For the purposes of this example it will be assumed that a disk that is 8 GB in size and represented by */dev/sdb* is available for addition to the volume group. The first step is to turn this partition into a physical volume:

```
# pvcreate /dev/sdb
  Physical volume "/dev/sdb" successfully created.
```

If the creation fails with a message similar to “Device /dev/sdb excluded by a filter”, it may be necessary to wipe the disk before creating the physical volume:

```
# wipefs -a /dev/sdb
/dev/sdb: 8 bytes were erased at offset 0x00000200 (gpt): 45 46 49 20 50 41 52 54
/dev/sdb: 8 bytes were erased at offset 0x1fffffe00 (gpt): 45 46 49 20 50 41 52
54
/dev/sdb: 2 bytes were erased at offset 0x000001fe (PMBR): 55 aa
/dev/sdb: calling ioctl to re-read partition table: Success
```

Next, the volume group needs to be extended to use this additional physical volume:

```
# vgextend ubuntu-vg /dev/sdb
  Volume group "ubuntu-vg" successfully extended
```

At this point the *vgs* command should report the addition of the 10 GB of space to the volume group:

```
# vgs
  VG         #PV #LV #SN Attr   VSize  VFree
  ubuntu-vg   2   2   0 wz--n- 83.74g <10.00g
```

Now that the additional space is available in the volume group, the swap logical volume may be extended to utilize the space. First, turn off the swap using the *swapoff* utility:

```
# swapoff /dev/ubuntu-vg/swap_1
```

Next, extend the logical volume to use the new space:

```
# lvextend -L+9.7GB /dev/ubuntu-vg/swap_1
  Rounding size to boundary between physical extents: 9.70 GiB.
  Size of logical volume ubuntu-vg/swap_1 changed from 980.00 MiB (245 extents)
```

```
to 10.66 GiB (2729 extents).
  Logical volume ubuntu-vg/swap_1 successfully resized.
```

Re-create the swap on the logical volume:

```
# mkswap /dev/ubuntu-vg/swap_1
mkswap: /dev/ubuntu-vg/swap_1: warning: wiping old swap signature.
Setting up swapspace version 1, size = 10.7 GiB (11446251520 bytes)
no label, UUID=447fb9e5-5473-4f2c-96f8-839b1457d3ed
```

Next, turn swap back on:

```
# swapon /dev/ubuntu-vg/swap_1
```

Finally, use the *swapon* command to verify the addition of the swap space to the system:

```
# swapon
NAME      TYPE       SIZE USED PRIO
/dev/dm-1 partition 10.7G   0B   -2
```

35.8 Summary

Swap space is a vital component of just about any operating system in terms of handling situations where memory resources become constrained. By swapping out areas of memory to disk, the system is able to continue to function and meet the needs of the processes and applications running on it.

Ubuntu has a set of guidelines recommending the amount of disk-based swap space that should be allocated depending on the amount of RAM installed in the system. In situations where these recommendations prove to be insufficient, additional swap space can be added to the system, typically without the need to reboot. As outlined in this chapter, swap space can be added in the form of a file, disk or disk partition or by extending existing logical volumes that have been configured as swap space.

Chapter 36

36. Ubuntu System and Process Monitoring

An important part of running and administering an Ubuntu system involves monitoring the overall system health in terms of memory, swap, storage and processor usage. This includes knowing how to inspect and manage both the system and user processes that are running in the background. This chapter will outline some of the tools and utilities that can be used to monitor both system resources and processes on an Ubuntu system.

36.1 Managing Processes

Even when an Ubuntu system appears to be idle, many *system processes* will be running silently in the background to keep the operating system functioning. Each time you execute a command or launch an app, *user processes* are started which will run until the associated task is completed.

To obtain a list of active user processes you are currently running within the context of a single terminal or command-prompt session use the *ps* command as follows:

```
$ ps
  PID TTY          TIME CMD
10395 pts/1    00:00:00 bash
13218 pts/1    00:00:00 ps
```

The output from the ps command shows that there are currently two user processes running within the context of the current terminal window or command prompt session, the bash shell into which the command was entered, and the ps command itself.

To list all of the active processes running for the current user, use the ps command with the -a flag. This will list all running processes that are associated with the user regardless of where they are running (for example processes running in other terminal windows):

```
$ ps -a
  PID TTY          TIME CMD
  976 tty1     00:00:22 Xorg
 1026 tty1     00:00:00 gnome-session-b
.
.
13217 pts/0    00:00:00 nano
13265 pts/2    00:00:00 cat
13272 pts/1    00:00:00 ps
```

As shown in the above output, the user has some processes running that relate to the GNOME desktop in addition to the nano text editor, the cat command and the ps command.

To list the processes for a specific user, run ps with the -u flag followed by the user name:

```
# ps -u john
  PID TTY          TIME CMD
  914 ?        00:00:00 systemd
  915 ?        00:00:00 (sd-pam)
  970 ?        00:00:00 gnome-keyring-d
  974 tty1     00:00:00 gdm-x-session
.
.
```

Note that each process is assigned a unique process ID which can be used to stop the process by sending it a termination (TERM) signal via the *kill* command. For example:

```
$ kill 13217
```

The advantage of ending a process with the TERM signal is that it gives the process the opportunity to exit gracefully, potentially saving any data that might otherwise be lost.

If the standard termination signal does not terminate the process, repeat the kill command with the -9 option. This sends a KILL signal which should cause even frozen processes to exit, but does not give the process a chance to exit gracefully possibly resulting in data loss:

```
$ kill -9 13217
```

To list all of the processes running on a system (including all user and system processes), execute the following command:

```
$ ps -ax
  PID TTY      STAT   TIME COMMAND
    1 ?        Ss     0:05 /sbin/init splash
    2 ?        S      0:00 [kthreadd]
    3 ?        I<     0:00 [rcu_gp]
    4 ?        I<     0:00 [rcu_par_gp]
.
.
```

To list all processes and include information about process ownership, CPU and memory use, execute the ps command with the -aux option:

```
$ ps -aux
USER       PID %CPU %MEM    VSZ   RSS TTY      STAT START   TIME COMMAND
root         1  0.0  0.2 225860  9540 ?        Ss   10:37   0:05 /sbin/init
splash
root         2  0.0  0.0      0     0 ?        S    10:37   0:00 [kthreadd]
root         3  0.0  0.0      0     0 ?        I<   10:37   0:00 [rcu_gp]
root         4  0.0  0.0      0     0 ?        I<   10:37   0:00 [rcu_par_gp]
.
.
demo     13924  0.0  0.1  28272  3836 pts/2    S+   14:57   0:00 man ps
demo     13934  0.0  0.0  16952  1048 pts/2    S+   14:57   0:00 pager
```

```
demo      14068  0.0  0.0  46772  3560 pts/1    R+   15:02   0:00 ps aux
.
.
```

A Linux process can start its own sub-processes (referred to as *spawning*) resulting in a hierarchical parent-child relationship between processes. To view the process tree, use the ps command and include the -f option. Figure 36-1, for example, shows part of the tree output for a *ps -af* command execution:

```
15289 15300 15300 15289 pts/3    15300 R+    1000   0:00 ps axj
demo@ThinkCentre-M92p:~$ ps af
  PID TTY      STAT   TIME COMMAND
15289 pts/3    Ss     0:00 -bash
15301 pts/3    R+     0:00  \_ ps af
10395 pts/1    Ss     0:00 -bash
14319 pts/1    S      0:00  \_ sudo su -
14320 pts/1    S      0:00      \_ su -
14321 pts/1    S+     0:00          \_ -su
13223 pts/2    Ss     0:00 bash
15178 pts/2    S+     0:00  \_ man ps
15188 pts/2    S+     0:00      \_ pager
 1604 pts/0    Ss+    0:00 bash
  974 tty1     Ssl+   0:00 /usr/lib/gdm3/gdm-x-session --run-script env GNOME_SHELL_SESSION_MODE=ubuntu gnome-session --session=
  976 tty1     Sl+    1:27  \_ /usr/lib/xorg/Xorg vt1 -displayfd 3 -auth /run/user/1000/gdm/Xauthority -background none -noreset
 1026 tty1     Sl+    0:00  \_ /usr/lib/gnome-session/gnome-session-binary --session=ubuntu
 1103 tty1     Z+     0:00      \_ [xbrlapi] <defunct>
 1230 tty1     Sl+    1:29      \_ /usr/bin/gnome-shell
 1295 tty1     Sl     0:01      |   \_ ibus-daemon --xim --panel disable
 1303 tty1     Sl     0:00      |   |   \_ /usr/lib/ibus/ibus-dconf
 1521 tty1     Sl     0:00      |   |   \_ /usr/lib/ibus/ibus-engine-simple
14074 tty1     Sl+    0:53      |   \_ gnome-system-monitor
 1382 tty1     Sl+    0:00      \_ /usr/lib/gnome-settings-daemon/gsd-mouse
 1384 tty1     Sl+    0:00      \_ /usr/lib/gnome-settings-daemon/gsd-power
 1387 tty1     Sl+    0:00      \_ /usr/lib/gnome-settings-daemon/gsd-print-notifications
 1388 tty1     Sl+    0:00      \_ /usr/lib/gnome-settings-daemon/gsd-rfkill
 1389 tty1     Sl+    0:00      \_ /usr/lib/gnome-settings-daemon/gsd-screensaver-proxy
```

Figure 36-1

From within the GNOME desktop, process information may also be viewed via the System Monitor tool. This tool can either be launched by searching for "System Monitor" within the desktop environment, or from the command-line as follows:

```
$ gnome-system-monitor
```

Once the System Monitor has launched, select the Processes button located in the toolbar to list the processes running on the system as shown in Figure 36-2 below:

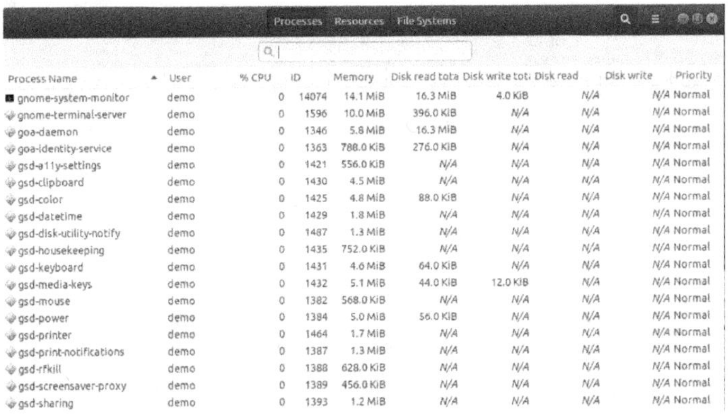

Process Name	User	% CPU	ID	Memory	Disk read tota	Disk write tot	Disk read	Disk write	Priority
gnome-system-monitor	demo	0	14074	14.1 MiB	16.3 MiB	4.0 KiB	N/A	N/A	Normal
gnome-terminal-server	demo	0	1596	10.0 MiB	396.0 KiB	N/A	N/A	N/A	Normal
goa-daemon	demo	0	1346	5.8 MiB	16.3 MiB	N/A	N/A	N/A	Normal
goa-identity-service	demo	0	1363	788.0 KiB	276.0 KiB	N/A	N/A	N/A	Normal
gsd-a11y-settings	demo	0	1421	556.0 KiB	N/A	N/A	N/A	N/A	Normal
gsd-clipboard	demo	0	1430	4.5 MiB	N/A	N/A	N/A	N/A	Normal
gsd-color	demo	0	1425	4.8 MiB	88.0 KiB	N/A	N/A	N/A	Normal
gsd-datetime	demo	0	1429	1.8 MiB	N/A	N/A	N/A	N/A	Normal
gsd-disk-utility-notify	demo	0	1487	1.3 MiB	N/A	N/A	N/A	N/A	Normal
gsd-housekeeping	demo	0	1435	752.0 KiB	N/A	N/A	N/A	N/A	Normal
gsd-keyboard	demo	0	1431	4.6 MiB	64.0 KiB	N/A	N/A	N/A	Normal
gsd-media-keys	demo	0	1432	5.1 MiB	44.0 KiB	12.0 KiB	N/A	N/A	Normal
gsd-mouse	demo	0	1382	568.0 KiB	N/A	N/A	N/A	N/A	Normal
gsd-power	demo	0	1384	5.0 MiB	56.0 KiB	N/A	N/A	N/A	Normal
gsd-printer	demo	0	1464	1.7 MiB	N/A	N/A	N/A	N/A	Normal
gsd-print-notifications	demo	0	1387	1.3 MiB	N/A	N/A	N/A	N/A	Normal
gsd-rfkill	demo	0	1388	628.0 KiB	N/A	N/A	N/A	N/A	Normal
gsd-screensaver-proxy	demo	0	1389	456.0 KiB	N/A	N/A	N/A	N/A	Normal
gsd-sharing	demo	0	1393	1.2 MiB	N/A	N/A	N/A	N/A	Normal

Figure 36-2

To change the processes listed (for example to list all processes, or just your own processes), use the menu as illustrated in Figure 36-3:

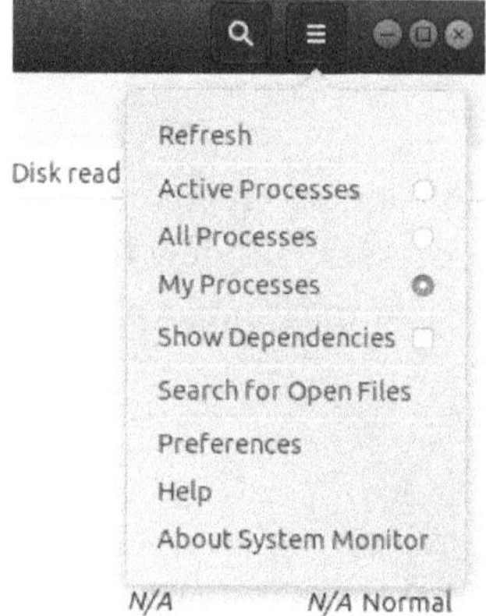

Figure 36-3

To filter the list of processes, enter the process name into the search bar:

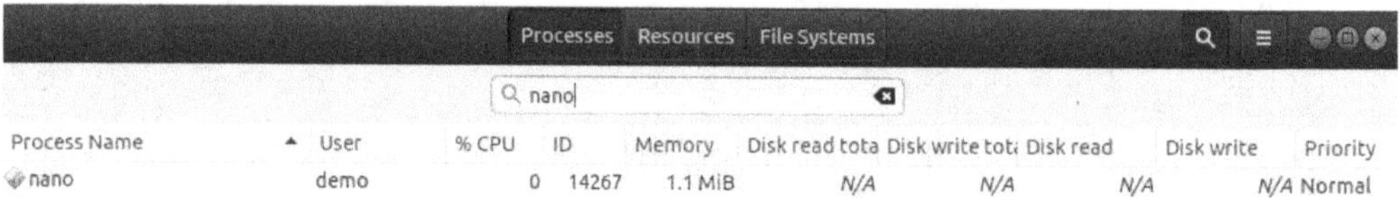

Figure 36-4

To display additional information about a specific process, select it from the list and click on the button located in the bottom right-hand corner (marked A in Figure 36-5) of the dialog:

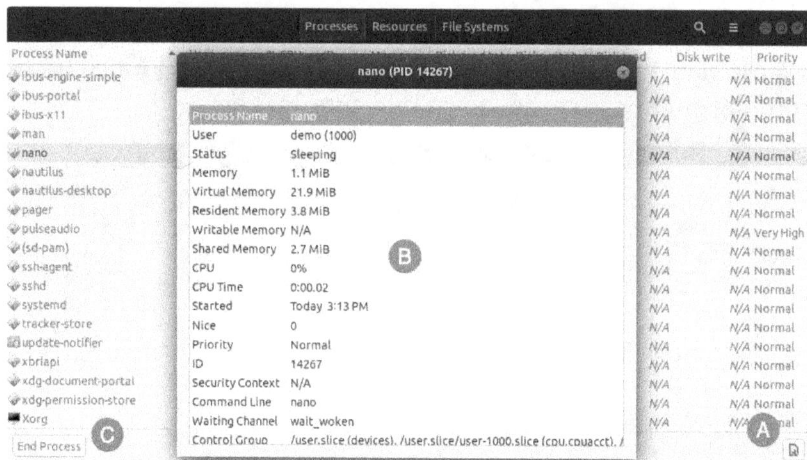

Figure 36-5

When the button is clicked a dialog similar to that marked B in the above figure will appear. To terminate a process, select it from the list and click on the End Process button (C).

To monitor CPU, memory, swap and network usage, simply click on the Resources button in the title bar to display the screen shown in Figure 36-6:

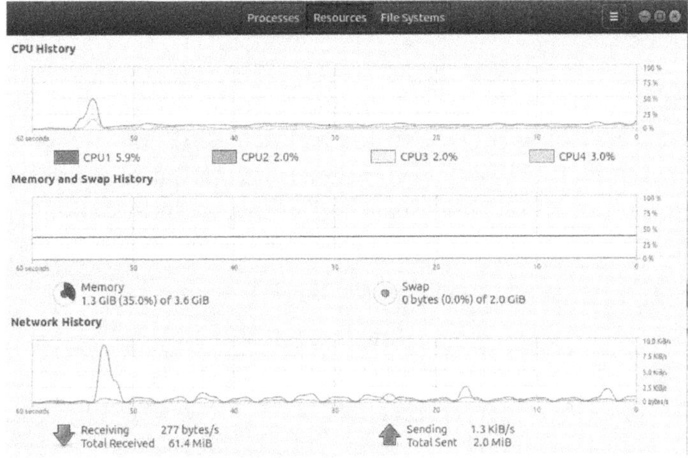

Figure 36-6

Similarly, a summary of storage space used on the system can be viewed by selecting the File Systems toolbar button:

Device	Directory ▲	Type	Total	Available	Used	
/dev/loop3	/var/lib/snapd	squash	57.4 MB	0 bytes	57.4 MB	100%
/dev/loop5	/var/lib/snapd	squash	57.7 MB	0 bytes	57.7 MB	100%
/dev/loop1	/var/lib/snapd	squash	98.4 MB	0 bytes	98.4 MB	100%
/dev/loop1	/var/lib/snapd	squash	98.6 MB	0 bytes	98.6 MB	100%
/dev/loop2	/var/lib/snapd	squash	168.0 MB	0 bytes	168.0 MB	100%
/dev/loop1	/var/lib/snapd	squash	254.3 MB	0 bytes	254.3 MB	100%
/dev/loop1	/var/lib/snapd	squash	4.6 MB	0 bytes	4.6 MB	100%
/dev/loop7	/var/lib/snapd	squash	2.6 MB	0 bytes	2.6 MB	100%
/dev/loop1	/var/lib/snapd	squash	15.5 MB	0 bytes	15.5 MB	100%
/dev/loop1	/var/lib/snapd	squash	15.5 MB	0 bytes	15.5 MB	100%
/dev/loop6	/var/lib/snapd	squash	1.0 MB	0 bytes	1.0 MB	100%
/dev/loop4	/var/lib/snapd	squash	1.0 MB	0 bytes	1.0 MB	100%
/dev/loop0	/var/lib/snapd	squash	3.9 MB	0 bytes	3.9 MB	100%
/dev/loop5	/var/lib/snapd	squash	3.9 MB	0 bytes	3.9 MB	100%
/dev/loop1	/var/lib/snapd	squash	57.5 MB	0 bytes	57.5 MB	100%
/dev/loop8	/var/lib/snapd	squash	65.1 MB	0 bytes	65.1 MB	100%
/dev/sda5	/var/log	ext4	98.4 GB	85.8 GB	7.6 GB	8%
/dev/sda5	/var/snap	ext4	98.4 GB	85.8 GB	7.6 GB	8%
/dev/sda5	/var/tmp	ext4	98.4 GB	85.8 GB	7.6 GB	8%

Figure 36-7

36.2 Real-time System Monitoring with htop

As outlined in the chapter entitled *"An Overview of the Ubuntu Cockpit Web Interface"*, the Cockpit web interface can be used to perform some basic system monitoring. The previous section also explained how the GNOME System Monitor tool can be used to monitor processes and system resources. In this chapter we have also explored how the ps command can be used to provide a snapshot view of the processes running on an Ubuntu system. The ps command does not, however, provide a real-time view of the processes and resource usage on the system. To monitor system resources and processes in real-time from the command prompt, the *htop* command is an ideal tool. Though not generally installed by default, htop may be installed as follows:

```
# apt install htop
```

Once installed, launch htop as follows:

```
$ htop
```

When running, htop will list the processes running on the system ranked by system resource usage (with the most demanding process in the top position). The upper section of the screen displays a graph showing memory and swap usage information together with CPU data for all CPU cores. All of this output is constantly updated, allowing the system to be monitored in real-time:

```
  1  [                                       0.0%]   Tasks: 126, 280 thr; 1 running
  2  [|                                      0.7%]   Load average: 0.13 0.06 0.02
  3  [                                       0.0%]   Uptime: 05:06:35
  4  [|                                      0.7%]
  Mem[|||||||||||||||||||||||||||||||||1.05G/3.65G]
  Swp[                                   0K/2.00G]

  PID USER      PRI  NI  VIRT   RES   SHR S CPU% MEM%   TIME+  Command
15306 demo       20   0 40828  4928  3888 R  0.7  0.1  0:00.22 htop
14074 demo       20   0  644M 49660 34836 S  0.0  1.3  0:55.59 gnome-system-monitor
 1230 demo       20   0 3820M  225M  108M S  0.0  6.0  1:30.26 /usr/bin/gnome-shell
  976 demo       20   0  594M 92300 72200 S  0.0  2.4  1:29.01 /usr/lib/xorg/Xorg vt1 -displayfd 3 -auth /run/user/1000/gdm/Xaut
  763 syslog     20   0  256M  4508  3476 S  0.0  0.1  0:00.06 /usr/sbin/rsyslogd -n
 1236 demo       20   0 3820M  225M  108M S  0.0  6.0  0:01.32 /usr/bin/gnome-shell
 1686 demo       20   0  583M 27076 21824 S  0.0  0.7  0:00.51 update-notifier
  823 root       20   0  182M  9432  8636 S  0.0  0.2  0:00.58 /usr/sbin/thermald --no-daemon --dbus-enable
  402 root       20   0 48028  6100  3124 S  0.0  0.2  0:00.86 /lib/systemd/systemd-udevd
 1238 root       20   0  314M  8600  7444 S  0.0  0.2  0:00.18 /usr/lib/upower/upowerd
 1297 demo       20   0  353M  8200  6432 S  0.0  0.2  0:01.16 ibus-daemon --xim --panel disable
 1295 demo       20   0  353M  8200  6432 S  0.0  0.2  0:01.85 ibus-daemon --xim --panel disable
 1425 demo       20   0  652M 22608 17696 S  0.0  0.6  0:01.13 /usr/lib/gnome-settings-daemon/gsd-color
    1 root       20   0  220M  9540  6624 S  0.0  0.2  0:06.79 /sbin/init splash
  383 root       19  -1  100M 22616 21612 S  0.0  0.6  0:00.58 /lib/systemd/systemd-journald
  691 systemd-t  20   0  142M  3396  2844 S  0.0  0.1  0:00.00 /lib/systemd/systemd-timesyncd
  674 systemd-t  20   0  142M  3396  2844 S  0.0  0.1  0:00.05 /lib/systemd/systemd-timesyncd
  675 systemd-r  20   0 70764  5268  4716 S  0.0  0.1  0:00.12 /lib/systemd/systemd-resolved
  702 avahi      20   0 47416  3852  3240 S  0.0  0.1  0:02.45 avahi-daemon: running [ThinkCentre-M92p.local]
  703 root       20   0  188M  9984  6924 S  0.0  0.3  0:00.10 /usr/sbin/cupsd -l
  705 root       20   0  4548   832   772 S  0.0  0.0  0:00.09 /usr/sbin/acpid
  706 messagebu  20   0 51548  6080  4044 S  0.0  0.2  0:02.72 /usr/bin/dbus-daemon --system --address=systemd: --nofork --nopid
  707 avahi      20   0 47076   344     0 S  0.0  0.0  0:00.00 avahi-daemon: chroot helper
  744 root       20   0  107M  3452  3132 S  0.0  0.1  0:00.00 /usr/sbin/irqbalance --foreground
  724 root       20   0  107M  3452  3132 S  0.0  0.1  0:00.52 /usr/sbin/irqbalance --foreground
F1Help  F2Setup F3SearchF4FilterF5Tree  F6SortByF7Nice -F8Nice +F9Kill  F10Quit
```

Figure 36-8

To limit the information displayed to the processes belonging to a specific user, start htop with the -u option followed by the user name:

```
$ htop -u john
```

For a full listing of the features available in htop, press the keyboard F1 key or refer to the man page:

```
$ man htop
```

36.3 Command-Line Disk and Swap Space Monitoring

Disk space can, of course, be monitored both from within Cockpit and using the GNOME System Monitor. To identify disk usage from the command line, however, the *df* command provides a useful overview:

```
# df -h
Filesystem      Size  Used Avail Use% Mounted on
udev            1.8G     0  1.8G   0% /dev
tmpfs           374M  1.7M  372M   1% /run
/dev/sda5        92G  7.2G   80G   9% /
```

```
tmpfs              1.9G     0  1.9G   0% /dev/shm
tmpfs              5.0M  4.0K  5.0M   1% /run/lock
tmpfs              1.9G     0  1.9G   0% /sys/fs/cgroup
.
.
```

In the above output, the root filesystem (/) is currently only using 7.2GB of space leaving 80GB of available space.

To review current swap space and memory usage, run the *free* command:

```
# free
              total        used        free      shared  buff/cache   available
Mem:        3823720      879916     1561108      226220     1382696     2476300
```

To continuously monitor memory and swap levels, use the free command with the -s option, specifying the delay in seconds between each update (keeping in mind that the htop tool may provide a better way to view this data in real-time):

```
$ free -s 1
Mem:        3823720      879472     1561532      226220     1382716     2476744
Swap:       2097148           0     2097148

              total        used        free      shared  buff/cache   available
Mem:        3823720      879140     1559940      228144     1384640     2475152
Swap:       2097148           0     2097148
```

To monitor disk I/O from the command-line, consider using the *iotop* command which can be installed as follows:

```
# apt install iotop
```

Once installed and executed (iotop must be run with system administrator privelges), the tool will display a real-time list of disk I/O on a per process basis:

```
Total DISK READ :       0.00 B/s | Total DISK WRITE :       0.00 B/s
Actual DISK READ:       0.00 B/s | Actual DISK WRITE:       0.00 B/s
  TID  PRIO  USER     DISK READ  DISK WRITE  SWAPIN     IO>    COMMAND
    1 be/4 root        0.00 B/s    0.00 B/s  0.00 %  0.00 % init splash
    2 be/4 root        0.00 B/s    0.00 B/s  0.00 %  0.00 % [kthreadd]
    3 be/0 root        0.00 B/s    0.00 B/s  0.00 %  0.00 % [rcu_gp]
    4 be/0 root        0.00 B/s    0.00 B/s  0.00 %  0.00 % [rcu_par_gp]
    6 be/0 root        0.00 B/s    0.00 B/s  0.00 %  0.00 % [kworker/0:0H-kblockd]
    9 be/0 root        0.00 B/s    0.00 B/s  0.00 %  0.00 % [mm_percpu_wq]
   10 be/4 root        0.00 B/s    0.00 B/s  0.00 %  0.00 % [ksoftirqd/0]
   11 be/4 root        0.00 B/s    0.00 B/s  0.00 %  0.00 % [rcu_sched]
   12 rt/4 root        0.00 B/s    0.00 B/s  0.00 %  0.00 % [migration/0]
   13 rt/4 root        0.00 B/s    0.00 B/s  0.00 %  0.00 % [idle_inject/0]
   14 be/4 root        0.00 B/s    0.00 B/s  0.00 %  0.00 % [cpuhp/0]
   15 be/4 root        0.00 B/s    0.00 B/s  0.00 %  0.00 % [cpuhp/1]
   16 rt/4 root        0.00 B/s    0.00 B/s  0.00 %  0.00 % [idle_inject/1]
   17 rt/4 root        0.00 B/s    0.00 B/s  0.00 %  0.00 % [migration/1]
   18 be/4 root        0.00 B/s    0.00 B/s  0.00 %  0.00 % [ksoftirqd/1]
   20 be/0 root        0.00 B/s    0.00 B/s  0.00 %  0.00 % [kworker/1:0H-kblockd]
   21 be/4 root        0.00 B/s    0.00 B/s  0.00 %  0.00 % [cpuhp/2]
   22 rt/4 root        0.00 B/s    0.00 B/s  0.00 %  0.00 % [idle_inject/2]
   23 rt/4 root        0.00 B/s    0.00 B/s  0.00 %  0.00 % [migration/2]
   24 be/4 root        0.00 B/s    0.00 B/s  0.00 %  0.00 % [ksoftirqd/2]
   26 be/0 root        0.00 B/s    0.00 B/s  0.00 %  0.00 % [kworker/2:0H-kblockd]
   27 be/4 root        0.00 B/s    0.00 B/s  0.00 %  0.00 % [cpuhp/3]
   28 rt/4 root        0.00 B/s    0.00 B/s  0.00 %  0.00 % [idle_inject/3]
   29 rt/4 root        0.00 B/s    0.00 B/s  0.00 %  0.00 % [migration/3]
   30 be/4 root        0.00 B/s    0.00 B/s  0.00 %  0.00 % [ksoftirqd/3]
   32 be/0 root        0.00 B/s    0.00 B/s  0.00 %  0.00 % [kworker/3:0H-kblockd]
   33 be/4 root        0.00 B/s    0.00 B/s  0.00 %  0.00 % [kdevtmpfs]
   34 be/0 root        0.00 B/s    0.00 B/s  0.00 %  0.00 % [netns]
   35 be/4 root        0.00 B/s    0.00 B/s  0.00 %  0.00 % [rcu_tasks_kthre]
   36 be/4 root        0.00 B/s    0.00 B/s  0.00 %  0.00 % [kauditd]
   37 be/4 root        0.00 B/s    0.00 B/s  0.00 %  0.00 % [khungtaskd]
   38 be/4 root        0.00 B/s    0.00 B/s  0.00 %  0.00 % [oom_reaper]
```

Figure 36-9

36.4 Summary

Even a system that appears to be doing nothing will have many system processes running in the background. Activities performed by users on the system will result in additional processes being started. Processes can also spawn their own child processes. Each of these processes will use some amount of system resources including memory, swap space, processor cycles, disk storage and network bandwidth. This chapter has explored a set of tools that be used to monitor the both process and system resources on a running system and, when necessary, kill errant processes that may be impacting the performance of a system.

Index

Symbols

A

B

C

Index

N

P

Q

R

S

T

U

V

W

X

www.ingramcontent.com/pod-product-compliance
Lightning Source LLC
LaVergne TN
LVHW080113070326
832902LV00015B/2557

* 9 7 8 1 9 5 1 4 4 2 1 6 3 *